ARE YOU TITTERING CENTURION?

Stephen D. Headey &
Tim Parker

National Library of Australia Cataloguing-in-Publication entry:

Creator:	Headey, Stephen D., author.
Title:	Are You Tittering Centurion? / Stephen D. Headey.
ISBN:	9781925497298 (paperback)
	9781925497328 (eBook)
Subjects:	Soldiers--Humor.
	Wit and humor.
Dewey Number:	808.882

Published by Stephen D. Headey and InHouse Publishing
www.inhousepublishing.com.au

INHOUSE PUBLISHING

Printed using Envirocare paper

This book is dedicated to the memory of Robin Flack and Steve Fearn for their contributions and help with launching our books. Taken too soon. *Per Ardua.*

The decision at age seventeen to go for a gunner shaped my life to quite an extent. To all my brothers in what remains a very unique Corps, I say thank you for the character and life that you show in adversity and at play that has allowed me to capture your collective spirit and your individual quirks with pen and brush and give something back to those whose adversities continue.

To everyone that ever remarked, "These should be in a book," thank you. Now they are.

To my loving wife Heather whose support is absolute and whose guidance is offered without frills. And to my parents, particularly Dad who passed on his own skill with illustration in diluted form to me. Finally to Stephen Headey for setting me the challenge and for your continued belief. Thank you all.

Tim Parker

CONTENTS

Foreword

The Royal Air Force Regiment, the Corps, the Rockapes; a few of the *polite* names we are known by. A band of brothers, and a few sisters, moulded by a common purpose, bound by friendship, loyalty, and perhaps most importantly, a wicked sense of humour. The kind of humour that only a serviceman knows. The kind of humour that gets us through the most harrowing of times.

Having contributed to the first book in this series, *Nice One Centurion*, I was most honoured to be asked to create the foreword for the second book, *Are You Tittering Centurion?*. In my twenty years with the Corps, I served with some of the finest people to walk the earth; the friendships carved and the memories made cannot be undone and will last a lifetime. To be asked to write this introduction was therefore an honour indeed. This honour became more poignant when two of our great contributors and outstanding gunners passed just prior to the printing of this book: Mr Robin Flack and Mr Steve Fearn. Their stories in *Nice One Centurion* have brought many a tear to a war-torn eye and we, as a Corps, celebrate their passing by dedicating this book, *Are You Tittering Centurion?*, to them and their loved ones.

By creating this series of books, Stephen and Tim have helped to reignite old, weary memories and bring back thoughts of all those wonderful times in Germany, Cyprus, Gibraltar, Belize, and some not-so-exotic locations. The stories and anecdotes in this and other books in the series span over sixty years of life in the Royal Air Force Regiment. Some of the tales may have been somewhat dramatised by time, however barrack room legal advice has been sought where appropriate to confirm provenance. What these books have also done, most importantly, is to bring many of us back in contact with old friends, comrades, and brothers. I would like to personally thank Stephen Headey and Mick Cundy for that.

I congratulate all of the contributors on such a fantastic team effort. In the words of that famous poet Vinney Jones, 'It's been emotional.'

Enjoy the tales that follow, they are true tales of service life; a monumental journey but the most rewarding course a man can set.

Neil Horn
Squadron Leader (retired)

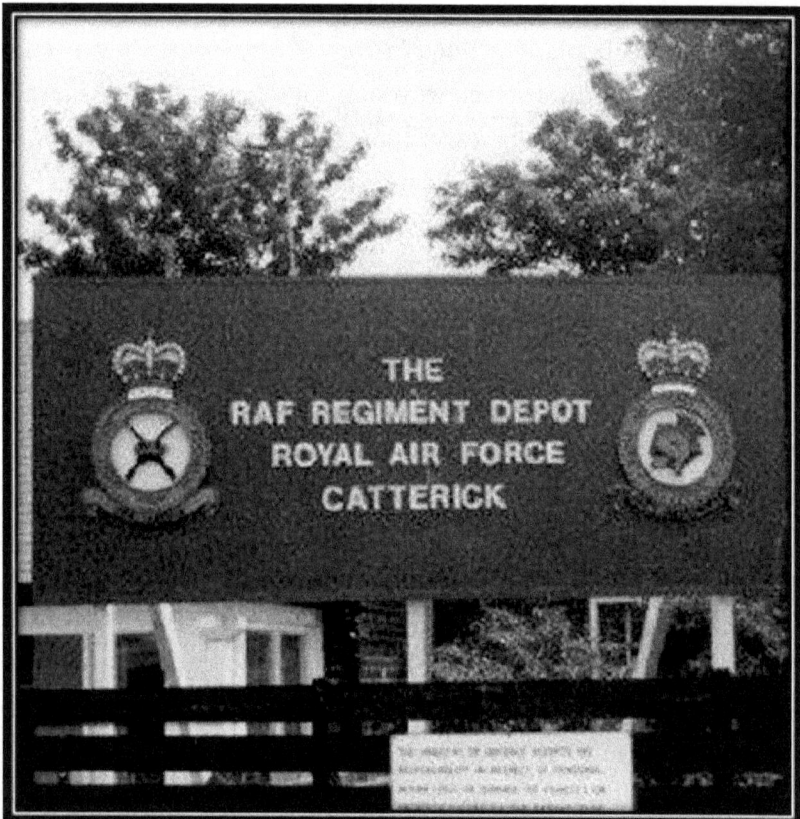

THE
RAF REGIMENT DEPOT
ROYAL AIR FORCE
CATTERICK

CHAPTER 1
FIELD CRAFT AND TRAINING

John Stowell

Another one from my time spent on basic gunner training. This time from my first tour. I was then a CPL. At the time, there were three young officers at Catterick awaiting their JROC course. As their course wasn't to start for several months, someone came up with the idea of putting them through a basic course to keep them occupied. This night we had them out overnight on Castle Hills on a trench digging ex. The course sergeant Geoff 'Chippie' Woods went around to each position and took an order for fish and chips from the chip shop in the village. He then went back into basics and wrapped slices of bread in newspaper that he duly took round the troops. It was then that, out of the dark, FO Burt shouts, "Sergeant Woods! You could have wrapped it in the Times!" I still chuckle every time I think of it.

Cliff Johnson

Back in '89, as a sergeant on RTSB, I had asked Al Paston on 4001 Flt to arrange a suitable excuse for the basic course that was dug in on omega exercise to bog out of their trenches and make for the ERV. The next morning at about 05:30 hours, I looked down from the hill we were on (can't remember its name but it was in north of the Catterick area and had a pillbox on top), next to me was Mick Rickards and Kevin Devine. From up the range road came a Land Rover driven by Al with a couple of gunners on board. We stood on top of the hill and watched Al and his men unload an empty 45 gallon oil drum and wedge it against a dry brick wall.

Nothing was said but we looked at each other in puzzlement at the scene unfolding in front of us. Al then proceeded to empty a couple of jerry cans of kerosene into the oil drum. They then climbed back in the rover and parked it next to the drum. A hand came out of the passenger's window clutching a TF, which had been ignited, and was then popped into the 45 oil drum. The rover sped off towards Gandale like an F1 racing car. Next the dim light of the morning disappeared as a bang, followed by a fucking big fireball (like a mini nuclear explosion) filled the area in front of us, topped by a ball of black smoke. We stood there stunned for a few minutes before we got the basics moving and for the rest of the day, I prayed that no one of importance noticed that fucking fireball. Cheers, Al, you mad bastard.

John Botterill

On basics at some range, I forget where, CPL telling decides to do a 1250 check. Oh shit, I'd washed mine in my denims after the assault course, quick thinking showed my rail pass instead since it was in my wallet, dodged pan bashing for that weekend certainly.

Fraze Barkway

Cambrian Training 51 Sqn. At Hereford, about to go out on the hills and I'm given some paperwork that needs copying and told my flight sergeant, he needs it fast. The guy is a legend and one of those people you just don't ever want to let down. Off I trot to SHQ and ask for a copier, I get waved off at a ball bag SAC sat behind his wall of power and explain what needs to be done. I'm stood right next to the world's biggest Xerox machine and I'm not allowed to touch it until he produces this plastic key thing and I fill in a form to use the photo copier.

I am getting increasingly angry as the wanker walks all the way round the office and plugs in this key to photocopy the form that I need to fill out! Eventually I get passed the form and, being unfamiliar with it, I start to read through it as I've never seen one before. The little shit says, "Do you want me to read it for you?"

"Errr no, why?"

"Because you lot don't need to be able to read, do you?"

That's it! I lose it and haul him over his counter and wedge his head in the photo copier. As I look around the room all I can see is a sea of faces with mouths hanging open, and the PSF warrant officer charging out of his office shouting, "Put him down, gunner!"

I end up with the little shit stood in the warrant officer's office and he calmly says, "Explain."

I do, I tell the whole story and when I'm finished he goes ballistic, not at me, at the Guin. Said Guin is basically told it's his fault for fucking with a gunner, and he's lucky to be alive and that it wasn't the end of it, and go do this lad's photocopying. He closes the door and explains he was a squadron clerk years ago and had a honking headache from being on the piss with Chiefy until daft o'clock that morning. Result.

Gareth Glover

On my basic gunner's course final ex, the call of nature got the best of me. Being a young, wet behind the ears teenager, I'd never had to do what bears do naturally but off I went, shovel in hand. Dug the hole, did the deed but I guess I must have missed the hole? Not until I got back to my shell scrape did I realise I'd actually shat back into my pants. It's all about angles. Lesson learnt.

Albi Pinnion

Ft1 weapons period, Tim Coad instructor. One guy was struggling, so Vince Ford and myself had helped him as much as we could. Anyway he does NSPS and then stands there. Tim asks him, "What's the problem, SACX?"

His reply, "I can't read Pinnion's writing."

The whole class, including Tim, started pissing themselves. Tim ordered everyone except SACX into the corridor, he followed us and proceeded to bang his head on the corridor wall, and then put his finger to lips, and went back in. SACX failed his FT!

Len Haimes

Rabbit shit. 1980/81, 58 Sqn. So we are on a one day exercise on Catterick Moors, Fieldcraft, camouflage and concealment, weapons handling, and all the rest of that field squadron shite. Anyway, after a long hard morning in a blistering Catterick Moors heat (you know—3 degrees), we take an infamous Catterick junior ranks mess packed lunch including the cold tea urn, and then a full half hour fag break. *Ahh luxury*, I hear you say. After our longer than usual lunch break, the order comes to fall in by Flts, so we all fall in as ordered. We are then split up into sections and are told we will be doing more camouflage and concealment, so off we trot, but before we all break up into the good old buddy-buddy system, we are told to hand over our camo cream, which we do so, with some bewilderment.

"Okay, use whatever you can to cam up with."

Some go for the good old mud mixed with cold icy water from the puddles, but some bright spark shouts out, "Wait!" (aimed at some of the younger lads and new Lac's just posted in) "Wait," the older experienced SACs says. "If you have no cam cream or cold wet mud, you could also use *rabbit shit.*"

"What!?" comes the exclamation. "Rabbit shit?"

"Yes," he says, bending down, grabbing hold of a load of said shit. Cupping it in both hands, he proceeds to spit in it two or three times until it is wet enough to make, well, a pile of wet rabbit shit. He then proceeds to smear it on his face in said camouflage way, covering his whole face and hands. By this time, one or two of the older guys have clocked onto what he is doing and proceed to copy him but with their backs slightly turned away.

Five mins later, after we have all supposedly cammed up, there are only around five or six guys properly cammed up, one being said instigator and the others the younger lads. The rest of us all turn round with whiter than white faces, pissing ourselves, and some uncontrollably spitting out the rest of the cold tea that we managed to keep.

When the younger lads realised they had been had, it was too late and were duly paraded in front of the rest of the flight. Moral of the story, never take any advice from an older experienced gunner, well, especially one called Geordie Wallace.

Johnny Ballantyne

Having a newly promoted JNCO posted into GDT, his qualifications required updating. First course available was first aid instructor, and I duly sent him on said course. On return, I explained the requirements on teaching our RAF students triage skills! He seemed happy enough to take on teaching the next course but admitted he was a bit nervous.

"No worries," says I. "I will sit at the rear in case you get stuck."

Course duly assembled, instruction began. Although starting a bit nervously, he soon gained confidence and all was going well. There is unfortunately always some wag who will try to interrupt the flow, and up he popped with the comment, "What you going to do about a broken back, CPL?"

I was about to stand up and sort out the problem when out came the reply from the instructor, "What type of broken back are you referring to? There are two types."

Sitting back down, I thought, *Ah, new information from the course.*

"You obviously did not know there were two types, did you?"
Silence.

"I will explain to you and the rest of the course. The two types of broken back are: broken back dead and broken back alive, and if you interrupt me again, you are liable to be the former."

I left the class at this stage a happy fight sergeant, with another able instructor in charge.

Michael Marsh

After disgracing myself on 16 Sqn, when I pinched a bike and, absolutely trollied, drove over a cliff and landed on the bonnet of one of Tenby's police patrol vehicles. After trying to get myself out of my predicament using the art of black magic—Abracadabra! Poof!—I surrendered to the police and suffered a £25 fine.

The OC 16 was not amused and, as he could not bust me, I was posted to GDT RAF Honington. Second week in a TACEVAL was called and I was put on guard in the bunker. Wing commander ops comes up and tells me he has no identity card and tries to bulldoze through me into the bunker.

He ends on the floor with my foot on his neck, the education officer comes out and asks why am I beating the shit out of wing commander ops? Well, you could knock me down with a feather. Wing commanding officer goes in and sends for me. I start thinking that I will soon be an SAC again, but there is my boss and flight sergeant beaming big smiles.

Seems the wing co was impressed and he wanted the whole station trained within the month, all personnel to be trained as close as possible to regiment standard. Tall order for the three of us, so lads from High Wycombe came over, one Sergeant Chris Penny and two of his lads came to help us. Dawn till dusk, we drilled the station personnel including 809 Sqn, Royal Navy. What a turn around, all for beating up the wing commander!

Steve Mullen

During basics, on one of the gallery ranges, for some reason the target mechanism got jammed. I jumped down into the small trench that the mechanism is mounted on and attempted to free the target, but somehow the large heavy metal wheel at the top came off and landed crack! On top of my head! The basics cpls took great delight in wrapping my head in a turban, complete with red blood dot. When I got back from DKMH with newly acquired stitches, I found that they had stuck my beret to a target and shot it full of holes!

Robert Booth

Laziness got us in trouble on the Brecon Beacons. After a day spent training on the SF role, live firing commenced. At the end, all the guns were cleaned except mine, as the junior gunner I had been volunteered to get rid of all the excess ammo and tracer after dark. After about twenty minutes of firing continuously clipping belt after belt together, the barrel was white hot and glowing in the dark on its own. So we removed the barrel and laid it on an empty ammo box to cool off. That's when the problem happened, the barrel had been so hot it drooped so we couldn't fit it back on the gun and the armourers wanted a proper excuse how we managed to do it.

Simon Pogson

On basics, I remember with great relief that the range would shut for lunch. Looking forward to a well-earned break rest in the sun, I became slightly disappointed when the instructors had us playing murder ball with a water bottle. One team in full NBC kit, the other team in respirators, all in webbing—at least at half time we got to swap dress codes!

Anthony Wells

Royal display. At RAF Catterick, 1979ish, and we were practicing exit drills from a Wessex heli for a heli deployment and attack on a position for the Royal visit of, I think, Princess Margaret. Anyway, we were using the four tonner to practice on, and going up and down the runway at speed. On one occasion, Brian Watson was driving and as we did a loop at speed, he yanked the four tonner around and we went up onto two wheels. All the opposite side of the wagons lads and kit, GPMGs, etc. came flying over to our side, and as the four tonner bounced back down, we all were thrown up and down.

When we came to a halt, we all jumped out the back shouting, "What the F!" etc. Inspected our injuries, which were teeth missing and cuts and bruises. We then all burst out laughing, as you do, and got back on for more!

The Royal Marine Band? Whilst based at RAF Cosford GDT in the early 90s, the Royal Marine Band were staying over in the sergeants' mess annexe. Over the few days, I got to know a few whilst in the mess and various drinking holes around camp. Oh, by the way, I was also in the annexe (separated as most Rocks will understand). One night on camp, I was drinking with a few of the lads, marines, and of course a few of the WRAFs. On route back to the annexe with of course a suitable WRAF in hand, I was having a bit of continued banter with the marines about them not being real marines, just trumpet players, etc. This of course got their backs up and four of them grabbed hold of me and threw me into one of those large skips. As they ran off, I got out quickly and took the short cut to the annexe.

Now, I knew their room numbers as I was IC the block. I got hold of their keys, which believe it or not, they left in the back of their doors, doh! I threw their keys into the block tumble dryer, and the WRAF and I went to my room. On arrival of the marines, all I could hear was an almighty noise about being locked out of their rooms, he he. They came straight to my room and wanted me to open the door, etc. I said their keys were on the grass outside the block (not!). As I looked out of the window, all I could see were five/six marines on their hands and knees looking for the said keys. I couldn't resist saying to them, "That is not the first time a marine has and would grovel to a Rock!" I gave then their keys after about an hour. The best bit was that in the morning at breakfast I noticed a marine in a sling. It was one of the marines who put me in the skip, and of course, I struggled and he broke his arm and only got back from A/E a few hours ago. That will teach them. He will never forget the night he met the RAF Regiment and not the band.

Frazer Nixon

On the subject of not leaving your camera lying about. Early 1990, RAF Stafford, an elite group of 20 Sqn. Gunners under the charge of Charlie Donnelly are to act as enemy for a five day TSW exercise. After a week of various shenanigans, including kidnapping and assaulting Guins, stealing weapons, NDs, amongst other things, the final morning arrives and the exercise ends in triumph for the enemy.

Back in the mess for breakfast after a long night in the field are all participants, prior to clean up and debrief, including wing commander, who had spent the week filming the exercise with one of those new-fangled video cameras, ready to proudly screen the show to all the station execs in the station cinema that morning.

Cue gunners stealing said device and skulking off to the bogs, where three willing volunteers each had a T, an S, and a W painted on their arse cheeks in cam cream. A nice panning shot of the arses with a soundtrack of giggling is in the cam, ready for the show. You can guess the rest but apparently three bare arses in full cinematic glory were the stars of the show later on, much to the amusement of the audience. We had long gone by then!

Chris Parkes Snr

I remember doing rolling dismounts from stripped down Landies for the same Royal Visit ('twas Princess Margaret). I got my boot entangled in some of the cam netting that adorned our vehicle and when my turn came to dismount, I ended up going out head first, but as luck would have it, the momentum carried me through an impressive forward roll and came back up on my feet, slotting in nicely in my position in the formation!

Ted Harte

I remember watching our first demo on how to do this. It was at the back of RAF Abingdon (now Dalton Barracks). The CPL instructing was going to great lengths to explain how fiddly putting the pin back in is. As he proceeded to demo to us, of course the ruddy thing went off. Cue us falling around and him cursing.

Unbeknownst to him, the trip flare had set fire to his helmet cam foliage. So now he was running around, screaming, with flames coming from the top of his lid. This made us fall around in fits. Wasn't until one guy grabbed him and threw him in a large puddle (very large) were the flames extinguished.

The flight was in bits, rolling around laughing. Hence demo cancelled and much running up and down the airfield commenced.

Adrian Walton

A lowly AC (later to become an officer) while on his BG in the early 80s was point in a night time nav ex while bimbling on the Yorkshire moors. One moment said AC was in front of us doing his leader thing, next minute we lost sight of him. After deciding being all quiet and tactical was not going to find him, we called out and found him wedged by his CEFO, nearly submerged in a deep water-filled hole. The tac side of the nav ex was ruined as all that could be heard was one AC squelching with every step and half a dozen lads sniggering. Just goes to prove officers and maps/compasses do not mix.

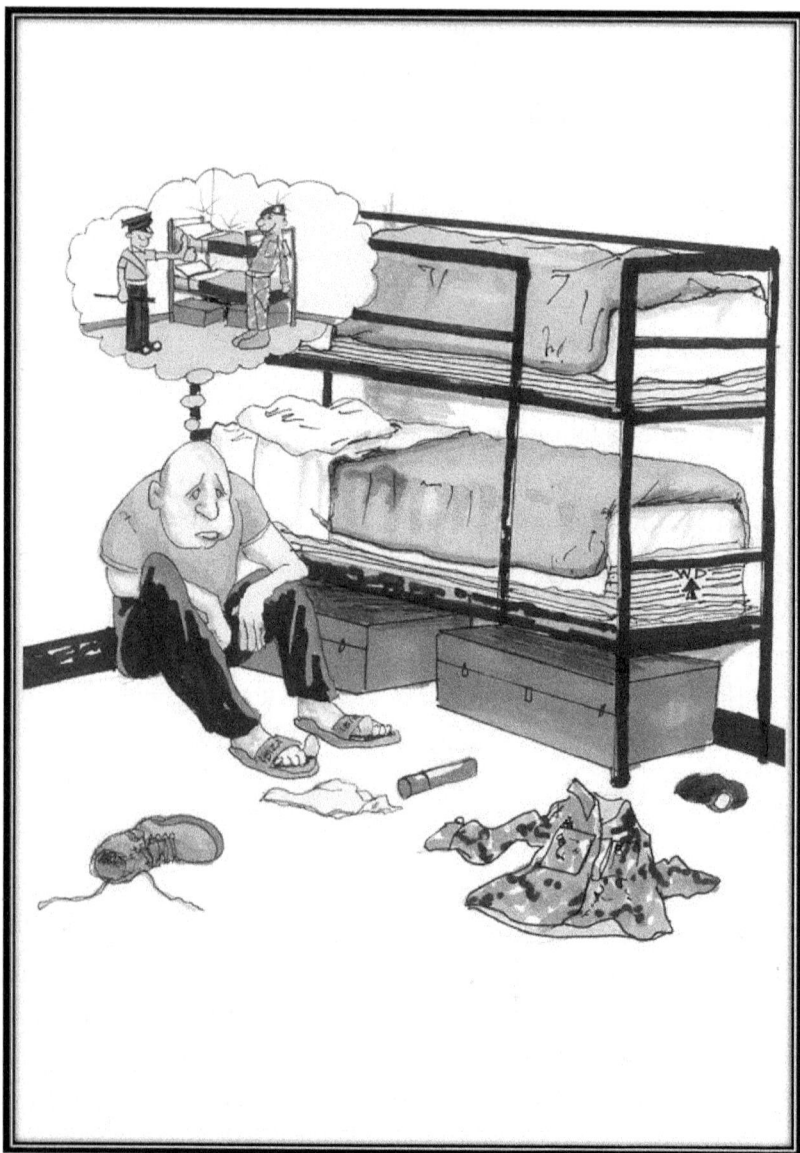

Glyn Jones

Following on with the Pentland exercise—you can fool some of the people some of the time, especially Rocks. It had been a dry time up in the hills and the local beck wasn't up to a lot but a bit of a dam downstream increased the water level sufficiently. Now

Paul and I knew damn well that there were no trout in the beck, but there was a fish farm in the valley so a plan was hatched. Dam up and down stream, buy some baby trout and set them free.

Next lesson was going well and a small trout was sighted, tickling produced nothing (funny old thing) so we went into making fish traps and left them in overnight. On checking the traps the next morning, they all came out empty except two, yep, mine and Paul's. We each had a rather large Rainbow in ours, much to the consternation of the troops. While setting the troops on building a signal fire on top of the hill, Paul slipped away to the fish farm and got us a couple of nice ones which we put in our traps.

All in all, we had a good week and we bought the troops a massive steak dinner before returning to base—never did get Rab Reid to eat worms though.

John Corr

Whilst on 26 Sqn on exercise in the 80s, the squadron had gone rogue and decided to do some field type training, away from the usual Rapier exercises. I was on stag in the early hours of the morning, in my hole on a lovely moonlit night. In the next hole along, just a little way away from me, was Gunner Chris Jones. I heard a, "Psst, psst," coming from Jonesy.

I whispered, "What?"

He said, "I can see a couple of guys pushing a Land Rover towards us." I was trying my best to look through the mist that had covered the ground. He said, "Shall I call stand to?"

I said, "Go for it."

He then let out a mighty, "Stand to. Stand to, enemy front!" All the squadron was up and ready for whatever followed. Various shouts for more information was asked for and Jonesy was there.

Then as the mist cleared around the two sets of legs and the bulky shape of the Landie, the shape transformed into a cow, which then, to add shame to it, all gave a defiant "Moo!" which drowned out the voice of Harry calling Jonesy all the names he could think of.

Glyn Jones

In the 80s, on 27 Sqn, Paul Stockton (RIP) and I were tasked to run a survival course up in the Mendips, above Glencorse Barracks. Took a while to set up, and food on the ground was fairly scarce at the time of year. So we made a couple of false provisos to help us along. We did a pre course recce, and after visiting several local hill farms, found a kindly old gent who had a knackered ram with bad foot rot that he was going to put down. After a bit of bartering, he let us have it for a bottle of whisky and would keep it alive for us.

The course started in spectacular fashion as the troops didn't know where they were going, and were flown in by 22 Sqn chopper. The pilot played the game and did an emergency landing, which as far as the troops knew was real. After we had calmed them down, we set off for the area we were camping in. On day two, Paul and I went to the farm to get the ram, boy did it stink with the foot rot. Anyway, we got it to the camp and got the troops to build a pen for it. Well no one wanted to kill it, but the plan was to bleed it, so Rab Reid volunteered to stun it first and walked up to it with a large tent sledge hammer. He gave it a massive wallop on top of its head, which by rights should have killed it outright—not this tough old fucker, it just shook its head, looked one of those looks, and promptly tried to headbutt Rob and chased him round the pen. We eventually got hold of it and it was quickly despatched, hung up, and bled, ready to butcher next day.

Unfortunately, and unknown to us all, this had been seen by a dog walker (who shouldn't have been there). She had called the RSPCA and 'The Sun', who had printed the barbaric training being given to soldiers on next morning's front page. The commanding officer—Sammy the Pig—was hopping mad, and I had to do some fast talking. The RSPCA were happy with the kill method though (might have lied a little itsy bit) and the course was allowed to continue.

John Berwick

On 63 Sqn in Sennilager I, just drove back to camp as the exercise had just finished, the Sqn 2IC walks passed me. I said, "Fancy some fresh meat, Sir?"

He said, "How fresh?"

I said, "Still walking fresh."

He said, "Go for it."

So Tam Lundy and I set out, as there was a pen with sheep on it on the training area, Tam and I jump over the electric fence and start chasing the sheep, who start running in circles. Tam and I are fucked, drive back to camp with no meat, and we bump into George MacDonald, so the three of us go back, but we forgot to tell George about the electric fence, which he touches with a machete. Anyway, we all jump over the next electric fence and try to block the sheep in a corner. Suddenly, the fence goes down and the sheep go everywhere, and we all split up. I bumped into George, no sign of Tam. Then suddenly, Tam walks over to us with a sheep over his shoulder. Was like out of a movie with the twilight. Anyway, we get the sheep in the back of the rover and back to camp, and we wonder who is going to kill it and gut it. I think George had worked in a slaughter house or something. Next minute, an axe comes out the back of a four tonner and handed to George. Sheep is lay there, I put my foot on it, George swings the axe, and I chickened out, as

I don't want to walk like Chicken George from *Roots*. George goes down arm around the sheep's neck and knocks it out with the axe. We tie it to a tree and start to gut it. Young Hector walks round see the carcass, we told him it was Rex, the sqn mascot, and we were going to eat it.

Anyway, big sqn fire, sheep is thrown onto it to cook, we all get pissed and forget about said sheep. George comes up to me in the morning and tells me he regrets killing the sheep and just burning it.

Robbie Robinson

In '84, when I was GDT at Hereford, I was asked by 22 if we could help out on a CP course they were running. We were to provide a suitable sized crowd as they escort a VIP from car to building and then back. The stage was set, the crowd would be a little noisy on the first trip and more hostile on their return to the car.

Up come one of their DS and gives me a large knife and an instruction to attack the VIP. My response was a sharp, "Fuck off!" and I passed the knife off to a supply trainee, and off he went, feeling like a chosen one. It was messy.

Bill Espie

Cyprus, back in the day, with the beach borne 34th of foot. The med and half of creation were kicking off with each other. Gadhafi was rattling several sabres, and it was decided that we needed some snipers to deal with the threat. Being the man, I get lumped to run an on island sniper course. There is some competition from the flights and for the purpose of this little ditty they will all remain anonymous except the two A Flight stalwarts—a mad papist who answered to The Nom De Guerre of Padraig, and a sun bronzed Adonis from Leeds with the nickname Gorgeous.

The course went well, lots of help from all the guys on the squadron, excellent range phase at Dhekalia, but all the troops were well above average. The final ex could not be a live fire but I tried something new—a sniper cordon IS ex for int gathering.

I enlisted the help of a particularly stunning nursing sister who agreed to being the suspect and to having her picture used. Observe and report was the story line. Troops got inserted after last light with section support to cart away spoil and stuff. There were six locations chosen as the cordon positions, around TPMH, working on the usual theory that three would be occupied.

The bad guys would know they were under surveillance but would never know which fairly obvious areas was being used at any one time. The A Flight gang constructed a fairly good short-term hide in a big rhododendron bush behind TMPH. Cut into it with secateurs from the rear, and cut most of the inside of it out, just leaving the front and then reinforcing that cover with scrim. DS retired to a reasonable distance so that there would be no opsec breaches.

Settled down in the Rover to watch the area after getting comms and night fell, with us perched somewhere on the hill over-looking the hospital. Well around 2 am, up came the wind and one of those storms out of nowhere sprang up and boy did it spring up. Water was coming down in sheet form horizontally and cascading down the road. Pretty soon afterwards, click codes for emergency evac were being sent. B and C were sensible and got back to their ERV where they were picked up and taken back to the squadron compound to be dried out. A Flight, however, had a much trickier task, being much closer to the actual hospital and almost in light. I knew they had a backup and they signalled they were going to their back up.

About an hour later, they confirmed firm at the alt. I took the decision to insert the other two teams back in before first light into their alts and extract the A Flight team at the same time. We asked for a PUP and were surprised to get one in the car park behind the hospital. Anyway, we moved in, and sat and watched a stream of highly attractive army and RAF nurses turn up for the day shift. About 7:20, a Cypriot orderly came wandering across the space with a longish thing bandaged up. He headed for a door that I knew to be the incinerator and so immediately assumed that he was going to dispose of some poor unfortunate's body part. He gets to the door and turns the handle to enter and pushes. Result—nothing, nada. The door doesn't budge. He looks up at the door and shakes his head and sets off back to get the key. This is a small distraction of getting P and G out of TPMH without the hospital boss finding out we are running anti-terrorist sniper exercises in his hospital grounds. We had had a slight problem previously getting permission. Bambi is on the net asking where the A Flight gang are, and having comms problems or nobody talking problems. Five minutes later, our good friend the orderly comes back with a key, proceeds to unlock the door, and tries to open it. It opens about three inches and then is slammed shut from the inside.

Pennies start to drop in my head, and I check with my good driver signaller Bambi, whose face is incapable of any lie, and one glance is enough to tell me that the missing pair are inside the room. There then entails some minutes of push-pull warfare between the orderly and P who has jammed an SLR into the door handle.

Eventually the orderly starts to witter away in Greek. There comes the most evil response from inside in a strong Irish accent, "Fuck off, you poisoned runt, before I burn you in here."

Like a Hanna-Barbera cartoon, he is frozen to the spot and gazes fearfully at the door, then turns and runs screaming back to the main door. All this pantomime is being relayed via the net to the two loons inside. As soon as the orderly moved, I slammed the Rover close to the door and the two of them leapt out and stuffed all the gear in the back of the Rover and pulled the back tilt down.

I started to exit when I saw the orderly coming out with a sergeant (male) nurse rabbiting on forever. The sergeant spots me in the Rover and says, "Excuse me, flight, this guy recons the door is haunted and that there is a demon inside. See anything?"

Forced laughter and my response was, "Get the name of the stuff he's been on and we will have some for the end of course do." Good laughs all round, he goes his way, I go mine. Back to the compound and a slight amount of muscular counselling applied—a brew and breakfast is in order so Bambi gets the order to get the Rover ready and we will break our fast after an eventful night. P pops his head into the office door and says quite quietly, "Chief, what do we do with that punter's leg?"

"What punter's leg?"

"The one the guy was going to burn and he dropped when he pissed off. We sort of scooped it up with all the rest of our kit and it got into the back of the Rover." They never cover stuff like that on the sniper instructor's course or the FT2.

David Matthews

My FT1 midway. Not doing so good, not had a lead and pissed off big time. Coming to end of midway camp last thing flight in attack. Sammy Snake giving out leads at brief, all names for sections given, now me thinking, *That's it, Spike, you're out.* Then I hear HQ flight IC Matthews. Big grin but short lived, as I remember, HQ is miles behind everything. So pissed off that when I went back to give orders to my HQ section, all I said was, "Follow me."

Well off we go strolling along, right out of it. Heard bang-bang! from up front but it was nothing to do with us. Radio crackled to life, signaller told me, "Spike, you are to report to prearranged location for battle orders." *What fucking place?* I thought, as I had not bothered to listen.

Well it will be somewhere near the bang-banging going on. I double away (as if you could with the kitchen sink hanging from you), went up this incline, tripped over, and rolled down the other side in a clump. Then I heard Sammy Snake say, "Well done, Matthews, for getting here so quick, now listen … Blah, blah, blah, re-org on the white light. Okay, now go."

There I was all on my own. Went back and found section. "Right, lads, there is enemy up front, we are going to attack, so follow me." Racing up this hillside we got to the top. I peeped over and there was the enemy. How the fuck I got there, I do not know.

Anyway, we won, and charged through to those 100 yards beyond location, go to ground, and start to re-org section. Everybody else is now coming to ground at our location. All of a sudden there is a 'whoosh', as a very pistol goes off and this white flare goes off in the sky.

"Right!" I shout, "Up and follow me." Up we get and start running.

After about five mins, Sammy Pig shouts, "Stop, Matthews! Where the fuck are we going?"

"Sir, you said re-org on the white light. I am just following it." Well that was it everybody was on their backs just pissing themselves with laughter.

After about five mins, Sammy Pig says, "Right, Matthews, point section, take us home." *Oh fuck, where am I?*

Now I had Taff Donavan on my section. Great friend of mine who just happened to be on TSF at this time. "Put me scout, mate and watch me." So I did.

Sammy Pig says, "Why do you need a scout?"

I said, "It's my patrol, Sir and I want a scout."

"Carry on," he says. So led by Taff, we got back. Now I know for years after there was a painting in 159 with a spotty four-eyes following a white star. I wonder what became of it.

Albi Pinnion

Cattcrick training area FT 1, freezing and wet as normal, orienteering phase pitch black, SAC V F was in charge and had a man in front of him who was lighter.

Suddenly, we heard a crack of ice and splosh! Di shouts, "Turn lights on!" All you could see was a weapon in one hand and a map in the other, and the top of his head. We pulled him out, changed clothes—how his map and weapon stayed dry was a miracle. The first man had walked across a tank trap and got away with it. Many have heard the story, but being there was so funny, DI's comment, "Good drills, SAC VF."

Steve Mullan

FT 1, was in a linear harbour, bivved up with Keith Vosey. One man in each position had to be awake and alert on stag. I was fast asleep in my maggot when I had a strange feeling, "Quick, Keith, get out of your bag! Quick!"

Seconds later, the poncho gets ripped back by an extremely irate DS who has found the whole harbour position asleep, except for me and Keith who were 'alert, weapons in hand, and stagging on!' Skin of the teeth!

Chris Taylor

58 Sqn, 1979, and we were tasked with providing the squadron for the defensive phase of the JROC course, and dug in at Cordilleras Wood. It was freezing cold and several squadron members suffered from exposure and trench foot. End ex was finally given and we began the task of filling in the trenches and preparing to move back to Catterick. A full weapons check was carried out and it was discovered that a Very pistol had gone astray.

After much passing of the blame from officer to officer (and them trying to blame some of the troops), we ended up having to start opening up the trenches again until it was finally found! That is the bad memory of this type of incident because wind forward about twelve years to an exercise in Germany and an officer dropped his pistol into about ten inches of shit in the communal training area shitters. He tried to order some of the troops to retrieve it, only to be told in no uncertain terms to get it himself!

During my time as the regiment sergeant on TCW, the wing had in place a course for all new members which culminated in exercise Brutus, which was a week-long field exercise held at Proteus training area near Ollerton in Notts.

During one such exercise, where the newbies had to dig and live in a full fire trench, complete with IPK, one of the support staff, who was a very good artist, stapled a load of tri-wall boxes together, drew a full sized elephant on the boxes, which was then cut out and painted pink! Several tent poles were added and the elephant was sent out into the bondoo, carried by about four guys. Last light stand to is given, and the DS are behind the trenches watching to see what went on. Radio message, "Elephant up," is whispered, followed by, "Move left."

Troops in trenches rub their eyes several times before calling out, "Enemy front!"

"What enemy and where?" says I.

"A pink elephant to our front," is the reply. This goes on for fully twenty minutes with the elephant appearing and disappearing several times. I have never sniggered quietly so much as I did that night!

Dave Capps

To set the scene, Catterick, mid-80s and mid-November. It's blowing a blizzard, the thermometer has bottomed out, and it's an FT1 final exercise. The students are on a recce patrol with a FS DS in attendance, they have reached the FRV, and the cover group go firm as the recce party move onto the target. An hour passes and they return, pick up the rest of the patrol and retire. At a safe distance, the FS stops the section and questions the recce team as to what info they had gleaned.

The answer, "Two blokes, dressed in ponchos and sombreros, sitting in armchairs with their feet on a table, watching TV in the middle of nowhere, in a blizzard at midnight."

The FS shook his head and muttered something about, "Fucking TSF …"

Gareth Burton

First arctic warfare survival week in Bodo. We have been out for three days. So we have spent a night in a ten-man Canadian tent, then a four-man tent to square our admin away. Anyone wanting to go to toilet did it in front of everyone on a cardboard and bag set up affair.

I've been chomping on Snickers to bolster energy and wouldn't use the bog. The last night seen us digging snow holes as our finale. They took our stuff from us so we only had what we were wearing. During the digging I had the immediate urge to go. So I grabbed our shovel and ran up a bank. Dug a hole and discovered it was just peanuts, ha. So to get rid of it, I tried to spread it. Well, it instantly stuck to the shovel and couldn't get it off. I went back down and borrowed a lad's machete and chipped as much as I could off. Ha ha, that night they issued a fish for us to eat. Well, they used that shovel not knowing and complained about it smelling sweet. I didn't have the heart to tell them until we got home.

Rob Andrews

34 Sqn NAAFI, a handful of scruffy individuals sporting beards stood at the bar drinking, minding their own business. Drunken Rock decides to go tell his life story to said bearded gentlemen. "Please go away, mate, we are just hear for a quiet drink."

Did the Rock leave? Oh no, he had more stories of daring do to impart. Faces of said bearded gentlemen begin to darken and the atmosphere thickens. Fast forward an hour or so and we realise that bearded chappies and the Rockape have disappeared. Thinking nothing of it, we all retire to the blocks to get some kip, ready for Monday morning parade.

On parade the next day, no sign of the Rock from the night before, and no one has a clue where he is. Gradually news filters down that someone has been discovered in the officers' mess strapped to a radiator. It would appear that the missing Rock had been found.

The moral of this story? Don't piss off the SBS when they are taking a sabbatical from a particularly gruelling exercise.

Stephen Andrew Knight

In about '87, 34 Sqn. Myself, Gordon, Ricky, and I think Steve, maybe some others, went off up Troodos for the day, armed with some maps marked up with a few way points—first mistake—for a bit of walking.

All went well for the first half of the day, then at some point we stumble into a Cypriot/ Greek National guard base. Instantly we are met by the end of a rifle and detained as possible spies. After searching us and all our gear they came across the maps, which were marked up with way points—that was it—"Definite spies!"

We were all conveyed separately in vehicles to Limassol Police Station for interrogation and questioning. After several hours of detention, released and returned innocent to Akrotiri, and ground ops, where we were met with rapturous applause, and shown the local Cypriot newspapers. There we were in black and white. I think we put a stop to all adventure training in Cyprus for a while. Oops!

Andy Divine

On FT 1 '86 with Tony 'Rico' Ryan. After a night in the Angel, we head to the Catterick Chinese. I places my order, and Rico says to the lady, "Nagasaki special and fried rice ... Oh, and go easy on the sunglasses."

Robbie Robinson

FT 1. My final patrol, came to a fence, so one guy starts to go under it as a second guy pushes the wire down with is rifle to step over it. So when the electronic pulse came, it was a surprise to both of them. Derek Hawk, who was marking my patrol, had to stop and let everyone settle down before we could carry on.

Andy Ramsay

1984, after completing the FT2 course, I was acting sergeant on RTSB. CPL Dougie was an instructor on the same training team—Dougie was a born comedian and good with the one liners.

One morning Dougie was walking from RTSB towards Trg Wg HQ, coming the other way was the SWO, accompanied by a WRAF officer from Newcastle CIO. As Dougie passed the SWO, he said, "Good morning, Sir."

The SWO said, "CPL, don't you pay compliments to WRAF officers?"

Dougie apologised and said, "Ma'am, that's a lovely hairdo."

Mark Minary

Piddington training area, I was SNCO IC the Guin recruits field exercise—used to be MFT. We were wrapping up the exercise and had done the declaration and were waiting for the transport for the crows back to Halton. Bob Smith *(The* Bob Smith) gets a Bedford four tonner stuck in a bit of soft ground. Thinking he would use four-wheel-drive and reverse out with no problem, I wandered off to do something else. Next thing I hear is a Bedford revving its tits off, and watch Bob get it bogged in down to the axles. I kid you not, the driver's step was at ground level. For fuck's sake.

Johnno and Bob tried various methods of getting the wagon unstuck, and snapped most of the ropes on site in the process. It was painful to watch.

Finally, in despair, I sent Bob back to camp. Johnno and I went to the fire station on Bicester Garrison to get some chains and proceeded to pull the four tonner out with a 7.5 tonne DAF flatbed. Came out a piece of piss once we could concentrate on it without much buffoonery going on. Ha, poor old Bob.

Dave Capps

Honington, mid 90s, the Tonkas are still occupying the haz site, but at night Rocks roam the area in Land Rovers. A boring and mundane task made more enjoyable by culling the local rabbit population with an air rifle from a moving vehicle.

The OC of one of the flying sqns has his vehicle DIed each morning by one of his urks, and reports to MT this morning that there is a burning odour coming from the engine compartment. The mechanics duly open the bonnet to find a well-cooked bunny with a single hole in the head laid across the top of the engine block. The carcass had welded itself in place and required heavy cleaning to remove, the aroma apparently lasted a few more days. Words were spoken to the gunners but nobody knew anything (shock!). The urk was threatened with action for falsifying the DI sheet, as MT reckon the carcass had been there at least three days. The vehicle was henceforth parked in MT overnight.

Richard Devlin

4001 flight, 1992, flight sergeant's first day, first morning parade, inspects us all and basically tells all to get a haircut. But to a few, including me, he said, "Estimate." After parade, the estimated ones asked the CPL, what the fuck this estimate thing was. We were told it was basically the same, and get a haircut.

All to parade at half one for inspection again. So at said inspection, he says to me, "I told you to get a haircut. What the fuck is your excuse?"

My reply, "I beg to differ, Flight Sergeant, but you told me to get an estimate, the station barber told me it will be 3 quid, and can fit me in on Monday afternoon."

Straight to his office for a classic bullocking, and then cup of tea as he thought it was funny as fuck I had the balls to do it, I was shitting it though.

Phil Swales

Our corporal on my basic training whilst on the ranges got bored one day and decided to have a 'live' game of this (not with a gun and live ammo though) but with a sandbag full of stones/pebbles. He sat on the Land Rover bonnet, us 'aliens' lined up in three lines in front of him at throwing distance. We had to all in unison take five paces to our left then one pace forward then five paces to the right, one pace forward, five to the left and so on, and so on. He lobbed the small pebbles in the air in our approach. We had tin lids (helmets) on, if the pebble hit an helmet, as the 'clunk' sounded said 'alien' had to 'die in a dramatic fashion', then fall to ground, kicking his legs in spasms, then 'croak' it. Happy days!

David King

16 Sqn Wildenrath field firing, pretty certain a lot of lads will fill in the details, squadron trg off, who went by the name of Flight Lieutenant Smith, yet another waste of space (reminiscing in my head). Anyway, he was to teach us how to cross a minefield. He very discreetly laid the mines, those little blue things, first man was appointed to cross. Out comes the prodder, the tape, and away he

goes, long time passed gunner successfully gets across minefield, thinking that was a fluke, another gunner gets nominated, again with equal success, yet another gunner but this time is told to take a different route, again, crossing successfully.

Getting pissed off by now, the trg off orders us to cross in pairs, this time applying more pressure to the 'mined area', and not to use the ground that had already been cleared. The whole flight was then ordered to go through in one go, this time told to jump up and down, again these mines failed to detonate. We all knew by now that these things had been put in upside down, a walking disaster if ever there was one. I believe he was initially posted in as the squadron inspector general, but if my memory serves, he just became the trg off by default. He went out with the doc from SMC, I think the song played for him on a regular basis was 'Oh, doctor, I'm in trouble', very appropriate really. As I say often, couldn't make it up.

Stephen Snellgrove

34 Squadron, SW flight did a demo in the mid-90s for the chief of the air staff. Demo over and time to meet the troops. The CAS is introduced to a SAC by the nickname of Alf. The CAS stated that, "It is very hot today."

Alf replied with, "Yep, it's hotter than a snake's ass in a wagon rut, Sir."

Chris Pacey

During a FT Weapon TP, Rod Jones was doing the L2 and didn't get the description quite to the SI's liking. (Any Kent) So Ady says, "It is not green, it is *deep bronze* green and it is not a yellow band, it is a *yellow filler band.*"

Turning to the rest of us, he asked, "There are plenty of other things that have this colouring in service, name one. Pacey?"

"RAF bus, Sergeant? Helipad?"

"GO!"

Bill Hayes

The Carl Gustav lovely thing to rope with 120 feet from a Belvedere into the farm at Gemas, or live firing TPTP at Imber. And as the NAAFI wagon drew up, the two mad kicks Irish Rangers put one through the side of the van—crisps and stickies everywhere .

Doors fell off, and the old lady that drove it had to have her hands proved off the steering wheel, she had a mighty roar.

Phil Rowe

I did once find a RAF copper with a sense of humour. My GST2 course head instructor was a fly sergeant copper. We were learning to take orderly rooms, forgetting the fact that most Rocks had probably been both accused and escort on various occasions.

I was the officer hearing a charge against an airman accused of speeding on camp. All of the process was duly recorded on video and played back for the course to watch, learn, and comment on. All went perfectly with the said fuzz stopping at regular points and allowing discussion, he himself was well pleased with the professional manner in which the process was dealt with until the camera panned to me for the sentencing.

I had the black cover from the video on my head and said, "You will be taken from here to a place of holding and then to a place of execution, where you will be hung by the neck until you learn to stick within the speed limit."

By the end of the video, me, the accused, the escort, and the SNCO were pissing ourselves in front of the camera. As I waited for the eruption, the flight sergeant, with tears in his eyes, said, "CPL Rowe, don't you take anything fucking seriously?"

John Stowell

Whilst on basic gunners back in '82/'83ish, we were on the grenade range at Catterick. As was the norm, once the trainees had thrown their grenades, the instructors threw any bombs left over. On this occasion and on my turn, Bob, then a CPL (he later took a commission), stood in with me as safety supervisor.

As we were preparing, he says to me, "Bet you can't drop your grenade in that hole (which was full of water) at the far end of the impact area."

So on the throw, I gave it a little bit of effort and was rewarded with a splash as it lands in said hole. As we take cover behind the wall, I'm treated to the usual 'well done' calls of, "Lucky cunt and spawny bastard."

Now the book says that the killing area is determined by how hard or soft the ground is. That may be so but, as we found out, the amount of and distance that the debris that is thrown out is also affected, as shortly after the detonation, the now foul-smelling contents of the hole started to deposit itself on us in the throwing bay. I now received the same accolades already mentioned but without the prefixes. The officer on the range that day also caught it in the tower as well.

Nick Day

Then there was the officer on 48 when deployed on ops in 1986 who was sat in the entrance of the ACP opening up the tins of L2s, think there was four per tin, and he was saying how he, "Loves the smell of these tins." I should have told him we have plenty of Bostick on the FRT.

John Bailey

Think it's about time you had a medic's post! Byron heights, 1994. As an ex Rock, my other life in the RAF was an aeromedical/field medic. One night after being up the mountain, four Penguins didn't like me and desired to ask me outside. Now one of the civvies that was up there knew me and said to them, "I don't think you want to do that!"

They then started to laugh and said, "He's only a medic." The last words when I had all four of them dangling off Measles Point by a rope was, "We didn't mean it." Measles Point was 2000ft up shear drop. I was asked by the commanding officer that day, who was a squadron leader, "Will you please let them go?"

I said, "With pleasure." He shit himself, lucky I tied them off. I was on RandR next day. Now that was fun.

The same tour Byron Heights, 1994, after serving as a Rock for ten years and then being a tactical medic working with the army navy, and my brothers again, which kept me going. I was deployed to Byron Heights radar unit to be there medic/dept adj. Well, on my forced RandR, I was sent to an island off the mainland but there was a brilliant hike around a big mountain. Well I was quite content to stay in the bothy and cook because that was what chilled me out. Oh no, some Arsenal wipe of a techie FS decided no, we are all going for a walk around the mountain. Fair to him, so I decided to pack my Bergen with what I need. He said, "No, you don't need that, we will be back in three hours." Well things went tits up two hours in, I had the only resources, plus med kit and survival clothing. He had bugged me for hours that I was lagging behind all the time. Now one of the guys was hurt so medic mode went into action. He decided we would carry him over the mountain as it was the shortlist way.

Then my Rock head came into life yet again. The last words were, "I'm a FS, you can't hit me."

God, I hate mending broken noses. The PTI back at base camp was concerned that we had been gone too long and was on watch. Luckily, I had also taken a pocket mini flair pistol. I saved the guys leg, rank doesn't know best, needless to say my RandR was cut short. But there's more. That's another day. Once a Rock always a Rock.

Albi Pinnion

Falklands '83 with 63 Sqn, someone had the bright idea to let the squadron Guins throw twelve grenades, cannot remember who was the guilty bastard, but it was decided a tac range would be good all Guins had two grenades. Guin was assisted with priming his grenades and off they crawl, gets to firing point and had not lost one but both his bloody grenades. Stop! Gunners now looking for said grenades, and Guins stopped from doing the tac bit! Someone will remember who it was no doubt!

Andy Orhard

I spent hours one night, crossing and recrossing RAF Wittering runway as ZB298 'targets'. First time across was in stealth mode—nothing (us well chuffed). However, by crossing number six, we still hadn't been picked up despite stamping and jumping up and down on the concrete strip. Useless crap, still didn't get us. Barely, managed to pick up the LWB sent to pick us up!

Turns out that where we were crossing the runway was in a slight dip. That's okay then—training exercise was deemed a success (WTF?). Lesson learnt being to site ZB298 correctly (no shit!) and for us 'targets'—get seen ASAP, get to go home early!

Geoffrey Herschell

When I went on my FT1, Rapier squadron didn't have the SA80 (as we called it then) and field squadron did. It meant the FT was extended for a week for training on this new rifle.

On day one, we were being instructed by Sergeant Ally. When he had gone through the parts of the weapon, he was pointing to bits for us to repeat. He pointed to a part and asked me. I answered, "DTMH, Sergeant."

He said, "Repeat that."

I said, "DTMH, Sergeant."

He said, "What does it stand for?"

I answered, "I'm sorry but I've forgotten what the D is, but the rest is trigger mechanism housing, Sergeant."

By now everybody was sniggering and saying things like, "The flack's off us, he's the one."

Ally said, "It is DTMH."

I said, "Yes, Sergeant, DTMH."

Ally said, "Are you a racist?"

"No, Sergeant," slightly stunned at the question. And then the light bulb moment.

He had been saying, "*The* TMH," accented to 'dee' TMH.

Not a good start! He did see the funny side, but during the rest of the day, other DS were interrupting lessons to ask which one is Herschell before going away smiling to themselves.

Alan Trevest

B Flight 34 Sqn early '82, if I remember, taking part in the island-wide exercise Venus Rock. Final day and we dealing with the 'riot' down at the gate by the ARABS Club and Ladies Mile Beach. Picture the scene—OC B flight wearing a 351, with the whip antenna fully extended, is walking towards the beach next to a high wooden fence (6–7ft), when suddenly from the other side comes a roll of barbed wire. It sails through the air in a perfect arc and hooplas OC B perfectly and lands at his feet. The expression on his face was priceless. The lads and I just pissed ourselves laughing!

Fraze Barkaway

Bored! Spade, Adam, Chris, and I are left all alone in the flight harbour. Anyone that served on 1 with us would know that C Flight had a thing about flames.

I decided to do a trick I had done hundreds of times before and filled my gob with petrol, lighter ready, and spy Tuffer making a brew. So I blow huge cloud of petrol mist and light it doing a huge flame, for some reason, I burst out laughing and, that's it, game over. Head is on fire, all I can see is flames and feel the burn, and hear Tuffer pissing himself. Fair play, he smacks my head around until I'm extinguished. Much giggles and piss-taking ensues until the pain kicks in.

Only way to get to the med centre is to nick the dispatch bike and the pair of us hoof off down there for first aid, which ends up with us abusing the medic because he's on the phone to a doctor asking how to treat a burnt head.

Danny and Ray now know the truth! Peak stove backfire my arse!

51 Sqn. We get dicked to put on a demo for some foreign visitor. It was to take two parts, a very slick rehearsed demo of an attack on Castle Hills with a shitload of pyro for good effect and weapons stands with the armour parked up after. Ace! So a day of rehearsals later and flight sergeant asking us all questions about range, characteristics of weapons, etc. Warning us not to make him look like a cunt.

The big day arrives and from the start you know it's going to be an epic. The car pulls up and a midget, I think Chilean general, gets out and is wearing full dress uniform with enough gold hanging off it to pay off Mexico's national debt, and wearing issue wellies. It makes his trousers look like a cross between Herman Goering and the American Army character from Kenny Everett.

As soon as he's out and stood straight, we get called to attention and the flight cdr salutes. A voice from the back says, "Round them up, put 'em in a field, and bomb the bastards," in Texas accent. We all lose it, Jimmy goes nuts.

Anyway, demo happens, all great stuff. Weapons stands, Jimmy doesn't trust us to speak and starts picking up weapons with us stood behind and grinning like idiots and explaining in pigeon English what they are.

He picks up the 66 (throwaway portable anti-tank weapon), extends it, and gives the run down, ending with, "I believe this has been used to great effect in your country, Sir."

To which the reply comes, "Yes, the terrorists killed my wife with one."

Don't fuck up? Don't make me look like cunt, he said? I think Jimmy dined out on that one for a while!

Johnny Ballantyne

FT 2 and buggeration factor. Deploying for the field exercise week, I was nominated as duty student, this I think because I was the only student familiar with the newly introduced 12 x 12 tentage.

A half mile from the site, the instructors introduced a simulated four tonner breakdown, this now entailed manhandling all of the equipment across country including tentage, field equipment, and, worse of all, a 500gal water bowser. Having completed this task, I was asked by staff how many men I would need to erect the tents. "Two per tent minimum," I replied. I was given one. This indicated to me that I and one other would erect five tents.

We were coping quite well until the wind suddenly got up. Asking for more staff, I was allocated one other, not to mention names, this individual came with full field equipment complete with steel helmet. We pushed on but this steel helmet clad individual was causing more problems than help. Flapping canvas, wind, and webbing were all hindering our progress.

Starting to lose my temper and ready to say, "Fuck it."

My other assistant came to me and said, "Christ, he is lucky."

"Lucky?" I screamed, "What are you on about?"

"Well," he said, "he forgot to bring his combat cap, so the staff made him wear that steel helmet. He is lucky, he did not forget his water bottle else they would have tied him to the bloody water bowser!" The ice broken, we managed to complete the task.

Robbie Robinson

We had a new officer arrive on 1 Sqn in '83. He very soon wants to establish he is in charge, the colour sergeant RM told us cpls, "Just let him have as much rope as he wants." Well, Mr Officer announces we are doing a night exercise in the large wood just out of the main gates. We try to express our concern but was told very sharply, "Shut up and get the flight ready."

The night is a disaster, troops being chased all over the place by wild pigs. At the debrief he was very shocked about the wildlife. I asked what he expected in an area called Boarwood. He thinks for a moment then states, "I thought it was BAORwood ... British Army Of the Rhine wood." We were speechless. He did not last more than 4 months.

Sid Wright

I have a cracker. 1992, 50th anniversary of the corps. HM is coming to Catterick, so basically if it didn't move, paint it. If it moved, wait until it stopped, then paint it. I'd just arrived from III, was supposed to be on the wing but only as 'war' strength. So they palmed me off to 51, who didn't have any spaces. So, feeling the love, I was delighted when I got told I'd been selected for special duties during the visit. I was then told I'd be NCO IC red carpet squad!

A crack group of troops armed with tape, hoovers, and approximately 25m of royal red carpet. Which was only one of two on station. So my team had to roll it out, tape it down, hoover it, then hide while HM and all the VIPs, and the great and good of the regiment walked in on it, then walked out ready to move onto the next item on the walkabout. Once the VIPs had left and went down the rank structure to squadron leader, we'd magically appear, push them off, roll up the carpet, and make a mad dash through the buildings to the next location. Repeat the process before the royal entourage came round the corner. So, picture five gunners in No1s, which are covered in red carpet strands, running around with carpet, hoover, bass broom, and tape, laying carpet then running off behind a wall. Yet again, regiment pave the way for others, ha ha.

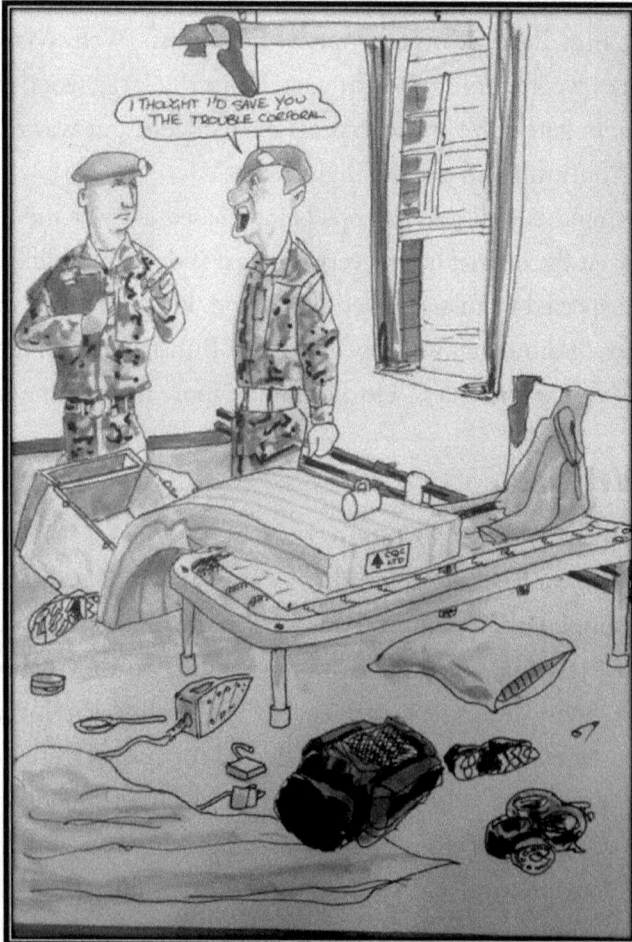

Fraze Barkaway

Squadron 2 IC was an absolute horror of a man. For some reason, this guy had a passion for fucking me over. On keys, I had secured the hanger and walked around the building about three times to make sure the place was locked down properly, it all was, apart from the officer's door. So, as per orders, I handed him the keys and clearly told him I was off and that the only door he had to lock was the officer's door.

Hours later, I'm on my pit when I'm kicked awake by a grinning RAFP and told the hanger is insecure. Yup, it's the one door cunt face was supposed to lock. I open up the next morning and am promptly charged by the CPL admin under instruction of the 2IC.

That night I'm locking up again and it's the same scenario, but the difference is OC catering is in the office with him—she's married to him and an absolute stunner. I get the Land Rover keys thrown at me and told to take OC catering home to Brompton on Swale.

I dutifully say, "Follow me, ma'am," and start to drive her out of camp when she asks me what I did to piss of the 'ogre', so I tell her the whole story. She sympathises and asks that we stop off to pick up some bits from the village. This I do and then I'm asked not to take her home but to take her to her office on camp. I then get told to come into her office and she sits in a comfy chair opposite and basically spreads her legs and asks me if I like the view. I bang her senseless and then drive her home, as I drop her off, she stuffs something in my pocket and says, "Wear these to work tomorrow for me."

So, when I get back to my room, I find her knickers in my pocket, and dutifully wear them under my uniform to work.

I open the squadron and am pretty much marched straight in front of Rigby to be charged for leaving the hanger open. So there

I am accepting the lying prick's punishment, wearing his wife's knickers on a promise to do it all again.

Stephen Williamson

Summer adventure training. 26 Sqn style. Someone thought it would be a good idea to canoe the Ardeche River, don't know how I got involved, I can't canoe and I didn't like getting my hair wet. We left camp in two Sherpas, full of kit, towing some canoes. Quick stop at the families NAAFI on the way out to get provisions steaks and beer, and off we head. The script was we would take it in turns to share the driving. I think the squadron cook had the first shift. We had hardly left the main gates when the bottled were cracked open. Ended up the cook had to drive the whole way, we couldn't stop for a pee so ended up using empty bottles and tipping them on the autobahn. We eventually pull over for a pit stop and one of the guys had held onto his pee for that long when he did let it go he fainted.

We eventually get to our first campsite and fall out of the wagons, totally drunk. No tents put up, everyone grabbing their slugs and dosing anywhere. What a sight the locals had when they woke up and found random gunners still in their slugs scattered about the camp site.

It should have taken us a couple of days to canoe the river. First day I was left guarding the kit, everyone returns, that's it, we done it, we're moving on. Where to, I wonder, Cote Azur. We sped south noticing signs like Cannes and Monte Carlo, eventually ending up in a campsite not far from the beach. Pitch up tents and have a good time for the rest of the week. Everyone found something to do, whether it was fishing off the pier or sunbathing on the beach, the sergeant PTI that was with us tried to get us out into sea with the canoes. After some persuading, we did.

One of the nights we get topped up in the campsite on our stash of spirits and head into town. Story goes, the back door of the Sherpa opens and I tumble out, next thing I wake up in someone's garden and it's daylight. So I make my way to the local tourist information office wait for it to open up so I can get directions to our campsite. A woman in the queue asks me what I was doing, I mentioned that I was lost and did not know where I was. She thought I had amnesia, she takes me back to her house, let's me have a shower and some breakfast, and rings up all the local campsites to find out if they have a group of eleven British tourists there.

Nothing local, she rings further afield and it seems we had come to another town the previous night. She eventually finds the campsite and drives me to it. I thanked her and made my way down to the beach where everyone was chilling out, telling everyone I had slept rough although I was clean and fresh. Punishment was that I was confined to the campsite for the duration of the stay in the evenings. Well, the first evening, I had a rendezvous with a daughter of one of the French families on the campsite, and word got out and I was allowed back into town the following evening. The sergeant PTI hated all of us, it was his worst nightmare. Until that is, 26 Sqn winter adventure, the same guys turn up in Bavaria for a skiing excursion and it's the same sergeant PTI. You should have seen his face, that's another story.

Neil Horn

Barrie Griffiths eluded to the story a little bit ago. 15 Sqn tour of the FI in 98. Barry was lucky to be in command of some enterprising officers. I will not name them, they can feel free to step forward. One fine Saturday, obviously after a Friday DandB, the OC had to attend, I think, the Goose Green memorial, unfortunately leaving the JOs unattended!

The JOs had also finished the Friday night (as per) in the Aircrew block bar 'The Goose'. Seemed every detachment had these big bars except the RRS officers, something had to be done, the boss would be proud. We had two crappy single rooms as our 'bothy'. So the adjt and I jumped on our Armstrongs (another tale that didn't impress CBFFI!) and whipped around the sites to see what could be had. We then despatched OC Eng and OC A to collect all the available construction materials. If memory serves, it consisted of: two felling axes, a couple of hammers, a saw, four paint brushes, ten gallons IRR Brown, tengal IRR Sand. Result, all the pikey tools we needed.

We then spent the next three or four hours constructing the RRS officers' lounge. Adjoining wall gone, everything painted desert cam, kind of, even the wardrobes, sinks, and taps. We dumped the evidence, sat back with a beverage and a movie, just in time for the boss' return from 'Goose Green'. You should have seen the look on his face, to say he was impressed with our initiative and construction ability would be well … a lie! I mean, it was not as if it was an engineered building, constructed to withstand the rigors of the FI weather, and all walls being structural or anything like that! I am not sure how much shit Barry got in for our shenanigans back then, but I have no doubt he sheltered us from a whole shower of shit.

The irony being that, for the last two years, I have been the borough code enforcement officer here in Alaska and taken people to court for illegal demolition and construction.

Roy Ives

Okay, let's do officers, let's face it, there are some that should be fragged at an early age, but most are okay, and a few I would follow into battle anywhere. And as an ex-army man, before I got better, most good ones are Rocks.

Anyway, I had been away from the squadron for a while, and when I came back, we had a new commanding officer, had said hello a few days ago, and now we are on an exercise with HG flight in a wooded area. We are non-tac and I am teaching the HQ Guins how to set trip flairs. As I am finishing the lesson, the new boss turns up and watches me. I finish and walk over to him, "Everything okay, boss?"

"Well, flight, you were not here when I took over and I have decided that one of the things I want to do on my squadron is to stop all the swearing that goes on."

I look at him as if he has gone mad, he wants a Rock squadron to stop swearing? I look him in the eye, look at the Guins who are looking at me, so I think I will try to make a joke of it, so I says, "That's a fucking good idea, Sir," as sarcastic as I can.

"Well thank you, but you have just sworn again, and you were swearing through your lesson."

So I says, "You must be fucking joking, Sir."

He says, "There! You have done it again."

"Done fucking what?" I say.

"Swear," he says. "It's every other word."

"Well, I had not noticed, Sir, but I will try to stop all these cunts fucking swearing cause some of them are quiet bad."

He looks at me, wide-eyed, I think he is going to burst, but he just turns around and walks away, muttering to himself. I look at the Guins and they are in fits—they got it!

I look at him muttering to himself still as he walks away and think, *My god, one day that prat could lead us into battle!*

Dean Montgomery

Remember being on Haltern trg area in Germany, Rick Haynes was the complimentary cabbage 'colours' IC. We put in a night foot flight attack on a bunch of pongos and their 432s. Thing was, they were non-tac and all asleep, and had no idea we were even on the area when TFs, smoke, and all hell broke loose. Did a right job on them, cutting down the tank tents and well and truly trashing the site. We do a rapid withdrawal on foot back to the patrol harbour and could hear the 432s out and about looking for us!

Anyway, as usual Roy's sect don't show up, turns out he decided to set his own section harbour (non-tac) and get the lads heads down for the night, used the excuse he couldn't find us in the dark! You could tell the cabbage didn't believe him but what could he do?

RIP Roy Taylor, you are a legend, my friend ...

Simon Stanton

Was watching SAS programme last night, it reminded me of an exercise we did one winter in the 70s. We had the SAS TA who were trying to get from A to B, without being caught. I was assigned to the interrogation, we had the prisoners in their shreddies, their hands and eyes bound by their socks. I then led them to the huge ponds, breaking the ice before putting them in, getting them out, then whipping them with stinging nettles whilst asking questions. The warrant officer shouted, "Careful, Stanton, you're being watched."

Looking up, I saw a regular SAS guy writing down all I did. Later, looking out, there was a RAF copper with his dog nearby when another TA broke cover. The copper let his dog free to chase him down, only to have the dog go to the nearest sheep and tear its leg clean off. I looked that copper in the eye and said, "That dog gets too close, it's dead meat."

Leslie Barnes

I remember that exercise, Iron Chariot, it was '87. I had just flown in and was picked up in one of the strip down Land Rovers, only problem was my kit was still in transit and I only had summer uniform on. "Don't worry, we will give you a parker when we get to Xanten." I jumped in the back under the cam net to keep a little warm. Don't remember arriving! Do remember waking up in the med centre in a bath of ice with some medic telling me I was lucky to be alive. "Hyperthermia."

Welcome to 26 Sqn. Who was the Rock who shared my slug on the way back to keep me warm? Thanks.

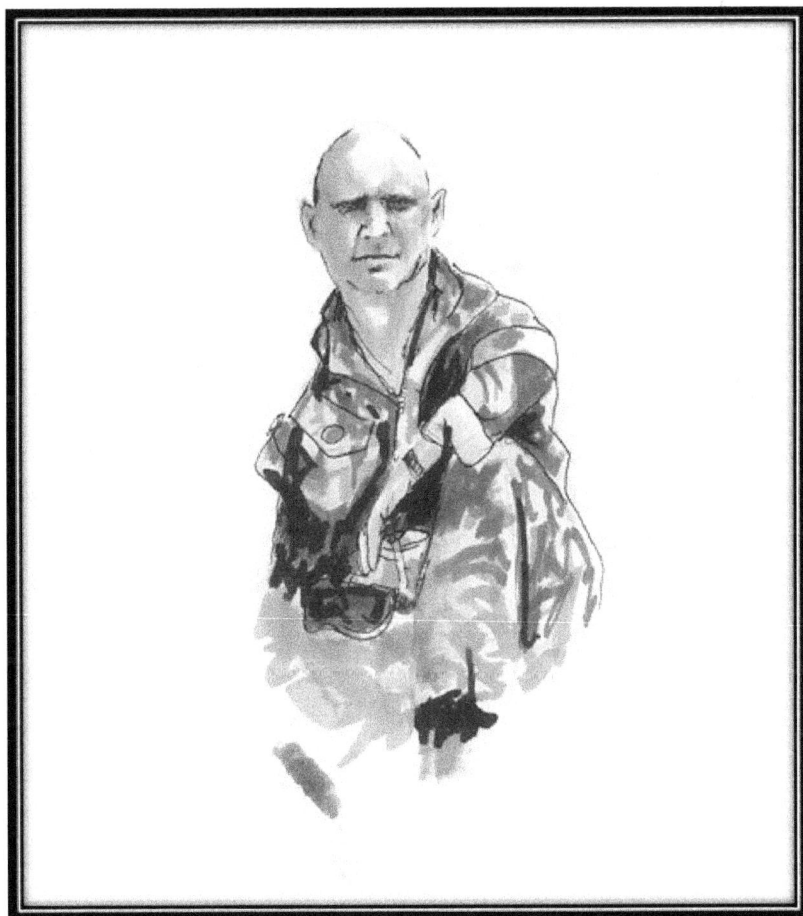

Rob Finlayson

We had such a laugh on 19 Sqn, HQ flight had some very 'special' gunners in its numbers. On one of the many piss-takes, I remember (only bits though) we were on patrol on Salisbury Plain. Our first trick to confuse the Russians ... and the zobs was to move the radio frequency down a few clicks. The infamous Italian Stallion and I had the radios at the time, and after stating a prearranged code word, we moved the frequency down, out of the window few call signs and BATCO in came nicknames and slang ... our logic was that nobody could work out our unit, its size, or our task if we did that.

We were in two sections and as we came through a bit of un-dulating ground, and as the sun hit our faces, the radio came alive with, "Dum de dum de dum ... summer loving, happened so fast," which ended up with both sections singing Summer Loving whilst on patrol ... we got away with it.

The reason why we had split into two sections was because we had a disagreement about cows (enough said). But the highlight of the day was when we suddenly heard this death defying scream. I got on the radio to find out, through the hysterics, that a certain certified sane gunner had rested his GPMG on an electric fence and electrified himself. Oh, we laughed.

Rob Andrews

On basics one morning, and someone has come up with the blinding idea of a stretcher run. So off we trot in all our enthusiasm, as usual the weather was dull, grey, and a little pissy with a little more pissy thrown in. Anyway, we are all trotting along quite happily—well when I say happily ...—when someone has another bright idea, "Right, chaps, we are going through the Swale, keep those stretchers above the water."

In we plunge, and a might chilly it is too, when all of a sudden, the man on the front right stumbles and loses his footing. As one well-oiled machine, we spring into action instantaneously thinking, *Fuck it*, and let go of the stretcher. In plunges the bod on the stretcher, disappearing under the water, coming up again looking a tad wet.

We would have helped him but were too busy pissing ourselves laughing. We should have done more really shouldn't we? Oh, and sorry Guy 'Red' Lester ...

Andy Ingham

Akamas range early 1980s, field firing. One evening went to the 'long drop' riggly tin shed before bed. On arrival, saw a light coming from the pit of doom (about 6ft down a mass of shit and soiled toilet roll; it stunk in the Cyprus heat). There were no doors to the traps, just a raised plank with half a dozen holes where you sat and took aim! Anyway, hanging from the rafters was a rope down into the pit with a Tilley Lamp on the end of it.

From another trap, a couple of lads had lowered SAC 'Alf' Hitchcock down on another rope into the latrine pit head first, suspended like someone from *Mission Impossible*.

Had to ask the question, "Lads, just what the fuck are you doing?"

The voice from the deep replied, "Boss, I was having a crap, and my wallet fell out of my fucking pocket—it's got a week's wages in it!" Needless to say, he found out who his true mates were that night as he surfaced with his trophy and only one shit covered hand—it could have been a lot worse!

Andy Duffield

BG11 '83. Monday morning block inspection by Sergeant Pat Patel. On the Friday, I had made the most of a free weekend and had made my way to Stockport to see a WRAF who I had met at Swinderby, and had recently been trying to turn her Welsh by giving her as much DNA as possible! I should, this weekend, have been melting the dimples out of my DMS with the spoon and candle method. However, instead, I had been giving as much loving as possible to the Manchester miss, I hadn't thought about consequences!

So on Sunday evening on return to block, I had done the toes and heels and they were gleaming but boots still dimpled! Monday morning and Pat was in front of me after decimating a number of bed spaces. His eyes were bulging and he was feigning madness as only he could! "Duffield, your boots, they are still full of fucking dimples! Why, you fucker?"

The reply I had came from somewhere but not rehearsed or thought about! "Well, Sergeant, I spent bloody ages, see, on trying to smooth the boots. I got the spoon and went round and round in circles over them and I have done it all weekend to no use! I didn't know what to do, see, Sarge. But when I came back last night, see, I saw JJ Sharp and told him my problem that the spoon wasn't smoothing out the dimples and that sharpie had told me that I had to heat the spoon up," looking straight into his eyes and trying not to look at said sharpie, Steve Butt, or J Taylor, who were sniggering like naughty school boys!

Pat rolled his eyes and asked, "So how long did you spend on your boots?"

"Hours, Sarge!"

"With the spoon?"

"Yes, Sarge!"

"But you didn't heat the spoon up?"

"No, Sergeant. I didn't realise, see!"

A smile sneaked onto his face which he tried to hide and then those immortal words! "You sheep-shagging Welsh fucker." He turned and went, muttering about the spoon and anti-Welsh expletives! But I got away with it! He knew though and said at end of course, best excuse he had heard for a while!

Damien Fisher

All right here goes. While on basics, I spent a weekend with Nick in Newcastle, coming from Cornwall, this was a huge culture shock and a lot of beverage was supped. Comes to Sunday, Nick, who was driving us back to Catterick, says, "Fuck it, we'll leave early in the morning."

Me, being a tit, says, "Okay." So we can get back to the block around six with the lads already up shining stuff and things, etc. A busy place of work, as you all know me and Nick slightly hungover, he looks at me, I look at him as we start getting our kit ready for inspection. We then hatch our now infamous plan to do one, so out the window we jump, no idea why, seemed like the thing to do, and run past another flight, up to the car park, and off we race out of camp. We stop off to phone the camp and tell them Nick's car broke down and we'll be back as soon as possible.

Four o clock arrives, we've had a great day doing nothing and get back to camp. Funny thing, the CPL doesn't believe our story and promptly charges us. The officer heard the charge and managed to keep a straight face as mine and Nick's stories didn't match, needless to say we were introduced to jankers at a very early stage in our regiment careers. Happy memories.

Andrew Burke

It's 1981ish, 34 Sqn, Akrotiri. Squadron warrant officer calls me over as I'm passing his office, "Airman, have you ever been on a charge?"

"Yes, Sir."

"Have you been an escort on a charge?"

"Yes, Sir."

"Good, get in my office."

"Yes, Sir."

"You're doing escort in fifteen minutes with SAC (no names, because they read these stories) and SAC is the accused, right, you lot, we'll have a practice before going into the adjutant's office." Anyway, he marches us all in, the adj reads the charge (another alcohol-related incident), then asks if he had anything to say.

"Yes, Sir," he says.

"Well, speak."

"Well, Sir, you can do me for what I've done, but not for what I'm thinking."

"What are you thinking, SAC?"

"Well, Sir, I'm thinking you're a cunt."

How the fuck we stayed nearly composed was probably through fear of the warrant officer. The charge ended with a massive fine and restrictions, I was so glad to get out of there.

Richard Chapman

Chris Pacey, you mention what about our warrant officer, well, we had some fantastic characters in that department. I'm sure the RAF in general would benefit from such good men. A quick one on warrant officer Clouson 'Mitch' Mitchell. He and I were teaching on El Al RTSB, we were both coming up to FT 1 time, Mal got us together and said, "Right, you two, meet me at the sergeants' mess tonight, I'm going to introduce you to mess etiquette."

Well first of all, we knew straight away, we were not going to be the winners at this game. Mal, a drinking establishment can only end in pain. We pitch up smart as a carrot five minutes early, waiting at the door is Mal and several of his clan, welcomed us in shook hands with just about everyone, they made us feel like lords. It was also, as it happened, a whisky tasting night. After about two hours, Mitch and I discussed leaving while we could just about stand. "No, not hear a word of it," said Mal, "Here, try this Dura, it's a lovely blend."

We finally escaped when Mal disappeared to play the slot machine, holding each other up, we headed for the main gate at

Catterick—as those of that era will know on the right just outside the gate was a bofar gun—we had managed to pick up another gunner on our way to the gate (also drunk). Mitch says, "Let's have a go." I was on these guns, well, carnage in the making. He put us in the pos of the no 1 bloke who fills the hopper etc., etc., and then starts teaching us the gun song. We had about an hour and as you will know the guard room is about five mtrs away, looking back any other station, you would have been locked up for doing that at a front gate. It was the following day that we found out the orderly sergeant was one Davy Lappham and he just let us play out our little game until off we staggered into the night. To this day, Mitch nor I can remember how or what time we got back to the Garrison. Some twenty-five years later, as civvies, Mal, Mitch, Scouse Johnson, and I are in the bar at Cranwell doing the same thing. Great people …

Ian Boyce

1978, young Ian is now a sergeant at Swinderby, I am in charge of twenty-three regiment cpls, who conduct the two weeks regiment training for the recruits, passing through. My office is first on the left from the main entrance, next door is the FS, John Kennedy, an old school jock Rock, hard as nails and a hard drinker.

Between our two offices is a small hatch, upon which our shared phone sits (obviously too poor to have one each). One morning, I am sat at my desk doing something really important, as regiment sergeants do, when I hear John pick up the phone and say, "Yes, Sir, yes, Sir, yes, Sir," he places his hand over the mouthpiece, hands me the receiver, and says, with an awed expression, "Ian, it's the Air Commodore for you."

Fuck what have I done? I gingerly take the handset and say, "Sergeant Boyce, Sir?" I then hear this uber posh voice waffle on at me, so I reply, "Mick, stop fucking about!" Next door, John nearly fell off his chair, thinking I was talking to near royalty in such fashion. When I had finished talking to Mick Gant, who had recently been released from nick and had been posted to Wittering (where he no doubt was station commander or some such), and invited me down to his place for the weekend, John went ape. He was going to do all sorts to Mick for impersonating an officer, he just did not understand that was what Mick was like.

Matt Webb

One very cold, dark, icy morning on basics, we're all lined up at the armoury, waiting for the water fairies (firemen) to pass by. All tooled up for a day's weapon training, we're quickly away at the double, round the perry track in front of the 58 Sqn hangar, heading back to RTS(B). We suddenly encounter a few patches of black ice. I dodge, slip, and slide all over the shop. True to form, I gobbed off all too quickly, "Almost went over then."

Then, putting any break dancer/epileptic to shame, I go arse over tit with my GPMG, eventually coming to a halt, with a face full of asphalt, twelve feet from where I impacted the floor. Turning round, I see the man, the myth, the legend that is Dougie Meadows, looming over me. I thought, *Bless, he does have a heart, he does care about us.*

He looked at me and shouted, "Fastest you've ever got into a fucking fire position, you wanker Webb, get the fuck up and fall in!" Ah, bless him.

Paul Johnson

Exercise gazelle Arabian. One of my final exercises with 1 Sqn was exercise gazelle Arabian in December 1985 at Soltau Training Area. During this exercise, we were staying at the infamous Rhinesehlen Transit Camp, which is in the middle of the training area. The whole area was always written as the SLTA (Soltau and Luneburg Training Area), it's amazing when you ask one of the guys who was there with you what it was called, because the old grey matter is lacking and the crap that he can remember (Dutch Hollands). Now this camp consisted of lots of Nissen huts with a pot-bellied stove in the middle, and it was also not far from another infamous place called Bergen-Belsen. This was the site of the German concentration camp during the Second World War. Not far from Bergen-Belsen was another camp we regularly stayed at and that was Bergen-Hohne, this camp was used by the SS during the war for guarding Belsen, and the accommodation blocks were great. But our wish didn't come true because that was not where we stayed during this exercise.

We all remember our days at Rhinesahlen. The exercise started in thick snow and ended up in thick mud! The first night at the camp was sodding freezing trying to get the stoves up and running. However, the camp did have one good thing and that was the communal shower block, it was lovely, hot showers every time.

We hated this place at Rhinesahlen, it was called 'Moon base Alpha' by the lads on the squadron because the area resembled the surface of the moon were naff all grows. The training area was used extensively by the army of all nations and all their main armour; during the exercise you would be given a map reference and told to go to a location and park up. However when you got out of the living area and into the training area, things changed massively. You were told to follow the tracks and these tracks were clearly marked on the map!

The thing was, when you got to the training area, there was tracks all over the place and none of them resembled anything that was on the fricking map! None of them was going to the place that you wanted to go, it was just a sea of mud and tank tracks all over the place. Everybody did eventually find their directions by using the SWAG method (Scientific Wild Arsed Guess).

The other problem that we encountered was that the area was used mainly by Challenger tanks and other main battle tanks, their track marks were a lot wider than our little sewing machines. Consequently, we kept throwing tracks as we couldn't fit in theirs. Plus some of the tracks were full of deep and muddy water and, as you didn't know how deep it was, you just drove in it, and the next thing you knew the water came over the bows of the tank and straight into the driver's hatch, almost bloody drowning him. Some of the tanks didn't have their belly plates on and wound up with a flooded engine bay and stuck in the deep water.

The training area was vast and was separated with a main German road right through the middle of it and tanks were not allowed on the road. So, to get to the other side, a tank bridge was built and was of a very sturdy construction; it could easily take 100 tons. The other side was mainly of woods and areas that you could park the tanks in. This area was called the Luneburg Extension and stretched right up to the East German border.

I'm sure that some of you will remember the Church Army sticky bun wagon coming around the sites. This guy was a German local working for them and you could be in the most camouflaged place in the woods and he would find you, he would drive through the woods shouting, "Coca Cola, Haribo, hot dogs, and sweets." It was amazing how he could find you hiding in the woods but others with a radio and maps couldn't.

The culmination point of the exercise was an airborne attack on the tank bridge with 1 Sqn tasked to defend it, and 2 Sqn RAF Regiment which has parachute capability and also one of the sister squadrons, was also tasked with trying to take the bridge from 1 Sqn and parachute in from helicopters.

This proved to be a bad move because the weather had affected the ground near the LZ, and I believe they had a few accidents on landing. The day before the attack, 1 Sqn was told to assemble by the bridge and try to dig in your tanks if possible.

Now on this particular day, the weather was quite dry and the digging in of the tanks began in earnest. Watching the guys trying to dig a hole for a tank with small trenching tools was quite funny, they just weren't getting anywhere. Now we had on the squadron a certain CPL. No names are mentioned. He was a CPL on 'B' Flight and during the digging in of his tank, he noticed a local German with a small JCB under the bridge, digging in a cable of some kind along the road.

Now this CPL had an idea that if he could persuade this guy with his digger to give them a hand things would be easier and he could have nap. Now armed with a ten-man ration pack, he made his way down to the driver and, with the help of the ration pack, cajoled him into making his way up the side of the road and dig in his tank. This local made a bloody good job and all you could see was the top of his turret when you drove into the hole. The others were impressed by his ingenuity. The problem was when the war was over, we had to fill in these holes and this CPL's was a big one.

That night, we all bedded down and waited for the fireworks to begin the next day. However things were not going to go to plan, because that night the heavens opened and we were deluged with rain. The area was a nightmare and was a quagmire of mud and slop up to the front of the bridge. The CPL was bedded down in his tank with his crew and they closed the back door, they also used the inside clamps so that nobody could get in the back door during the night. But these clamps also made a good seal on the door. The rain just kept coming down and unbeknownst to this CPL, the water started to fill his hole, plus all the surrounding water went to the lowest point—the CPL's hole.

The time for the attack started to creep up and the CPL told the boys to unlock and open the back door, ha! They had a struggle to push it open, due to the weight of the muddy water behind it. When it finally opened, the water that had collected in the hole flooded into his tank and covered everything in muddy crappy water. The water didn't come in during the night because he had his belly plates on and the door was sealed from the inside, all the kit inside was piss wet through and muddy. The boys were killing themselves laughing at them trying to extricate themselves from the quagmire of mud and slop.

By the time 2 Sqn was ready to put in the final attack, all the cooks, clerks, bottle washers, and mechanics had been drafted in to fill the gaps, plus they wanted to get in on the act. Everybody was digging in along with two other SACs Mark Allen and 'Scouse' Jones, and another CPL that I can remember and he was Duncan Hollands, the Sqn clerk. However he soon got christened 'Dutch', obviously because of his surname, and to this day, he is still serving the Queen and still goes by the name 'Dutch'. This guy had a wonderful character about him and he would help anybody within his remit. He was a Guin pretending to be a Rock! Everybody loved him because if you had a problem with any money claims, he would sort it out toot sweet; he was the Rock's best friend. If anybody asked him if he would like to move from the Sqn to a cushier job in SHQ, you would more than likely get a typewriter in your gob (we didn't have computer screens then). He loved the squadron and all the exercises that we did.

The whole exercise was made more realistic as we had Harrier Air Strikes from RAF Gutersloh, plus plastic explosive charges to simulate the bombs going off. In all the excitement, someone fired a Shermully flare at the wrong trajectory and hit one of the MT techies right on the back of his helmet; what a lucky bastard he was that day. It went off at an angle into the woods. It left the techie with a bruised ego, and plus he kept his head well below the parapet after that.

Now CPL 'Dutch' Hollands had been given a few packs of mini flares to get rid of as we had loads on the squadron, and he was busying himself launching these things off in all directions. He was thoroughly enjoying himself, blasting these things off, when the next thing he knew was a directing staff member whacking him on the side of his helmet, screaming his head off and, as he puts it, nearly ripped him a new arsehole.

Unbeknownst to 'Dutch' and a few others, there was a Puma chopper parked just outside his line of sight, tucked behind a small pine plantation, and the mini flares that he was blasting off went zipping towards the chopper, just missing it, and sending the crew diving for cover. If it had hit the chopper, we would have had a great ending to the battle. The moral of the story is: never give a Guin dangerous things to play with. It was a fitting end to a good but hard exercise.

The ghostly apparitions. One of the sites we used at Sennelager for the aircraft was an old hospital. This was used during the war as Sennelager was a RandR site. This hospital was called Heimatof. It was in a bad state of repair but some of the rooms were still usable, and a lot of the engineers stored their kit in them.

On this particular night, we were all bedded down for the night in our bashers, fast asleep, when we were abruptly woken by this blood curdling scream. We all jumped out of our slugs with our weapons and ran to the stand to positions, thinking we were being attacked by the enemy. However, we eventually found out it was one of the guys an SAC, Colin Weston, who got out of his slug for a midnight piss and as he was looking around, he saw these ghostly apparitions rise up out of the ground near his basher and walk over to the hospital.

On seeing this, he screamed out, unaware that he put the whole camp on stand to. We later found out that the area where he saw the ghosts was consecrated ground and the patients that died in the hospital during the war were buried there.

It was amazing how many men moved their bashers away from that area during the night, and ended up so close together you could walk over them for 50 yards without touching the ground.

CHAPTER 2
NORTHERN IRELAND: WHEN IRISH EYES ARE SMILING

Dave Pascoe

Whilst on a tour of NI, we were due out in the Makrolon Land Rovers. A certain Chiefy J had tasked our patrol with removing the road sign 'Randox Road' not too far from Aldergrove. Presuming this formed some part of a strategic plan, our team set about hooking up chains to the rear of the vehicle and lashing them to the two concreted-in posts that secured the road sign in place. After much revving, pushing, and shoving, the pavement started to crumble and released its grip on the two posts. So sign, two posts, and two large blocks of concrete still attached were placed in the rear of one Land Rover, along with crew members crammed in, and a hasty retreat was made back to GDOC where said sign was deposited at the side of the loading bay.

Chiefy J came out and we were met with a torrent of expletives that I'll not repeat. Apparently it was just the sign he wanted, as to stick a Y in it would leave RANDY OX, which may look amusing on the mess wall.

Needless to say, we were then tasked with returning the sign back to its original location. No spades but a few hands and lots of boot stamping; good as new!

Would love to have seen the look on the council officials trying to figure that one out. Patrol members, you know who you are!

Si N. Becks Lloyd

Picture this: sitting in GDOC one dark evening as one of the signallers. Radio crackles into life and the handset is retrieved.

"Go ahead, over."

Reply: "Ooo..." followed by hysterical laughter.

Cue quizzical looks and bewilderment in GDOC. Several attempts follow, again followed by hysterical laughter from the other end.

Eventually it transpires that the foot patrol decided to cross what they thought was a concreted farm yard. Wayne 'Legs' Lemar leading the patrol. Third man in patrol steps onto said concrete, which starts to crack, and thinks, *Fuck this I'm going back*, quickly followed by the second by-now-sinking-in-the-quagmire man.

Legs however is too far to save and ends up in the shit, literally, to his chest. Needless to say, everyone collapses in hysterics as he gets dragged out.

Once they asked for and got the QRF to collect them, Legs was made to sit on the naughty step on the way back.

Steve Mullan

Again on 3 Sqn, mid-90s. While on OP Pennant, the squadron had carried out field firing at the beautiful resort of Sennybridge. CPL C, in an effort to cool down after a hard section battle drill, decided to jump into the pool at the end of the assault course. Unfortunately for him, he landed on a rock and cracked his coccyx.

Anyway, back at Aldergrove, I was sat in the mess, and in walks CPL C, walking like he's got an ironing board shoved up his ass. I couldn't stop laughing as he walked towards me. From around thirty feet away, he saw me laughing, leaned over onto the Scuffers' table, picked up his cream bun, and launched it at me! Hitting me square in the face! Excellent shot from a broken-bum man!

Robin Flack

The scene: Aldergrove GDOC, late 70s. In attendance: CO (who had walked over to GDOC), Flight Ossifer (attending briefing by CO), duty FS and sergeant, two signallers (including moi), and CO's driver.

Suddenly, the radio crackles. "Contact! Wait out!" It's the static VCP at the airport.

CO shouts, "Let's go! Dispatch stand-by unit!"

As lead signaller, I'm up and running. Duty sergeant shouts, "I'll drive and grabs the keys to the CO's special LWB Makralon Land Rover fitted with 2 x c42 radios."

CO's driver: "But, but ..."

Duty sergeant: "Never mind, get in the back!"

We leap into the vehicle, sergeant turns key ... nothing.

"Get out and bump start it!" he shouts.

"But, but—"says CO's driver.

"Do it!" is the reply. (Note: it is extremely difficult to push one of these, even with two of you.)

Several failed attempts later, the CO's driver is getting extreme GBH of the earholes for it.

"Explain yourself, airman! How did you let a vehicle so important get to this state?"

CO's driver reaches into his pocket, pulls out some keys. "Sir! On the vehicle DI this morning I reported to MT that the alternator was fucked and the batteries were flat. Shall we use the replacement?"

When we finally arrived at the VCP, all was calm. Local farmer had been out shooting rabbits (prat!), fired a cartridge full of pellets towards the VCP by mistake. He was leapt on by four hairy-arsed airborne Rocks who were a tad miffed. The CO? Embarrassed. The sergeant? Bollocked. The CO's driver? "Well, I was ordered to shut up, Sir."

Not another one! (Did I ever have time to do a proper job?) Bishops Court, mid-70s. Police club. Fan in the ceiling going full chat to clear F2F (friend-to-friend) the smoke-filled air and we are having a sing-song. The Music Man. After several unfunny Feds had done their apparently hilarious turns, they pointed at one of ours, who I shall call Tim.

"What can you play? What can you play?"

He declined.

"Fooking sing, Rock!" a voice shouted.

Tim shrugged, and began to sing. We all know the words so I won't bore you ... ending with 'I can play the stupid twat' ... blah

blah ... finishing by picking up a tray of empty pint pots from the table and launching them at the fan! Glass, Feds, and us going everywhere!

"Told you I didn't want to sing," was his final comment.

Not him again! Bishops Court, mid-70s. Section commanders were issued with dictaphones (hey, modern, eh!) to record any unusual sightings. In GDOC, playing back one tape, a familiar Scottish voice said, "Now at the pub in Strangford Lock, there are two oars in the pub doorway—that is oars as in rowing, not as in at the NAAFI bop ..."

Duty officer nearly spilled his tea!

Steve Mullan

On 3 Sqn, mid-90s, Aldergrove, a certain SAC and CPL were practising the dark art of 'skiffing' each other whenever they could.

We were sat in the QRF room watch footie on the TV when the aforementioned SAC jumped around in the background blowing his whistle, which he kept in his smock pocket.

Oh how we laughed and laughed as the penny dropped that we weren't laughing with him, but because the whistle had been right up the CPL's arse not moments before when he was out of the room!

Ian Moon

51 Sqn, either '84 or '85, RAF Bishops Court. Our section signaller was asked by the section commander to inform ops that we had broken down. We duly calculated our location and requested a recovery vehicle.

After a short while, the CP signaller came back and asked us to check the grid reference given and send it again. Having checked it was correct, we sent it again.

After a short while a rather smug-sounding CP signaller came back on and advised us to check the grid reference again as the one we had given was in the middle of the Irish Sea. To which the prompt reply was given: "That is correct, over."

By the time the recovery vehicle arrived, all that was visible above the waves was the cheese, wire-cutter, and the spotlight due to the speed of the rising tide on the shallow beach. I don't know at what point the FS on duty exploded and snatched the handset from the CP signaller, as it all becomes a bit of a blur after that. Bollockings on the radio, bollockings when we got back, and bollockings for some considerable time afterwards. I think we were 'grounded' and dry for a while too, if my memory serves me right.

How did we get into this predicament? When we had first gone onto the beach, the intention was just to drive up and down the huge empty expanse of Ballyhornan beach. However, in true Rock fashion, one vehicle had dipped a tyre in the water, then the other one went a bit further in, and the ensuing game of 'dare' continued until the inevitable happened and the engine on one of the vehicles cut out.

You can see Lenny 'One Punch' Carlyon's obvious delight at seeing the vehicle recovered from Neptune's clutches. Paddy Boswell is less impressed on kit guard.

Robin Flack

Op Banner, a time-hardened section has a new lad. He's young, keen, and a pest!

After a week of him leaping about keen as mustard at VCPs and various searches, we are getting worried that someone might get hurt trying to keep an eye on him. Action needs to be taken.

We drive to a remote wood, stand said individual against a wall, tie his hands behind his back and his feet together, and line up in front of him. He looks at six SLRs with full mags and giggles nervously. IC section then blindfolds him. Giggles stop. Quietly we remove mags.

IC section (name withheld as he became a well-respected SWO) then says, "Cock weapons! Aim!" Walks up to him and quietly says, "Someone's going to get killed if you don't calm down. Shall I cut out the middle man and do it for them now?"

He became a very good friend and a credit to the section. Forty years on and we still laugh about it; well, he giggles.

Russ Price

3 Sqn returning from four weeks in Germany in '89 to Aldergrove (during which we got released due to the Berlin Wall coming down) to find the commanding officer believed that our skills needed refreshing at Ballykillna before we were released back into the province.

D Flight had already done the journey as Advance Party, the rest of a very pissed off squadron were waiting in air ops for the Chinook, when we were informed that unfortunately the bird was unserviceable.

Thank you to a certain junior officer regiment who was on very good terms with a certain flight crew Chinook.

Spike Davies

3 Sqn, late 80s, Aldergrove. Waiting in my room all packed and ready to go on leave the next morning, flight time 6 a.m., after looking at the clock for the hundredth time decided it would be a good idea to visit the squadron bar for a beer to help me sleep. While there, met a rather tall chap called 'Tiny' Stynes for the first time, got chatting, as you do, decided to have another beer …

A few hours later, Tiny introduced me to a drinking game called 'Spoof'. After that, a complete blur.

Tiny and I awoke the next morning, 7a.m., covered in frost in a skip outside the bar, clothes in tatters, and full of scratches.

Missed my flight, then lied my arse off to Mrs D that flight was delayed.

It was only a couple of years ago while me Mrs was talking to Tiny, he grassed me up and she found out the real reason. Swine Stynes. Moral of the story: never, never, ever play drinking games with said Tiny Stynes. Filthy man.

Chris Vipond

Two tales from three. First we had our Christmas do at a local pub cause of IRA activity so it was moved to Templepatrick, to a hotel on the Antrim road. Can't remember its name. So we are upstairs on our own for security reasons, then we all move down to the bar downstairs.

Well, two gunners get talking to two girls at the bar who invite them into a wedding reception, so it doesn't take long and half the flight are in there, photos taken, smiling faces, brilliant.

Next day we find out it was some P.I.R.A chief from the border area's daughter's wedding; couldn't make it up.

Always remember them saying, "Are you the Brit side of the family?" Ha ha!

Glynn Ford

Aldergrove, 1982, C Flight, 51 Sqn. Parade outside to be addressed by warrant officer Tam Cambell. Why? Tam tells us someone is using the bath as a latrine in the block and crapping in it!

Tam asks, "Any questions?"

Step up SAC Geordie George Graham. "I have a complaint, Sir."

"What is it Graham?"

"The baths don't flush!"

Cue look of sheer horror on Tam's face! Classic.

Bill Espie

Christmas in the Garage and Jock's Amazing Mechanical Sausage. Christmas when you are away on ops is a very difficult thing to describe to the outsider. You have to experience it to know what it is like and those who have spent time away from home at Christmas may think they know what it is like but really don't. To start with, you are alone, with 120 guys within an elbow's distance. There is no privacy but you don't need any; it gets locked up until you return to normality. And at Christmas that's even more testing, like being with 120 members of your family but knowing them closer even than family and yet at the same time missing your own family.

Confused? Didn't say it was easy, did I? Well, Christmas on the border was like that. We had failed in the attempt to tempt the male population of Enniskillen to engage in a little urban wrestling and to tempt the female half to engage in some horizontal PT, so the head shed decided to keep the enlisted shower under control. They would fall back on the old remedies: duty and entertaining ourselves in the time-honoured fashion of 'It Ain't Half Hot Mum' and having a review to follow our Christmas pud.

To me this would be a welcome distraction; my exploits with the pig had severely tugged at my strings of self-confidence and I needed to have a quiet day on Christmas day as it was almost 4 a.m. when we had eventually crawled into bed after weapons had been cleaned, patrol reports written, and vehicles refuelled and checked.

As around ninety of us lived in a drill hall, the only lights were the centre lights and navigating to your bed space could be a bruising experience. This wasn't helped by Dennis the Perve having acquired, from God knows where, a life-size cut-out of a bunny girl. This had various positions dependent on where and what Dennis wanted her to do and, to be truthful, she had more than one kicking after unsolicited collisions in the dead of night before now, but this Christmas morning he had left her in the alleyway between our bed space and

Rick and Frank's. When I crawled in after doing all the reports and weapons checks an hour after he was in dreamland, I got a wallop across the shins from her as she was laid across the entrance to the space we had. This was followed immediately by me putting the head on her and a major fracas. There can be few more unedifying sights in the eerie half-dark of that smelly pit than Dennis sans his front teeth spewing forth all manner of North Northumberland curses in idiomatic 'pityakker', clad in a skanky German grey vest and underpants of similar lineage. I guess I was in such a fettle that even Dennis was slightly taken aback and struck silent by the sheer venom of the look I gave him as I tumbled, fully clothed, into my bed, pulling a brown blanket over myself and becoming immediately unconscious.

The alarm clock only showed 8:30 when I was dragged back to the world by a cheery, "Merry Christmas, support weapons, it's a bright clear day and what would you like, young Espie, rum or brandy?"

It was a dream, right? The squadron commander, dressed up in Santa Claus kit, with a big mug and two bottles, serving gunfire? That was the myth wasn't it—officers and seniors serving you tea laced with some kind of strong drink on Christmas morning?

Well, yes, actually—we had coffee. Coffee and brandy in such a liberal quantity that I was sleep deprived, exhausted, and fuzzy one moment, and after the tin lip of my water bottle cup had been shoved against my lips and a decent draught taken, I was awake, alert, and buzzing. My thoughts went along the lines of, *Jeez, what did they put in that?*

I learned years later that it's not just tea/coffee and spirit, but the secret has to be earned so you lot will not be told.

What can one do after such an awakening? Normally, after a late patrol, breakfast would either be skipped or got by the unlucky LAC dispatched to the cook house for a pile of bacon sarnies, but today we decided we would have breakfast because it was obvious that the REMFs on HQ were so taken by their do-happy-things ganja that they would continue their incessant good humour until we found a way to pee them off big time.

The mess was in the old vehicle garages and pipe range across the yard from the main block. The cookhouse was folding flat tables, long benches, and an ever-full tea urn. The cooks actually did a brilliant job of delivering us good, plain fare. None of your Italian rubbish—it was meat and two veg and Chinese wedding cake for afters. Fill 'em up with bread and gravy, these sterling sons of Albion—or something like that. The greatest value of the mess was that it was the word centre for rumour control, stoked usually by the Rocks on squadron HQ.

These were the senior or most damaged guys on the squadron, with either the nous to get themselves out of the long, dangerous, and boring patrol tasking, or those teetering on the edge of being sectioned as a danger to the public.

One of the number was Jock, a massive pockmarked monster from Glasgow. Although he was never the sharpest knife in the box, he was blessed with such a store of low animal cunning that one was always wary. His accent was music hall Glaswegian, full of, "See yu," and, "Hey, Jimmeh." Jock could always be relied on, on a scheme or two, to lift the spirit, not cause it would work but because you knew the loon would try it.

Christmas morning appearance by patrol flight was greeted with some of the usual ribald comments from the orangutans on the field flights, who were obviously unable to conduct themselves in the presence of a technically superior race, and insult flew back and forth when I was confronted by Big Bill, our FS (the same one who had deserted us in the confrontation with the pig earlier that morning).

"Esp, we have to put on something for the review after Christmas dinner. The commanding officer has invited the lady mayor and her husband to the show and we need an act. The plan is that you, Big Ralph, Dennis, and Jock will become a ballet troupe and traipse around the stage doing pirouettes and stuff to the tune of the Sugar Plum Fairy, harmless fun, three minutes and you're done. And Esp, there is no refusing this one—you take one for the team."

The look on his face told me I was going to take one, one way or another, and this was probably the least painful. So I get the condemned four together and hand over to Ralpie who is a sergeant and gets to give the orders. We spend about two hours familiarising ourselves with the music and prancing about with a combined weight of around sixty stone. We break for a brew and get our tutus fitted by the store's sergeant (no comment here as there is no statute of limitations on libel) and return to our bunks to get the Christmas mail delivered.

As we saunter across to the mess hall for lunch, Jock sidles up to Dennis and I, and in pantomime Scots, tells us his master stroke. From out of his combat jacket pocket he pulls a huge sausage, stuck through with a length of wire, to which there are two lengths of string attached, one at each end. The plan is to do the routine and at the end when Jock is carried forward in a diving pose by the three of us, he will slowly pull on one of the bits of string and the sausage would emerge from his tutu like the Shuttle Endeavour having a good morning, in the full view of the lady mayoress.

"I understand she fancies mehave took her name a couple of times foe seeing the commanding officer and she always remembers my name and smiles at me."

The response he got from us: "Away you go, you get us the jail."

Throughout the meal he continued but eventually stopped and we assumed that it was done with. After dinner and a sterling speech from herself and the commanding officer, the mess was rearranged and the show was on. I warned Ralph that Jock had been on the laughing gas and to watch him.

We were last on. With attendant leers and jeers from the unwashed on the field flights, we took to the stage. Well, it was smaller than rehearsal, and Jock had not been drinking coffee in the meantime. Still,the sight of four big lads in tutus and combat boots was obviously entertaining to all, especially the lady mayoress.

The crescendo approached and we swooped to pick Jock up and I noticed he was frantically fiddling in his jacket pocket. The struggling suddenly ceased with a beatific beam and we moved forward to the edge of the stage where we were supposed to lower him to the ground and he would roll over like a dying swan. Trouble was, his hand was in his pocket, pulling frantically at the string controlling the 'mechanical sausage', and he failed to arrest his forward momentum. As he shot off the edge of the stage, almost onto herself's lap, he grabbed Dennis with his free hand and pulled him after him. Dennis, in turn, did the same to Ralph.

I was lucky or too quick and stood gazing down on the debris of all the good relations between us and the political hierarchy of Enniskillen. The mayoress's chair had disintegrated under the assault by Jock and she had fallen to the floor, almost onto his chest. Dennis had taken out her husband completely and Ralph was picking himself out of the commanding officer's lap.

Lady mayorwas shocked but pleased that she had been saved by a member of Her Majesty's forces and smiled at Jock until she felt some movement on her leg. Looking down, she was astounded, shocked, disgusted! to see the mechanical sausage jerking up and down for all the world like the money shot of a porn movie.

The shriek was Jock's confirmation that he would be on his way home the next day to his beloved Sadie in their split-level rancho in Catterick Village. It took some time to calm the lady mayor down and a trip to the AandE for something calming to be prescribed and for the inevitable food fight to subdue.

Strangely enough, it restored the street cred I thought I had lost the previous night.

It was rumoured that the lady mayor had lobbied for years with the GOC to get a regiment squadron returned to Enniskillen.

"I ONLY COME HERE FOR THE ATMOSPHERE!"

David Matthews

NI, 37 Sqn, '73, Aldergrove. On patrol round loch side. High banks to one side, open lake the other, bends all the time that you lose sight of Land Rover all the time. Not going to mention sergeant in charge but about 2300 hours the red transmit light flashes on C42. I am second radio op by this time. I picked up the headset to listen in. I heard something garbled about ambush. Next thing we had run into back of lead LR. I heard ambush left, muster right. Now what a cock-up happened!

Danny was our driver with about three weeks left in mob. He jumped out and ran away! Jonny was acting as our 2IC. Now he had the remote headset on his head with the trailing lead. He jumped out and started to run till the lead ran out and he went down, flipped back by the crack of the lead. Tears of laughter as I write this. I grabbed the A441 and my SLR and jumped out—where to go? Well, into the lake. I waded out holding SLR and radio up. Terry Glover was left in LR as he was writing a love letter to his beloved in Belize.

Now it all went quiet. I was pissing myself, thinking I should have sent a contact wait out as second radio man, but I had been listening to Late Night Extra on it. Should I retune it? How, with my SLR in one hand and radio in the other?

I then saw a dark figure coming towards me. I froze. IRA, I thought, and in all the war films the signaller gets shot trying to send a message. Not this fellow. I dropped the A41, cocked my weapon, and started to fire. Nothing was happening as I had forgot to take the safety off.

Then I heard our sergeant say, "Right, everybody back, good drills." He had decided to carry out a practice ambush.

They had held the transmit button down as they knew I would send a contact message so while we were on transmit I could not.

Now we spent a while looking for Danny Daniles, who said, "I am out soon, not going to get shot." Jonny Bolton had a sore neck. Terry Glover had a quiet chat with the sergeant. I put the shits up the sergeant when in unload bay a live round came out. He went white when I told him what I had done under the real ambush I was caught up in.

Matt Webb

A quiet night out at the Aldergrove NAAFI. Most of 3 Sqn were on ops and just a token few popped up for a sherbet or two. Well bugger me, the place was full of Army Scare Corps and other pond life. Cats away, mice will play and all that.

Anyhow, top of the bill, mud wrestling. I felt honour bound to represent the regiment, the squadron and volunteered to engage these six scantily clad buxom wenches in hand to hand combat.

I first picked two of the 'ladies' to warm up my finely honed athletic prowess fighting skills, one of whom whispered in my ear, "Follow my lead and we'll have some fun!"

Not wanting to embarrass the young lady, I did as I was instructed and indeed, it was great fun. I was having lovely succulent, full bodied breasts slapped in my face left, right, and centre. All was going well, the ladies were now naked and much writhing and squirming about was being had. Then a member of C flight, dirty boys, stuck his index finger, knuckle deep, up one of the girl's butts. Believed to be one Gnr Ady House. No sniff test completed at scene of crime.

Well, all hell broke loose. The girl screamed to her mates, accusing me of this act of violation. I pleaded innocence on deaf ears and promptly became under attack from all six girls and a female version of Giant Hay Stacks that appeared from nowhere. One of the girls slapped me in the face with a handful of mud, blinding me. I was slip-sliding on all fours trying to escape my pummelling in the mud. I was being kicked, thumped, and whipped with a tea towel when I received the biggest wedgie known to mankind ever.

Any thought of fatherhood disappeared with my pants, via my arse. The thought of this still brings tears to my eyes even today.

I was rescued, battered and bruised, by other members of B Flight and after many years of counselling, can finally pluck up the courage to tell others of the trauma suffered whilst serving my Queen and country in Northern Ireland.

David Matthews

37 Sqn, 1973, Aldergrove. On P1, we had come back onto camp and the section had gone to mess for meal. Being the LAC on crew, was told to look after LRs .Well there I was when the radio cracked up asking for our call sign. I can remember picking up the mic and saying, "Hello, who is there? Sorry, but I am not trained on radio. They are having their meal. I will ask the sergeant to call you back when he has finished. Bye."

John Crammond

NI, early seventies. Wessex dropping our section in a less than dry but not quite marsh. Geordie Wallace Malcolm Wallace (I think), last man out with the A41 on his back. Chopper goes down low enough for us to jump without him touching down, doesn't compensate for the loss of ballast as we jump and the chopper slowly rises. By time Geordie jumps it's well in the air ... Splosh up to his waist in mud! Laughed our heads off. Wessex pilot was a navy jockey on detachment, we could tell by looking on the flight deck when we boarded to see his tan coloured boots. Same guy, when we were doing 'quick' VCPs, dropped us on a fecking roundabout and flew off laughing!

Chris Parkes Snr

Felt a right idiot after calling, "Contact, wait out," NI and we'd just done the section change over at Delta.

Our two Macrolons hurtling through the staggered junction back to camp when I heard the loudest 'crack' I'd heard since being 'fired over' at Hythe Ranges—weapon recognition training—which had only been a couple of weeks previously and still freshish in my mind. Yes, I know there should be an accompanying 'thump'! However, both Macrolons screech to a halt and the section hastily debusses, take up fire positions, and observe. Nothing to see, nothing happening so we tactically 'mount up' (okay, we just piled back in vehicles—as it was dinner time).

It was as I was heading back to my vehicle that I noticed the rubber 'Marigold' glove our lead vehicle must have ran over, inflating then exploding it, hence the 'crack'. Much hilarity and piss-taking. So much so that I couldn't reply properly to the flight commander who was by now probably ready to deploy reinforcements. I'm pleased to say he saw the funny side.

Even nowadays as a bus driver, when I drive over a plastic bottle and it 'cracks', I still chuckle to myself. I do stop short of ordering a bus load of pensioners to, "Debus!" though.

Mark Minary

C Flight, 3 Sqn, circa 1988, Bishops Court Detachment. Our section was on standby, which meant that we were over on the admin site in the blocks and in kit. Most of the lads were on their beds kipping with just a hairy Mary blanket covering them. I was wide awake and the mess had just opened, so I decided to go and get some lunch. Now for those that know, you will remember that the shortest way from the block to the mess was straight across the grass (30 yards), rather than following the footpath round by the sergeants' mess.

Anyway I'd had my lunch and was walking back towards the block across the grass when, and I'm not sure why, I turned around to see the 'SWO's' car (a rusty orange Fiat Strada) coming through the main gate and heading towards me. The SWO was a FS Guin adminner with a bad attitude. I continued to saunter towards the block ignoring his presence, although I could feel his eyes burning the back of my head. Suddenly the inevitable happened, I hear the shout of, "Gunner stand still!" In that split second I had to decide what to do. Again, "Gunner stand still!"

So, doing what every good gunner would do, I legged it back into the block, hopped onto my scratcher, pulled a blanket over myself, and played at sleeping. A minute or so later I hear the clip clop of segs on the lino floor as the SWO comes into the room. The clip clop stops and he obviously can't work out where I am as there are another seven guys under blankets kipping.

"I'll get you," he mutters before clip clopping out of the block.

Some months later, the SWO kindly had a path built from the blocks to the mess to stop us from walking on the grass. It didn't last long though because when Paddy mortared the place the path took a hit. Good times, I enjoyed it at BC.

Anthony Wells

Northern Ireland. It was a 58 Sqn tour in, I think, 1979/80. I was signaller in the back on the old C42 with certain well known Rocks whose names I will hold back, and we were on our usual mobile patrol around Loch Neagh or near there.

Anyway, we were driving around and we pulled over to let a few lads have a bit of driver training on the Macrolon LR, and as we drove along the LR in front swerved and took out a telegraph pole, oops! *Explain this away, CPL*, we all thought.

Anyway an old lady came out to see if we were okay and we were. However, the pole was not and was hanging half across the road.

We moved back a little and decided to report the pole damage, saying it was of course already down and as there was no damage really to the LR, we carried on and until this day the story has never been told and we heard nothing the whole tour.

Steve Scott

A gunner and an officer were tasked to carry out a convert job in N Ireland. In the bog standard MOD Ford escort. Unmarked apparently. Off they went, did what they had to do, and were returning to Aldergrove. Stopped by the RUC, searched, and carried on. Just before Aldergrove they were stopped by the UDR. Returned to unit, started to unloaded the vehicle, normal wash etc. before hand over. Gunner shouts out, "Sir, is this yours?"

Sir turns around and says, "What's mine?"

There laying in the boot was a Sub Machine Gun.

Panic set in. Phone calls made to both RUC and UDR. Both denied it was theirs. We couldn't even give the thing away. A week later, special branch appear to collect said weapon.

Carl Carrier

I probably had one of the best bricks during my first tour on 2 Sqn in NI, as an LAC. Wilson, Paul, Martin 'Bonny' Bonnes, and myself. One night on patrol, Cockers suddenly shouts, "Stop!" Angel hits the brakes and we screech to a stop. We all look at each other (as the other brick drives off into the distance), and Cockers asks Angel to back up a bit as he thinks he saw a wallet lying in the road. Sure enough about 50 meters behind us was a black wallet lying in the middle of an unlit road, how the hell he saw it with those crappy Macrolon Land Rover headlights I'll never know.

Anyway, Cockers asks yours truly to jump out and scoop it up. Just as I'm bending down to get it, there's another, "Stop!" I think this time from Bonny, and some mumbling happens in the landy at which point they drive about 100m down the road, stop and shout, "Okay, pick it up!" Being a sharp LAC (apart from when I knocked the camp milkman over on my Macrolon familiarisation, and made it into NI Reps) I knew what they were thinking (attractive item) so I carefully, maybe not sharply, kicked it a bit. Just to be safe, right? After successfully holding aloft my bravely secured trophy, they sped back down the road, grabbed the wallet, and split the dosh. At least I got a fair share!

Robin Flack

The 'Thickwood Run'. A few of us at Colerne lived off camp at Thickwood. We came back from a long tour and the coach dropped us off at a central point. Smokey lived about three doors away and was first off, bags in hand. By the time Chris and I had got our kit off the coach he was already at his door.

He put down his kit, he knocked the door open, two large, black arms grabbed his lapels and he was gone! Chris lived five doors nearer the drop off point than me, we casually started the 60 metre walk, getting quicker with each step. Within 10 metres, we were sprinting to get to our respective doors first, cheered on by all on the coach.

Smokey? Well later that evening me and Err (wife) went up the families club for a drink, came back about 2300. Smokey's gear was still on the doorstep! Silly but tired smile on his face the next day.

Anthony Wells

18th birthday treat—it was my first tour of NI and it was with 58 Sqn in late '79. I was eighteen part way through the tour and not allowed off camp (Aldergrove) until eighteen, as you all know. For a lovely birthday present, I was sent on a two week spotters and muggers course (learn to recognise mug shots of terrorists) with the Royal Anglian Regiment based at the New Lodge part of Belfast. If you have been in a tin/portakabin city with the Army in Belfast then you will know it's corrugated housing and hot bedding with your doss bag. I would move from bed to bed like a nomad, as did all the troops. As you found a space to kip, you would be interrupted with patrols coming and going, some trying to do their admin, and some even fake tanning with a machine that looked like a heater and silver foil around the person's neck to reflect the rays!

A few minutes past midnight, I was 18 and told I am on the 0100hrs patrol—yipee, happy birthday. Our multiple patrol were briefed along with myself and a royal marine, and out we went to load up and await the burst out of the metal gate leading onto a side road. I was tail end Charlie, another present it can't get any better! We burst out a couple at a time to confuse the maybe-terrorist looking and we settled into our 5/6 hour patrol around the streets and alleyways of Belfast's back yards. Nothing much happened and the sergeant gathered us in and said, "Right blue job and the booty, get your heads down in the alley while we guard each end and wait for the other patrol to carry out vehicles checks, and we act as satellite, and we will swap over in half hour."

Sleep, I thought, you got to be kidding, right? Job nearly done and light was coming up and we woke the patrol commander and moved into the streets. It was at this point when I was in a fire position of a doorway that an old lady approached me and said, and I will never forget it, "I think a rifle is in that top window over there," dodging and weaving to the patrol commander who was near, I told him the story.

About a few moments later, we could observe a barrel popping out of the window through the lace curtain half way up the house. A patrol was dispatched as we watched on and after a crash-bang-wallop, the lads were in and nothing really happened except a few angry words between a few of ours and some locals. The commander came over to us and gave us the news. Wait for it ... The barrel was actually copper piping being passed up to the top floor and the only way to get the pipes up was to poke it a little out of the landing window (terraced houses) and then up the stairs, laugh or what, and my backside started to regain its normal shape. Happy birthday, Tony and I will always remember my 18th.

Ian Crash Stevenson

3 Sqn, Aldergrove. All the things we did to each other if you left your room door open. Sand into your kettle. Made a nice BANG! But you didn't get a brew. Super glued boots to your ceiling or nail through one of them. Cold beans poured inside. Nice feeling that. Various items that you discovered in your bag as it went through x-ray on your way home. The dildos was the best one. Why would a Rock have one? The old trick of a pint of milk hidden in your room or the fish in the back of the TV. Crest carpets too. The crotch cut out of your DP trousers. That took some explaining in stores. Just general practical jokes we played on each other to amuse ourselves.

One more springs to mind. Down at Bishops Court. New flight commander. Very keen and into his phys. CFT time. Kit weighed in, he pisses off to the bog. Somehow two Land Rover wheel jacks ended up in his Bergen. He struggled. We laughed, so did he at the end. He never left his Bergen near us afterwards, ha ha.

Robert Booth

51 Sqn at Bishop Court Christmas, '76? Anyway we are all having the singly Christmas meal in the mess served by the officers, when the Sqn leader education officer, a well-built lass, gets up onto the table and starts doing a striptease. Several senior officers grabbed her and dragged her out just as we got to the interesting parts, spoil-sports.

Not as bad though as the lad who was caught and charged with lewd behaviour with a local girl, when he was caught in the Sanger opposite the guardroom on the floor in six inches of rain water, pounding away. Think he got jankers and a fine, we thought he had done okay as he got her to lie in the water.

Steve Mullen

3 Sqn, Op Pennant, mid 90s. SW flight had broken away from the main squadron to go and conduct mortar firing at Salisbury

plain. We were billeted in an old RAF camp (RAF locking, I think) and John Paul finds some interesting reading material left in an old locker (40+, Razzle, etc.).

Anyway, exercise over and we jump in the minibuses to head to airport for flight back and as we reach the hire car return, John realised he needed to ditch the pornos. Stuffed them into a bag and hand, minibuses home, fly to province.

Next day Paul (sergeant) gets us all in briefing room, shit hit the fan! Flight Lieutenant wife has gone batshit because she started to unpack her newly returned husband's bag and finds the grotty magazines! Oops! Wrong bag!

Steve McNulty

Out of Bounds NI. 15 Sqn, Bishops Court, 1985/86, I think. Stranmillis College Belfast, we had gone up there to play basketball. Typical gunners, we were more interested in meeting female students after the match and exchanged bodily fluids and numbers with a few.

Got back to Bishops Court, no problems. A few days later, we contacted the said females and arranged to meet them. Now the problem was the college was not in bounds for an immediate visit, I think we needed to put 48 hours' notice in or something, but we were on a promise and didn't have 48 hours. So me and Tony (I was still a LAC and Tony a senior SAC) booked out to go to, I think, the Britannia Bar on Belfast Road, arrive at bar, meet women, few drinks, then get invited back to the college we had visited the night before. Anyway, we didn't know we had been followed by RAF Police so just about to get into the female's rooms for a bit of action and we are tapped on the shoulder by two plain clothed coppers and told something like, "Under the laws of SCRAFONI and the emergency provisions act 1982," I'm not sure if that was the real act but something like that, "I am arresting you for being out of bounds."

In our wisdom Tony and I decide to try and make a run a for it. We made it to the duty car, a yellow Ford Cortina I think, drive like a lunatic back to Bishops Court, Tony was driving.

As we arrive at the gate, the flight commanding officer an Irish PO whose name I can't remember, is waiting at the gate for us and we are duly arrested. We are then interviewed and Tony and I give our stories of we thought it was inbounds because we had gone there a few days ago, so what was the problem? The PO was from Belfast and told us we were stupid and what we done could have got us killed and we were going down for this.

So we are locked up, I was also told as I played basketball it was all my doing and I must of led the SAC astray, now those of you that knew Tony, you know that is hard to do and he wouldn't of needed much persuading.

Anyway, to cut a long story short, the commanding officer came down from Aldergrove to hear the charge and at some point either on route or upon arrival, he got a phone call from someone high up saying I couldn't get sent down as I played basketball for the RAF and we were due to play the army, and my skills were required. So we got off scot-free, apart from loads of shitty jobs around the sqn. Looking back, a stupid thing to do but a promise is a promise.

Steve Mullan

Again, 3 Sqn, mid-90s. The sqn was getting ready to deploy on op pennant, I was tasked to go and collect a trailer from the green vehicle park on the other side of the airfield. We were in a rush, so I bombed around to the other side, reversed up to the trailer, hooked up, connected the lights, then floored it towards the car park entrance. There were some runners going past so I had to slam the brakes on ... only the trailer didn't stop ... it shot past the rover, light cable still connected (not for long), and narrowly missed the runners as it scraped a gouge across the Tarmac with the towing eye ... always double check the split pin is in the towing lock!

Steven Isherwood

3 Sqn, 1988, new flight commander posted in. His first task was a single man overnight OP onto Lima barrier with an IWS. He was eventually named 'Tumbledown'. When he found out about his new name, he enquired if it was because he was, "Inspiring and led from the front?"

An SAC replied, "No, it's was because you are shot away."

Leon Littler

March '99, just arrived on 3 Sqn and doing the rounds of HQ doing arrivals. Just finished in the commanding officer's office, saluted, turned, and left. Walking down the corridor, the commanding officer's dog came out of an unnamed FS office covered in

Post-It notes with a phrase along the lines of, "My owner's a cunt!" and crudely drawn penis/penises/peni. Brilliant.

Scott Ramsay

Posted to 3 Sqn, Aldergrove and my first night there was a dress like a scouser night at the Bimble Inn. So there we are all dressed in our three stripe trackies, moustaches, and scouser 118 118 wigs. A couple of new guys undertaking some drinking game initiation and, as I was also new, I was tasked with knocking out a para reg sergeant who had been jumping a few of the 3 Sqn younger lads over the last few weeks after the NAAFI bop. Now those that know me, in my younger naive years, I was delighted at this initiation and para regiment sergeant was duly taken care off, however, I was also duly arrested along with a few others, all sat in the guard room with our trackies, moustaches, and wigs still on, giving it, "Alright, alright, calm down, calm down," to the duty RAF police, who, to be fair, didn't take it too much further.

Mac McCarthy

RAF Aldergrove, 2000/01, 3 Sqn had just moved into a nice spanking new ops building which we now shared with everybody else. One morning, I arrived in the QRF room ready to take over, to be met with a 3 ft tall stuffed tiger and some of my lads giggling. "Where's that from?" I asked.

"We found it downstairs in the aircrew place."

Found it? *Pinched* it! "What do you intend to do with it?"

And that's when their plan fell apart! After ruling out giving it back (because they wouldn't!), a decision was taken to hold the tiger hostage. An old Sun newspaper was meticulously cut up, hostage note created, photo of said tiger with a 9mm pistol at its head with a UVF flag in the background, photocopied, then posters distributed around station at 'really early o-clock'. Essentially, the ransom note asked for a thank-you letter from the charity of the squadron's choice for a small donation of around £100. Peanuts to a flying squadron, a charity gains, tiger goes home, easy. Oh no, the squadron (230) kicked off, they even sent their own Rocks round to see if we knew of its whereabouts.

Apparently 230 stole the tiger from an Italian Tiger Squadron previously and were due to give it back. Hmm, best pay the ransom then lads!

Well, the tight gits never did pay up, so they never got the tiger back. As far as I know, it retired back to the mainland to be used as a bed for one of the lad's dogs!

Stuey Rowbotham

3 Sqn Thai-themed night in the Bimble Inn, organised by Dave Pooley and Paul Hindhaugh. Full boxing ring erected, maybe not a great idea with a load of pissed Rocks. Recall Jerry Brown, a regiment boxer, beating the shit out of a very lightweight Paul Elvis Elvidge. Then it was decided to move onto tag team boxing. The Flight Lieutenant Jim (Magee?) and Bomber George onto two of the lads. Nobody liked the boss so all of a sudden, stray punches from outside of the ring began to rain down on him, before long it's like a riot, and he's had a right good twatting!

He's black and blue and walks down to the gate house to get the plastic police, who basically tell him they wouldn't dare go into the bar as they would get the shit kicked out of them!

The next day, everyone is called in by the boss who goes through everyone like a dose of salts. He then turns to Bomber and says, "And you, you cunt, you were my partner, why didn't you fucking help me?"

Bomber's response, "You didn't tag me, Sir!"

Everyone just pissed themselves laughing. Best night I had out on 3 Sqn and there were many!

Kurt Forster

So I was working in the JOC on 3 Sqn in about '93 when I overheard a grid reference over the NI-wide net of an IED. When I plotted the grid, it was the main road between Antrim and the Port Rush ferry terminal.

I told the IC and it was put out of bounds. For the next 12 hours, all traffic coming and going between Aldergrove and the port was really routed.

When we checked in about it, we found out that I got the first two letter identifiers wrong. Oops. I'm bad.

Mac McCarthy

RAF Aldergrove, 2000/01, 3 Sqn. We were tasked with a foot patrol from lima gate to kilo gate. No dramas, a nice easy job. I'm bored with these patrols, so I give command to my 2IC (Larry Grayson, if I mind right). I take up post on the flank with SAC X. It's a crap job because you're paralleling the tarmac but pushing through gorse, brambles, barbed wire, ditches, etc. SAC X is wanting me to use the road as it's easier. "No, we're doing it properly," says I. This goes on for the entire patrol.

As we approach kilo gate, we can see the wagons ready to pick us up. Even so, I break left through bushes to cover the flank and do it all right. SAC X grudgingly follows, but gets stuck in the bushes.

"C'mon, stop messing about, and get here."

"I can't, I'm stuck on the barbed wire fence."

"What are you on about? There's no barbed wire, I just walked through it."

Then SAC X starts howling and screaming in a non-pretend manner, I go and pull him clear of the bush and hear a loud buzzing noise. I'd only disturbed a wasp nest that was now getting fired in amongst SAC X waist parts, and having a right old go at him.

Leon Littler

3 Sqn, Xmas, '99. JRM Xmas dinner and the squadron (A and D flight, I think) had set up our own top table at the end of the mess nearest our block, beer is flowing and spirits are high.

The two civi trolley-dollies, Donna and Shirley, are being kept busy keeping us topped up with free beer. Crate after crate being destroyed by us. At one point they commented that even by Rock standards, we were knocking them back!

After the obligatory food fight (a few full cans may or may not have been launched towards the Scuffers' tables!), it was NAAFI bop, then party at Wessex block, courtesy of the twenty or so slabs of lager we'd been sliding out of the fire door behind our table and in through the fire door of Wessex block!

Sean Johnstone

Reindahlen, late 80s, I pop over from 3 Sqn (NI) to see my old mate NM who was on GDT there. Long story short, last night we are in the NAAFI bar along with DD, last orders and shutters are down. Two mystery men come up and start to talk to NM and DD, the big one is talking to the vertically-challenged NM and vice versa with the other two.

Out of the blue, big bloke takes a swipe and NM, bad move, as NM ducks the punch and lets fly with a cracking right hook, mystery man is then grabbed by the hair by NM who proceeds to batter his head into the bar shutters from one end to the other. At the same time, mystery man number two makes his move but DD is a boxer and his reaction is with lightning speed, first a left mystery man does a 360, followed by a right, a 360 in the opposite direction, but does not go down.

Leaving our two mystery men battered and bruised, we leave at speed, when we are clear of the incident I ask them, "WTF was that all about? They both said they had no idea."

I patted them both on the back and thanked them for an entertaining send-off, back to 3 Sqn.

Robin Flack

Sat in GDOC Bishops Court, phone rings, "Ah, Flack, glad it's you. Have got you records with you?"

"Err yes, Sir."

"Good, bit of a problem, got a party on Saturday at Aldergrove, need a DJ."

"But, Sir, I'm on shift Saturday."

"No, you're not, change in shift pattern."

"Oh. But how do I get there, Sir?"

"Well, by chance, a Wessex is on radio trials in your area at 1400, be on the helipad. Oh, by the way, it's back on mech trials on Sunday at 1300, strangely enough going back down your way."

"Err okeydokey, Sir."

I don't know how many misuses of kit men and service support were involved, but hey, it was an officer's birthday.

Chris Pacey

3 Sqn fancy dress BBQ at Aldergrove prior to an Iraq tour. One lad dressed as Hitler, another as an SS guard, complete with Swastika, partnered a group of AQ suicide bombers, with plastic AKs, hard targeted over to the officers' mess to cause some sort of levity. About fifteen minutes later, the mess manager come over to the BBQ to complain that the lads had formed a Guard of Honour outside the mess and were going into the present with the green plastic AKs each time somebody left or entered.

"Who is in charge here please?"

Mark Knopfler (Guss Powell), complete with guitar and head band, answers, "I am, why?"

"Can you control your lads please, they are scaring the families on an open day. One of the junior officers even returned a salute to a terrorist!"

"Okay, my 2IC will sort it out for you." He turns to a group of prostitutes (Dave Ford-OC B, Liam Mitchell-OC C) and says, "Guy Ford, can you sort this please?"

"No problem, boss." Off three whores go, wobbling on stilettos in miniskirts to retrieve the wayward menace to society collective! Top squadron with cracking lads. Work hard, play hard. *In Arduis Audax.*

Fraze Barkaway

1 Sqn, C Flight, NI, Alexander barracks. We are all in eight man rooms so privacy is non-existent and banging one out in the bogs isn't an option either.

I'm casually walking down the corridor when XXXX crashes through a door on the left into the corridor, he's wearing nothing but a tiny towel around his waist and carrying a TV/video combo. As I get closer, I notice he's not steady on his feet and drenched, and I mean *drenched* in sweat, he can't nearly hold himself up and is sliding along the wall towards me, leaving a sweat trail on the wall like a slug.

Genuinely concerned, I ask him if he's okay, expecting him to collapse any second when he explains between gasps that he's fucking great as he's just spent an hour in his homemade wanking booth with some of the best VHS porn known to man, grins, and slides off down the corridor, drained but happy.

It's only as I read the sign on the door he just crashed through I realise the situation: 'DRYING ROOM'.

Noel Robinson

I remember, whilst on 3, we had been volunteered to learn to drive the Tavern armoured vehicle (meant to be a snatch replacement). So the night before, like all good Rocks on a driving course, we got pissed. We turned up next morning feeling slightly under the weather. Next to where the snatches were parked there was these brand new Taverns. So we got introduced to our instructors, I think we were four to the vehicle. The four I was in had a female RLC corporal, straight away the smell of alcohol didn't endear us to her. So introductions over, she pulled the vehicle to the middle of the parking area. We got a famil of said vehicle, then it was time to drive. So up steps a young SAC Sheard to go first. So we all get in, now the Tavern was an American vehicle and had stick shift. Sheardy put into gear and off we went, unfortunately he put into reverse and we went into a 3 Sqn snatch. RLC corporal was going mad, to which the reply went something like, "Don't worry, love, it's one of ours." Found drive and off we went. The word charge got mentioned by the pongo, but was soundly laughed at. Good days on a great sqn.

Steve Bateman

On a quite Sunday afternoon patrol while on 3 Sqn, we were on the edge of TAOR near Ligeneal, heading down a very tight country road. But this was Nov, 1993 and live on Sky at 1600 was the Toon vs Liverpool.

Heading towards me down this very tight country road was an OAP in a Mini Metro. We ended up bumper to bumper and the lady was going nowhere. So we reversed back a couple of metres, and the lady tried to squeeze passed us, then stopped because it was too tight. So being a true gent, we move as far left as we could possibly go. The OAP beeped her horn to thank us, and at that moment the road gave way and the wagon rolled onto its roof in the field. We were upside down hanging by or seatbelts and yes, my OAP never looked back. There were no injuries to anyone only my pride. We had to wait for the Paras MT to pick us up.

And yes, I missed Andy Cole scoring a hat trick.

Sid Wright

Aldergrove, I'm driving down towards one of the hangers when padding across a flight line comes a bloody great German Shepherd. Thinking that someone's pet had got out, I did my responsible bit. Stopped the LR, got out, and whistled the dog over. Opening the back hatch, I told him to get in, which he dutifully did. Jumping back in, I drove round to the JOC to report said dog to the RAFP so he could be returned to his owners.

Arriving in the car park, I can see a lot of activity as the Scuffers are all in a huddle and looking like they have a job on.

I park up and go into the sergeant in the JOC asking what's up. "A patrol dog has chewed his way out his kennel and gone AWOL," he explains. "We're about to tannoy everyone to get indoors as he's a vicious bastard."

"German Shepherd, black muzzle?" I ask.

"Yeah, you seen him?"

"Better than that," I says. "I just picked him up, he's in the back of my wagon."

"Show me," comes the order.

Off we go, "Be careful, he won't let you near the Land Rover," at which point he shuts up as I open the back hatch, whistle the dog out, and then fuss it. I was not flavour of the month with the police after that ... right.

Kurt Forster

So whilst on 3 Sqn, we're off on foot patrol in Armagh after being dropped off in a puma. We do our stint and we are in a field waiting to be picked up and a chopper arrives. But it's a lynx. Well eight gunners with rucksacks and ammo are not light. Lynx pilot says, "Sorry, can only take four of you, and we don't know when we can pick up the next four."

I have never seen eight guys get onto a chopper so quick. He tried to take off and had to drag the skids for 200m before he had lift.

Again on 3 Sqn, about '93, the search team gets deployed to Armagh. We get told to search ammo that is in the area. So as time goes on more and more search teams are turning up.

It turns out that one of our glorious Wessex pilots, who had a green RUC officer in the back, decided to make him puke up. Well after hedge skimming and doing some other shit, he does a stall turn to the right. Needless to say GPMG rounds don't stay in the tin when turned upside down. They fell out the box and the link split. They then started to spiral out of the door and into the field below. The squadron search team and the on duty flight had a great day and night searching the fields.

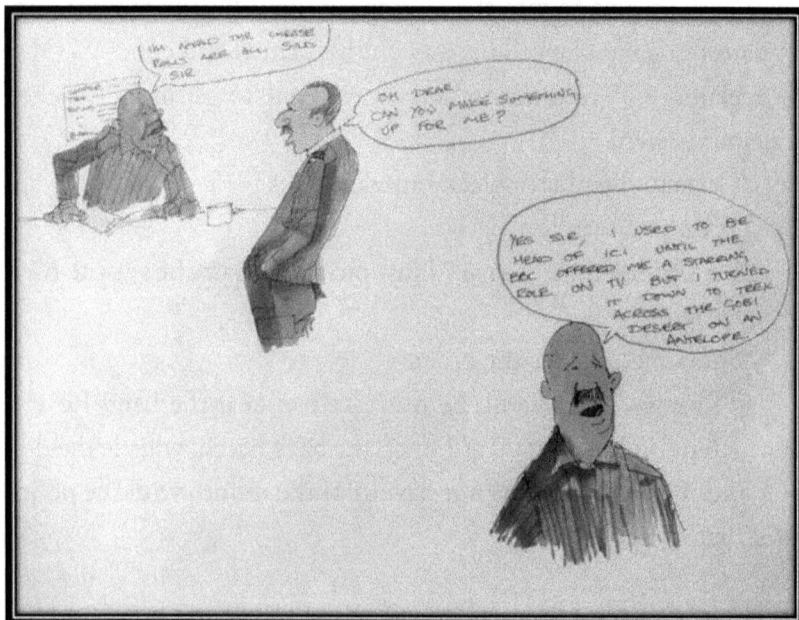

Robin Flack

Woohoo, it's him again! (Ohffs, thought he was dead). NI, late 70s, zoo night. A young civi lad is there giving it a bit large with the girls, God's gift, etc. Not many impressed as 2 Sqn were there (incoming!). He swaggers up to the DJ (ahem, moi!) "Oi! Play some Rosetta Stone, mate."

My reply: "I would rather poke my eyes out with a fork."

Him: "Why?"

Moi: "Cos you were crap in the Bay City Rollers, and you were crap in Rosetta Stone, go play with yourself."

He didn't ask again, last I heard he was a failed porn star (?) in the States. Must have taken my advice, the wanker.

Fraze Barkaway

So it's NI stories? I forget the year but it was late on maybe '98? 1 Sqn, C Flight. As the peace process took hold, we were doing less and less, and in line with govt policy, were being a bit cuddly in the approach. The troops were getting, shall we just say, danger bored?

Aldergrove is buzzing as President Clinton and what appeared to be his entire air force, and entourage are on camp, and we need to be kept at a safe distance, so C Flight are tasked to do riot training and that's exactly what we do.

Problem is C Flight are known for getting a bit out of hand, and that's exactly what happens, riot training gets brutal very, very quickly, with lads genuinely trying to kill each other whilst giggling that psychotic giggle that only a fired up Rock battering his mates can do.

Only one small problem, our discreet out of the way location has a very special visitor and his entourage transiting through it unexpectedly. So, there are the lads, battering guys dressed in civvies with batons, when the entourage passes by, shiny cars with faces of horror pressed up against windows. Mark Bottrill, I believe that day, proved that if his career as a flight cdr was over, he had a very bright future in the diplomatic corps or as a UN special envoy, as he blagged us out of that heat, which was considerable at diplomatic level!

Another Aldergrove tale of woe, I can't remember where we had been, but we had been and two of us were at the POL point filling the snatches with petrol. All of a sudden there is a screech of brakes and the sqn 2IC—who, if I'm blunt, wasn't a bad bloke, just tightly wound and a bit odd—screamed at us to get our berets on and report to his office.

So after a bit an, "Oooh!" and holding up pretend handbags, we eventually appeared in his office. The pair of us stood to attention and first, he went ballistic at the other lad and when he had finished shouted, "Dismissed!"

Sherlock duly saluted and left. Leaving me stood there thinking, *Dismissed? Fuck me, when did this become the USMC?*

My thoughts were interrupted when the 2IC suddenly pipes up and says, "Barkway, can I be frank with you?"

My reply, "Yes, Frank, as long as I can still be Barkway."

Flipped a switch in his head because he vaulted the desk and chased me down to the crew room kicking me up the arse calling me a cunt. Out of character for him and we laughed about it later.

Geraint Jones

Well, we never did catch the phantom bed space shitter on 15 back in '89, to the best of my memory, his last victim of that particular tour was Moggy Gardener. I remember being awoken to screams of terror one early November morning as the phantom had struck again, leaving his cylindrical calling card in Moggy's green slug.

For whatever reason known only to him, but it may be a case of mild PTSD being covered by the phantom's droppings, Moggy decides to blame a very intoxicated Dan Dare that proceeded to give him a very shiny black eye. The phantom's identity, to the best of my knowledge, remains a mystery, dirty bastard.

Ally Atkinson

Covering the Holy Cross Girls School incident we were operating out of Girdwood Barracks. Rolling around the Belfast AO when, as we are driving along Antrim Rd, I think, me (driver) and Georgie (sergeant) spy a couple of likely lads lingering on the corner. We both shout to the top cover lads, Pat and another (forgot his name) to keep an eye on said lads as we drive past.

Suddenly a large object is thrown towards the top cover lads and a shriek echoes from the back telling us that Pat is hit and is strangling himself on his sling. We go foot down through the streets to get to Girdwood back gate with frantic calls telling them to open the gate.

In we fly, with Pat being supported by another, we skid to a stop, leap out and help get Pat, who is unconscious, out and to the medic.

Pat comes round and looks at me and Geordie, "Why didn't you duck?" I asked

"We can duck?" replies Pat.

The object thrown at the vehicle turned out to be a snooker table leg, ouch!

Another time, our squadron is completing public order training at Newtown training facility. All personnel are given the rules and regulations covering what we can and can't do in the village.

Scenario 1: squadron completes a move through the village, securing areas, arresting scumbags (army guys playing terrorists), etc. We finally arrive at the field at the far end of the village, squadron is line abreast, two ranks deep, when the order to dress rearwards is bellowed out. The entire squadron in unison steps backwards about ten paces, all except one lad who is daydreaming. Georgie then, smart as a carrot and twice as big as an orange, strides forwards, wallops him on the helmet with his riot baton in front of the entire squadron, and then steps back into line. Sorted!

Geraint Jones

On NI tour, '89, we were all pissed up in the NAAFI with Chiefy, the bar shuts abruptly at midnight. Keen for another drink, we weigh up our options. Hmmm, severely limited. Chiefy pipes up, "Well I'm off to the sergeants' mess for a top up, you cunts can't come in, as you have no neck ties."

Obviously this was taken as a challenge, and with the promise of extra rations, we retire to the block to make some 'ties'. Armed with bayonets and green, issue cotton towels, fuelled with our belly full of ale, we proceed to rival any Milan fashion expert and make our way back to the sergeants' mess looking like a cross between tramps and refugees, but all in all pleased with our efforts. We were immediately bullocked and slapped when we arrived, and Chiefy in between hysterical, almost psychopathic rants and laughter gave us half a case of wobbly as long as we never came back again. We didn't.

CHAPTER 3
RAFP SCUFFER'S DELIGHT

Stephen Headey

I will start the ball rolling with the RAFP theme. I was on exercise with 33 Sqn choppers and we were just outside Newcastle on a training area. Well we also had a detachment of RAFP with us. As per normal guard duty was order of the day and we shared this with the Scuffers.

10.00pm at night a bit of banter with the Scuffers saying that you guys will never get the best of us, we are too good. Really?

Guard shift change completed and SWB Land Rover with blue light handed over. The Scuffers take their place and settle down in the guard room and watch TV, parking the Land Rover directly in front of them in the light and within their view at all times. Super alert as always.

Cue us early in the morning. We remove the blue light and replace it with an amber one all in front of them. 0430, a no duff situation occurs and zed victor one springs in to action. Lights on. Blue light on ... Hang on, why is it amber? Red faced coppers look stunned and can't work out how it was switched without any of them seeing it. Work that one out, Sherlock.

Next morning OC police blows his top and plod gets a bollocking.

Wildenrath, 1983, summertime. A party was being held at RAFP club and a few of us were invited. So everything going along swimmingly until one narky copper took offence to one of the guys who, let's be fair, nicked his girlfriend. That being said, the copper was getting worse for wear with drink and we were asked to leave. The disco was pumping and everyone was having a good time. So reluctantly we did so without incident and waited outside.

Unknown to me one of the guys had placed CS tablets in the ashtrays before he left. It didn't take long. First one then two complaining it was smoky in there. A minute later, it was a full on explosion of coppers, wives, girlfriends, and civvies pouring out of the club. No sense of humour them coppers.

Robin Flack

TV room, Bishops Court. Thursday night bop. LAC acting, SAC acting, CPl acting, Pratt of her Mages fines RAFP.

Trying to watch a program, suddenly shouts without turning round, "Will you lot pack it in at the back! I get one night to enjoy myself and you are ruining it!"

The reply: "So do we! Feck off!"

Bishops Court. Just finished my stint on the decks, get a message, "You are needed by the fire exit."

Off I toddle, full of anticipation. At the fire exit is a young lady. Result! Oh shit, it's my mate the doggie handler's girl. Oh well he's working, so then the fire exit door opens and said doggie man comes in c/w 90lb GSD. "Hi mate, can you hold my dog? She's up for a bit."

"Yeah, no problems, mate."

"Oh and Rob, please don't keeping calling 2s up, it puts me off."

So I take the dog walkies instead—ish.

So, we arrived back from a tour of Op Banner to Catterick, my neighbour and I both on the sqn with the deformed right arm. We both have GSDs. The day after getting home, a 4 tonner arrives by the back fence, out jump six sqn guys and start tugging at what looked like a shed from the back. Turns out to be a 10 foot by 6 foot dog kennel complete and ready to go.

"Where did you find that, mate?" I enquired.

"Aldergrove," was the reply. Turns out that he had seen an un-occupied dog kennel and hatched a plan.

"Do they know you've got it?"

"Nah, there was no dog in it and needed one, gissa hand."

So much for the vigilance of the RAFP dog men!

Graham Spike Thompson

Aldergrove Marching Season '99, and tensions were high due to another ban on the Drumcree March. RUC are manning Delta Victor PVCP and to gain experience RAFP are providing the vengeful operator. My multiple is about to deploy on a routine task and duty plod asks if we could drop off cpl plod to DV. Said plod was a very green and new to province cpl who had never been outside the wire.

"No problem," says I. "Put him in the back of my wagon."

"Mount up and go," said plod sat behind me.

As we approach Hotel CP, I start a fictitious radio conversation with Zero, winking at the two lads in the back, due to the earpiece, plod is oblivious.

"10B, confirm crowd numbering 100 plus massing on Airport Road? 10B, roger confirm crowd are becoming hostile? 10B, roger, petrol bombs sighted."

Plod has been registering all this and the colour is starting to drain from him.

"Right, lads, this is kicking off, close the doors and hatches. Plod, are you public order trained? No FS. Right you stick with me. Kit on, lads." Two lads in the back start to put on shin and forearm protectors. Plod is practically filling his pants now. "Right, check chin straps and CBA, that goes for you too, plod." He is whiter than his SD hat now!

"10B, confirm petrol bombs thrown at DV? 10B, roger, baton rounds fired. Feck me, lads, this is going to be fun!" Plod is crapping himself!!

Driving up to the Airport roundabout, "Standby, standby."

Turn the corner, lovely bright sunny day and not an orange man as far as the eye could see. The whole vehicle looked at plod, "Whhhhhaaaaaaaah?" He fekkin hated me for the rest of his tour!

Dave Capps

Honington, mid-90s again, a mixed flight of Rocks and RAFP were on a field ex at Barnham. Members of a sister flight provided the enemy and after three days of back and forth, the ex was to end with an assault on the old bomb dump area. Battle ensues and the blanks, smoke, and TFs are flowing fast and thick. The supposed hostiles dramatically succumb to the onslaught in a grotesque and military manner, as befits the bad guys. OC the flight (RAFP) slaps himself on the back for a job well done and gathers his troops for a debrief (note: no endex called). At this point, a female steps from behind cover and proceeds to empty blank automatic fire into the mass of troops. OC calls foul play and threatens the op team for using unqualified and unauthorised personnel with weapons. To which he is informed that the female is a WRAF, fully green carded and trained. Also the former lady of one of the enemy team. Lesson learnt? It isn't over till the lady with the SA80 sings, or endex is called ... and not all baddies are blokes

Wayne Holliss

Occasionally on 48 Sqn the odd gunner was given the opportunity by the station commander to par take in two weeks RandR, sometimes even three. This time I was chosen to be the lucky recipient, and only after a week from getting back from a four month det to Belize, so off I trot for an overnight stay at Kinloss before flying down to RAF Northolt and two weeks of fun, Brasso, and bullshit.

Now as luck would have it, all the screws and SWO were all old timers and loved Rocks, except one ex fat useless excuse for a copper, so muggings here had fallen on his feet. The SWO in particular pissed himself when told why I'd been sent down, yet another tale to tell, so he always made effort to have me help him out.

So I gets marched up to the officers' mess this day to help set up for the summer ball. The SWO starts by asking, not telling, *asking* me to set out the chairs in the tent outside. Which start doing. Anyway, there I am, doing the biz, when up comes this pig zob. Now I didn't take a blind bit of notice of the twat as he stood there looking me up and down. The next thing I know he calls me over and starts having a right go at me for being incorrectly dressed for my situation. So I give him the 'what the fuck are you on about look'.

He points to my regt shoulder slides and tells me to get them off as I'm a prisoner and have no right to wear them. This I flatly refused to do. The next thing I know he's gone off one threatening to have me shot, hanged, and all sorts of nasty things.

With that the SWO turns up and asks what's going on, so plod starts demanding that I remove my slides and all this bollocks, to which the SWO replies, "Why should he? For as a member of the regt he's earnt the right to wear them, plus he's an airmen under sentence not a prisoner, thus retains his rank," ... so piss off, Sir.

Well I'm ordered off to the mess bar, and walk away thinking one–nil, where the SWO joins me after putting the pig right. He then goes behind the bar and says, "What you drinking?"

Well I say, "I can't, Sir, I'm in the clink."

"It's an order, gunner."

"Pint please."

Chris Taylor

RAF Wittering Sgts' Mess in 1994. I was serving on the ASU and we were having exchange drinks with the officers, one of whom was a rather portly RAFP WRAF. She and I are stood at the bar waiting to be served when her pager starts bleeping in the back pocket of her rather tight OGs. Some wag in the bar immediately shouts out, "Watch out, lads, it's reversing!"

Paul Martin

RTU in the mid-80s and we were tasked with providing a kit for, I think it was Waddington Air Show. So we get there Friday night, park the kit up and hit the NAAFI. Several shandies later on the way back to the five star transit block, it was decided it was time to go souvenir collecting. Up a lamp post I go, and from nowhere appears the RAFP. I'm ordered to get down. So I rightly jump, landing on the police Land Rover roof, putting both feet through it. On landing I shout, "Leg it!" John Truscott, Gary Nealon and the rest of the crew do a star burst, I run off escaping the snow drop only to run into a dog handler and his GSD.

All I remember hearing was, "Stop or I'll release my dog." Then waking up in a cell the next day.

On returning to West Raynham, I was marched in front of Jake Edwards, charged with resisting arrest. Fortunately, the police submitted a written statement. So when it came to my turn, I looked at the sqn leader and said "Sir, I would like to remind the court that I am downgraded with hearing loss and didn't hear the police officer command me to stop."

Over the top of his glasses was a cheeky smile and the words, "Case dismissed."

Result! Cheers, Jake!

Dave McCallen

Can remember the end of '82 on 1 Sqn. The squadron had gone off to Sennelager for field firing (quite usual for December), I remained behind as I was clearing and leaving for the delights of 48 Sqn at Lossiemouth. I was tasked with being escort to one of the lads for his court martial. I can still remember his face but can only remember his name being Terry. He was accused of beating up three pongos but always maintained it was self-defence. Terry had got a smart London barrister in who was doing a great job but it still wasn't looking too good.

We were sat talking during one of the breaks and it was mentioned about the record of one of the pongos, said barrister picks up on this and says the prosecution were supposed to declare all this information. Barrister then has the officers removed while he argues the case to the judge advocate. Subsequent result, case dismissed as evidence from pongos can't be trusted. On way to the mess for dinner Terry just turns and says, "I done it just like they said."

Anthony Rodgers

On jankers at Honington, '99. Scuffers have me as duty bitch for the weekend. So one smart arse Scuffer tells me to go and hand wash the plod car, in he walks with a bucket and plonks it in front of me already full of water, obviously a task he had been dicked with but gave it to me. So I take the bucket and plunge my hand in to the soapy cold water looking for the sponge, and joy of joys, pull out some Scotchbrite, you fucking dancer. So I begin to scrub the car with the cleaning materials given,—lots of paint taken off the car.

Scuffer comes out to check work and goes mental, so off I go to see OC police and get away with it due to the plod giving me the cleaning material, as it was all I had, it's all I could use, of course I played the thick as shit Rock Ape card as well.

Oh and I found a Rolo on the seat in the car which I used to push deep into the ignition key slot and rimmed the steering wheel with my cheesy, post-wank bell end. Job done. Hope the twat could smell it on his hands.

Derek Wagle

Coppers raided Block 50 at Bruggen one night chasing a gunner and his girlfriend. Having locked himself in his room and refusing to come out or even acknowledge he was there, two young coppers continued banging on his door. Eventually they left to get 'back up'. By the time they got back, the girlfriend was already hiding in the loft and the gunner was in another room. We pulled the door frame off, ripped at the plaster, and put a hole in the door. A short while later the two sprog coppers turned up with sgt police and WO Phil Marcer (RIP. Sorry we made your life a nightmare, Sir).

Of course the two Scuffers denied they had caused the damage, but with a little bit of gunner indignation complaining about how they marched in and started banging shit out of doors, "And just look at the damage, Sir!" Both Scuffers were ripped into by Mr Marcer—the look on those Scuffers faces was a classic … all this allegedly, of course.

Derek Wagle

Blue light story—mine and Ricky Bedward's (?) going away do in Bruggen at the footie club. A packed bar and the lads are bored so they are outside nicking anything not nailed down and bringing it to the bar. Plod turn up to reclaim their stuff, which of course we deny having! I'm on the pool table in a fed dayglo jacket jam slinging a pint of curry from an upturned blue light—wasn't me, guv!

Geoffrey Herschall

After starting some 'bother' in the community centre at Wickrath, a RAFP locked himself in a toilet cubicle and shouted, "I'm not coming out until SAC (RAF Regt) leaves!"

Robin Flack

RAFP were always going on about how 'safe and protected' they were in their breezeblock tower on the domestic site gate, "unlike you muppets prancing about." We invited them down to the 25 metre range and showed them what a 7.62 round can do to a breezeblock at 25 metres. Formal complaint followed from IC plod for frightening his men, good job, but, for his own safety, after that we didn't have many dealings with the RAFP, except on the football pitch, but that's another story.

Chris O Gorman

1 Sqn Laarbruch, now I can't remember if it was my 1st or 2nd tour (done 3 altogether). But there was a right shit of a copper, he hated the Rocks something rotten, every time he saw you he'd tell you to get a haircut even if you've just had one. Now this twat was really pissing the guys off so one night a few of the lads waited for him to come out of the police club, grabbed him, took him to a nice quiet area, and explained their concerns to him.

After a few days in the med centre, he went to the compound with a flt sergeant and a couple of his cronies to see if he could recognise the explanation party; he had no chance as the guys were all camouflaged up when they done him in.

Anyway, after a couple of weeks, he was called to the station commander's office and told he was being posted back to the UK, not for doing a bad job, but for his own safety. After that we didn't have many dealings with the RAFP, except on the football pitch, but that's another story.

1 Sqn again, this time it's Aldergrove. Myself and other who goes by the name of Bob Clegg, we have just left the NAAFI a bit worse for wear and heading towards the main gate, and there they stand waiting for us, two coppers and a dog—yep, you know what's coming next. "IDs," says one, no please or anything. So I show the snowdrop my ID, he's happy so I go through the gate. Next it's Bob's turn, and yes, he shows the dog his ID, as quick as a flash the dog bites him on the nose. His nose pissing with blood, and me pissing myself with laughter. Who said police dogs haven't a sense of humour.

Jamie Quinn

Since I started the Regt Historic Flight, which shows the history of our Corps, we try to live up to the traditions of the gunner. At Waddington Air Show, we were in the airmens' mess queue, behind me is a snowdrop, we get chatting. I ask if F1 250 still gets shown to brain on a chain. He doesn't know as he is station plod. On exiting mess, he is stood in animated conversation with others. He chases me down the road, I stop and he says one word, "Yes!"

It's nice to hear that tradition survived all changes the service has been through

Tony Tom Sawyer

RAF Brüggen 1986/87. Rugby game between 37 Sqn vs RAF police. Some pig gets nailed in a tackle and they need the bucket of water and sponge. The police don't have one so they call on John Grieves with ours. He runs on, puts the bucket down, takes a photo, and tells the pig "Fuck off, you're not having the Rocks' water," and runs off with the bucket again.

Michael Hobbs

Was at St Athans doing the driving course, and as expected, go for drinks in the NAAFI later that night. I had a few too many sherbets, and got into an argument with a firemen who says he was ex REG. Turns out he never passed basics, but went around telling people he was an ex Rock. So, after a few buckets of wobbly water, he starts slagging off the regiment, so me, being all new and shiny, stand him up and knock him sparko on the floor.

Naturally the Scuffers were called, and because I didn't go quietly, had to be dragged to the guard room. I got a bollocking from the guard commander, and sent back to my pit.

I finished the course three days later, but was up in front of OC A FLT and a guinzob back at 66. Boss gave me a right chewing out in front of the zob (OC FIRE). With that done, the OC FIRE left, and when he was out of earshot OC A FLT says, "That was just for show, next time you hit someone, please make sure they don't get up again."

Anthony Wells

RAF Gatow before the wall came down. Whilst on 1 Sqn at RAF Laarbruch in the early eighties we were sent to Berlin to take part in the Freedom of Spandau and I drove the four tonner there and back with the No 1s in the back (that's another story and many more on this trip). Anyway, one venture into Berlin centre had us getting the early morning bus back, about 4 in the morning (practice parade at 0800) and we were on a curfew, which of course we mostly ignored.

As the word was out that the Rocks were on camp, the RAF Police and guardroom staff were to be on their best eyes peeled vigilance. Me and a few lads crept along the floor through the Gatow entrance and just near the guardroom door were a couple of bikes, of course we nicked them and 2s up along the road to the transit block at the end of Gatow.

However, we were rumbled and the Snowdrops were on route. Right we said, ditched the bikes, and off into the woods to hide and move. Suddenly the feds arrived with dogs and lights a flashing! We kept still and quiet and slowly made our way to the block, got in just as the feds arrived only to find us all in the block fast asleep. Thinking better of it they did not search the block and if they did they would have found us semi-clothed in bed. Another great escape!

The next morning we were briefed on behaviour and curfews with the iron curtain only being metres away and we survived capture.

Glyn Jones

The Great Escape. Back in the distant mid-70s I was based at Neth-eravon and, as it was a sort of dead camp, we used to go to the bop at RAF Uphaven, which was full of WRAF. One night, at chucking out time from the NAAFI, myself and Ray Kyle got into a slight altercation with some Guins and taught them some manners (okay, we pasted them) which resulted in us both being arrested.

We were taken to the guard room and handed over to an aging RAF GD Cpl, who was quite a nice chap. He took our wallets, 1250s, etc. off us and put us in the cell. Ray and I had a quick chat and decided we could probably play on his niceness, so shouted him and asked if we could have some water as very dehydrated from the beer. It worked and he unlocked to give us our drinks—ooops mistake. We grabbed him, took his keys, and sat him on the bed before locking him in his own cell. Our 1250s, etc. were still where we had put them and he hadn't even written our names down.

A quick look outside and there was no one around so to add insult to injury, we stole his station bike and I gave Ray a crossbar out of the gate and onto Salsibury plain, eventually getting back to Netheravon. We never heard another word about it but didn't go back to the discos.

Robert Booth

Curious how many cons/gags on Guins went too far? My own incident concerned the Snowdrops in NI in the 70s when our flt cdr at Bishops Court started the rumour that the RAF Police were to be issued white berets. The rumours spread quickly throughout NI. So much so we started getting phone calls from very senior officers in the UK asking for publicity photos when they arrived. Cue embarrassing fess up that it was an April fool's joke.

Chris Booth

So it was Sennelarger, 58 Sqn, early 90s. Awoken is the small hours by the German police. "Sqn on parade!" Someone knocked a local's door asking to borrow a phone to ring a taxi and did a runner with the phone. 0200hrs, quiet as. The police rings the phone. The ringtone echoed around the parade. You're nicked.

Robin Flack

Gibralter, '74, our first time out there relieving 3 Queens (oh don't go there, I'm being serious!) from their hard (the gates were shut ffs!) border patrol duties. Sqn assembled in the gym for briefing on dos n don'ts by Snowdrop Sgt, including places/bars not to visit. At the end of the briefing said Snowdrop leaves. CO clears his throat, "Ahem! Okay, men, please give a round of applause to the Snowdrop, he's saved you a lot of time looking. You now know where to fight, fornicate, and get pissed on the cheap without having to ask." Well done and thank you Sgt *Prat*!

Darren Crosby

I was posted from 27 to 63 but 63 only had rear party so us lads would go for drink. Well, wobbly got the better of me and I ended jumping out a two storey window and running around the camp naked.

Woke up in morning in guardroom cells by RAF Police. They took me back to the block to see if anyone knew. All I got from Ally that urn was a laugh. Went to my door, locked, but found out I had left my keys in door and jumped out. An angry CO had me on jankkers.

Andrew Dobbin Horobin

On 26 Sqn return from Laarbruch in 1998 to RAF Waddington. Bearing in minds a lot of aircraft use RAF Waddington that's when the RAF had planes. I was on HQ Flt at the time and went into the porta-cabin where a couple of gunners were rigging up a naiad alarm to a battery to which the two gunners asked me to hold so they could bodge tape it easier, to which I replied, "I'm having nothing to do with this."

So after rigging it up they put it under OC Engs office (por-ta-cabin) and then they walked away. Next thing we knew the whole squadron was getting evacuated, we all knew why. But when the cordon went in, if you could call it that. A CPL came up to me and asked me if I had anything to do with this bomb to which I replied, "No, CPL."

He said to second gunner, "Go and get Ben," as he was in the shitter. As you can imagine, the camp had never had a sqn of gunners before and every RAF policeman was on scene. So out comes Ben with the said bomb swinging it in his hands saying bomb defused, then he was quite quickly arrested and off he went to the guard room. Two Sentries, one Tornado was grounded. One Nimrod and a Sentry couldn't land, and the station commander briefing next to our hangar was stopped, as it was station execs briefing so he was in the shit big style or so you think. OC police thought it was funny and he got away with it—spawny twat.

Robbie Robinson

My first charge was a GBH. I'm a very fresh faced LAC in the court and was being asked about the bruising up the side of the injured party. "Did you kick this man when he was down on the floor defenceless?"

"No, Sir," I replied. "I prodded him with my foot, wanting him to get up and fight like a man."

Even the judge sniggered.

Steve Mullen

Again on SD814 duties, there were such a thing as OSPs (off site patrols), up to this point there was always a copper and sometimes a rock on this, but never two rocks. Two things happened that stick in my mind, 1st was when I asked the Scuffer boss if I could go and take my stereo to SSVC as it was faulty. "Yes," he said, "But that means there's two rocks in the police wagon so take it easy."

Long story short, speeding (doing 60+; speed limit 30) round the ring road, bit of arsing about with the hand brake, the Land Rover ended up rolled, and thanks to a bit of careful repositioning of the gears into third, got away with it with nothing more than a bollocking!

Chris Vipond

How to wind a Scuffer up. Well yours truly is being interviewed for something he didn't do. Honest, as I was on leave at said time. So the Scuffer is giving me an eight going over and I'm getting a bit pissed off to say the least. So I said to him, "Glad I'm a rock and didn't get into RAFP."

Now he's laughing, "How long did you want to be RAFP?"

I said, "You misheard me, I said RAFP dog."

He says, "Dog, how long have you wanted to do this?"

"Ever since I was a puppy." Big laughs from the sgt rock and thunderous looks from Scuffer, then I said, "By the way, I was on leave when this happened so get your facts right." *Ouch!*

John Stowell

On my sunshine tour in Gibraltar, the Regt section was an officer and myself, they decided to do a rare event, a station call out in the early hours. Whilst at the planning meeting, it was suggested that this would be a good time to catch the lads that were using the WRAF block on a regular basis and that if SNCO Regt were placed outside the entrance to the WRAF block, he could take names as they came out.

When the alert sounded I am there and sure enough the lads started to exit like rats leaving a sinking ship so I gave them directions to avoid getting caught. As things were developing, our boss, OC admin, turns up, a rather well-endowed sqn ldr WRAF and expressed surprise that I had no names.

I then said, "Ma'am, I'm an RAF Regt gunner who a few years ago was doing this myself. This is the job for a policeman."

To which she replies, "Point taken, Sgt," and walks away. I never heard any more on the matter. What a girl.

"HELLO SON, WHEN ARE YOU GOING BACK?"

Andrew Paul Jones

I had completed a last shift of four and had looked forward to my four days off, only to get a call from one of the NCOs to come back in immediately and to bring in all my kit I had on shift with me. Everyone was being called in. Shit the balloon must have gone right up.

So I get in to Honington and go to the old Police HQ and there I find the rest of the flight just corralled together doing nothing but waiting in true 'on the wagon, off the wagon style'. Long story short, SLP Browning 127 had gone missing!

Now a few days later, P and SS turn up to interview all involved in the HO/TO. The copper (I think his role was good cop) says to me, "Look, Andy, we're not all that too worried about the loss of the pistol but it's future intent we are concerned with. Do you know anyone who has ammunition? Who could use the pistol? I mean, come on, we've all taken rounds from a range, just in case we lose some and need a spare."

Gift, thinks I. My response, "So then, Sarge, you've just confessed to me that even though you will have made a declaration, you have stolen live ammunition from a range and withheld it in your own personal possession."

"Erm, no, I never said that."

"Oh yes you did."

Interview terminated!

David Nicholson

Tale from '84/'85ish whilst on 51. We'd just done a two week sqn exercise somewhere up around Gutersloh, then the sqn was to move to Bruggen for a TACEVAL. A small group of us were picked to play enemy at Larrbruch, I think it was about a dozen of us, so we set off and headed for Bruggen. You can imagine the state of us after two weeks in the field, not a pretty sight.

So we duly arrived at Bruggen guard room about 2100 hrs, no accommodation, so they stuck us in the changing rooms at the swimming pool, I kid you not! So it being pitch black and after a quick chat the words, "Fuck it, I'm going in," all of us dived in bombing, screaming, and other shenanigans soon aroused outside interest.

Well the pool was surrounded by married quarters, so before long a Rock's favourite person arrived—you know them, the white hat gang, RAF Police. Now to be fair, they were quite good in actual fact, they kind of stood and watched guys diving off the high board and were laughing, not the usual greeting from them. Quite quickly we all noticed them and they politely asked us to get out the pool. On us all gathering round them, we asked what we'd done wrong, they said nothing, so we asked what was the problem?

It was then that they explains to us that the pool had been closed for a couple of months, some problem with the water filters. They'd asked us out for our own good, the water was boggin, we came out of the water dirtier than we went in and that took some doing after the two weeks we'd just spent rumbling round in the CVRT. Now you have to remember it was at dark so we never noticed the slime, holy fuck the next day after showering for hours we saw the water in the pool, well I think it was water. I think the two week exercise had prepped us for the minging pool as nobody got the shits and we duly played enemy for the station, the old saying, "Look before you leap," comes to mind.

Garry McCormack

The 26 Sqn BBQ/block parties were legendary, you could probably fill the book. I'm sorry if this particular saga is slightly blurred around the edges, but I'll try my best, take it as a given that Dunning and Swales were there and, of course, a block party wouldn't be a block party without Gonzo walking around with his never ending bucket of punch, to name but a few!

The theme for this block party was 'Great war movies', the dress possibilities were endless. Geordie dressed as a Korean soldier in Chinese fighting suit, complete with red star in the front of his hat (we are in West Germany!) and yours truly as a character from Bridge on the River Kwai, with the essential hoops in the bottom of my shorts, are cycling down Singley Strasse from the mess towards the block. It's 2200hrs, pitch black, neither of us had lights on our bikes (offence) and we nicked the bikes from the Guin block next door (offence). Geordie has a massive tray of chicken across his handle bars, I have a tray of chips that you'd need rope and crampons to get over–how we managed it after the skin full of 'wobbly' we'd already consumed, in itself deserved a CO's commendation!

Not far from the block we are passed by an RAFP Sherpa van, driver and passenger mouth agog as they passed us. "Oh crikey, Garry, what ever shall we do?" Or words to that effect, shouts Geordie, more like, "Fuck, let's get in the block and warn them quick before the bastards turn round!"

Unbeknownst to us, another series of events are beginning to unravel within the block so more pretend police officers were on route to that location! Geordie and I race into the block with not a chicken breast or chip dropped "Quick, the five-o are on their way down ... where did all that blood come from?"

Now I must say, the 26 Sqn entertainment committee always did a crackin job of decking out the block for a party, indeed the TV room complete with bar serving hatch would put the 'Old Mill' down the road to shame, it was like a night club. Reacting to our shouts of alarm, every WRAF and female guest are jumping out of the two TV room windows faster that a Sim 20 over Frog Hill DZ! However, flashing disco lights inside, pitch black German wood outside, it was obvious these ladies had not had field craft lesson 4, 'night vision: why things are seen', because one minute they're all leaping into the unknown, the next it's Russian Roulette with pine trees—ouch!

Just then, in walks the 1 Sqn and 26 Sqn nemesis, Sergeant Norman Bailey RAFP, or more commonly known as Norman of the Yard! This clown is a legend and I'm surprised that he hasn't appeared, as yet in, other tales of Flugplatz Laarbruch! The tales of this idiot's campaigns to fight 'crime' on the mean streets of Goch, Weeze, and the camp would put Inspector Clouseau to shame! He was so dedicated to his cause that he never ever wore a white police cap, no, he only wore a blue one, that way he could sneak up closer on his prey! However, on more than one occasion, he was seen on the MQ bus dressed as a J/T, complete with beret, in order to catch the scaley brats who'd been vandalising the bus.

Norman is standing in the middle of the 'dancefloor' and is holding out his ID card and sweeping the room like it's a handgun, shouting at the top of his voice (there is still bedlam in the corridors and ablutions as other guests that really shouldn't be there are trying to escape), "TURN THAT MUSIC OFF NOW! I AM SERGEANT BAILEY, ROYAL AIR FORCE POLICE. IS ANYONE NOT SATISFIED WHO I AM?"

Now picture the scene, there's drunken Rocks all over the place, flashing disco lights, and everyone in fancy dress, from Ceasar to Judge Dredd, Douglas Bader to Action Man. When up steps a body in green overalls, a 'Planet of the Apes' gorilla mask, and tank commander's helmet similar to the one worn by Donald Sutherland in 'Kelly's Heroes', it could of been anyone. It's Chris 'Spunky' May, the place goes quiet, you could hear a pin drop.

The gorilla walks up to Norman, grabs the ID card off him, and as cool as you like says, "I'M NOT, WHAT'S YOUR LAST THREE?" Norman actually starts to answer him before he realises what's happening and grabs his ID card back as the congregation fall and roll around in laughter! Never one to miss an opportunity, the leader of 26 Sqn escape committee (we'll call him 'The Cat' to protect his identity, a Cpl on A Flt) remembers his training and decides the best form of defence is attack; quickly gathering a few of us together, leads us outside to where the other RAFP that arrived left their unattended, unlocked Sherpa van—brilliant!

Within minutes, shitfaced drunk, we manage to make use of the 748 kit, jack it up, and begin taking the wheels off whilst Noddy Rodgers is on the police radio shouting, "Hello, Hello, that's a big ten-four, good buddy!" I'm sure the other escapades of the evening will come out on here and it's only right that those involved put their spin on things.

Nearly 30 years ago and like most other tales I've read, if you were involved, seems like only yesterday, keep 'em coming, boys!

Per Ardua.

David Matthews

26 Sqn Larrbruch. A Flt Lt Police walks into disip office. "My Land Rover has gone missing, Cpl."

"Oh, I say, better call the police."

"I am OC Police," he says.

"Where did you last see your L/R and did you leave the keys in it, Sir?" Just then I see it coming into the compound. Two Lads jump out and go about their way.

"I left it parked outside, Cpl," he says (nothing about leaving keys in it).

"Have a quick check in yard again, Sir, I say you might have missed it."

He was so red faced. He never came back into the office. He must have found his L/R.

Simon Pogson

When 58 got disbanded in the early 90s, a lot of us were posted to the dreaded 814 at Marham.

One night I was in the Sybar and for some reason was the only Rock in there, in fact I was the only person in there apart from the barmaid, who was the wife of one of the lads. Just before last orders, six coppers from my shift come in the bar and order a round of drinks. As I get on with coppers, so well, I just totally ignore them.

The night is coming to an end and my mate's wife calls over to the coppers and asks, "Do you want another drink before I cash up?" They answer no, they were fine and so she starts cashing up. As she is finishing, one of the coppers comes to the bar to try and order another round to which he is told he's too late as she had finished cashing up. Then came the immortal words. "You fucking Rock slag!" So, always the gentleman and a very proud gunner, I headbutt said copper, which starts a massive brawl that lasts for a few minutes.

I see the blue lights appear and make a fighting withdrawal to the fire exit, out the door, I go, and suddenly a police dog and handler appear at the bottom of the fire stairwell. Unfortunately the dog is on a long lead (I say unfortunately as I like dogs). Anyway, I had to give the dog a kick to keep it away from me and re-enter the bar where the on-duty Scuffers have arrived and as tradition dictates I get locked up for the night.

The next morning I'm charged with six counts of assault and assaulting a police dog (which I didn't even know existed). The boss hears my charge but because I had a bit of form and over eager police sqn cmdr it goes to summary of evidence. Boss gets me in and tells me the CO is worried that I will intimidate the witnesses and so I get sent to RAF Odiham (which opens a whole new chapter of tales). This is already a nice one centurion for me but it gets better.

At the summary of evidence, I have Boss Dobson to represent me, as he was a top bloke and had some legal knowledge, and Stevie Gamble has my friend as he'd been charged more times than anyone else I knew. The coppers came in one at a time with well-scripted stories, which all pointed to me being a guilty bastard. Each stated that they had only had two beers and so were sober and little old me was being aggressive to them as soon as they walked in the bar.

They also denied saying anything to the barmaid. Until one of the less bright Scuffers came in and said he had drank about eight bottles of Stella. The boss got me to ask him if he was drinking in rounds, which he admitted, then he was asked would it be fair that the others had drank the same, which he agreed with. Many raised eyebrows from the senior officers and the judge advocate.

My mate's wife played a blinder as you would expect from a good Rockette as she told how she was so upset about the copper's behaviour and how grateful she was that I was there. Turned out I was found to have no charges to answer nice one centurion, but gets nicer.

The six coppers were charged and found guilty of attempting to pervert the course of justice. One was found guilty of disgusting, perverse language likely to incite violence, even the dog handler got kicked off the dog section and put back on the gate and I got a posting to 34 in Cyprus! Now that was a nice one centurion!

Gus Dunning

This might come under: 'how I escaped jail'. While on 26 Sqn, about '85, air trooping flight from Brize to Germany, got there early, so lots of hours to kill as an early morning flight. Booked my bags in and off to the spotlight to see who from 19 Sqn was about. Then it all went wrong, got soundly pissed until I was called to the bar at late o'clock as NAAFI Doris shouted out my name and one of the lads pings me. WO from the air terminal on the other end, "Dunning did you by any chance leave a bag of 12' records in the terminal?"

"Oops, yes. Forget about them, Sir, leave them at the desk, I'll pick up on my way out," and hung up and back on the pop, can imagine his face as was pretty pissed off on the phone. What I didn't know is my bag left unattended triggered a bomb scare and cleared the terminal for about an hour.

Come the morning I slipped in the terminal, spotted a copper with my bag of records at departures, so I kept quiet and blagged it, left the records, and boarded unchallenged. Daft twats thought I would step up and claim them so they could nick me. They had all my details, but for some strange reason it never followed me to Germany and I got away again scot-free.

Albi Pinnion

RAF Gutersloh, early eightie. Saturday night, Rock walks into the police guardroom, and says to the duty lac, "Cpl, I want to report an assault!"

"An assault on who?" chirps the Snowdrop.

"An assault on you, you bast—!" The rest is predictable!

John Berwick

1980, 15 Sqn, out at Aldergove, phone goes in GDOC from an RAF copper who is manning a Sanger, Rock answers phone. RAF copper say he needs to be relieved as he has problems. Rock says, "Sorry no can do," and hangs up.

Ten mins pass, phone goes again same copper saying, "If I don't get relieved, I will shoot myself." Rock laughs and hangs up. Suddenly over the net, 'Shots fired'. IRF are sent to check the RAF copper in the sanger.

He had shot himself in the gut, the 9mm ran down his thigh bone and exited. RAF copper is on floor screaming like a pig (pardon the pun). Next day, Rock patrol leave main gate singing the theme tune to M*A*S*H, changing the words to suicide is painful. Came up on SROs that no personnel are to sing any TV theme while leaving the camp.

CHAPTER 4
TARGETS WILL FALL
WHEN HIT

Kevin McGee

1980/81, 34 Squadron at Dhekelia ranges, we were living in a tented camp and the hierarchy had decided that it would be a good idea to bring the wives and kids up to see us perform.

To ensure we were seen at our best WO Jim Richardson had the whole squadron in extended line across the camp for a FOD sweep. His order was as follows: "Walk in extended line through the camp and pick up anything unnatural." I think it was Jim Satyanand (someone can correct me if not) ran forward got the WO in a fireman's lift and ran off towards the bins.

Those of you who knew WO Richardson would have expected him to explode in fury but in fact he burst out laughing.

John Stowell

16 Sqn, Wildenrath, 1978/79ish. 21 Sigs Regt held a skill at arms competition and threw out invites to all and sundry. Lots of other army units attended. Four of us got volunteered to go from the sqn. Stu Drury, myself, Steve Baker and, apologies, I can't recollect the last guy's name.

So, following an afternoon on the 25mtr range to check zero weapons, we arrive for the shoot. A two day event during which there are lots of sniggering and pointing. After all, to Percy Pongo, we were just another bunch of ill-disciplined blue jobs out for a wizard picnic.

Following the final shoot (falling plates) and the scoreboard tallied, the snide comments such as, "Watch out, Crab Air is about," and, "Break out the Brylcream and nice fluffy cushions on the firing points for ya lads," turned into cries of, "Oh my god," "Golly," and, "WTF!"

When it dawned that 'Crab Air' had won the competition. Not wishing to be outdone, Percy then refuses to award us the winner's trophy. So after some loud telephone calls and some table slapping from the late Flt Lt John Tunnah, 21 Sigs hastily make the shield shown and award us that as champion visitor unit. We never got invited the next year.

Robin Flack

On a range one day and our CO for once had removed his best blues and wellies (yes some will remember him). Anyway I've down tested and adjusted with my SLR, he lays down on my right side to see fall of shot. "Sir, that is not a good place to lay."

"Airman! I am observing your aim and fall of shot!"

"Yessir." Bang! First round goes down the range, empty red-hot case ejects slightly right and backwards, hitting him on the upper lip. How do you get a good grouping when you've got the giggles?

Steve Mullan

On 48 Sqn in early 90s, I recall a visit to Fort George ranges for annual APWT on the rifle (sa80) and APWA on the LSW. A certain chiefy has the great idea that if you take your zeroed SUSAT off your rifle and place it on the LSW then it should be zeroed to you! So, complying with this bizarre logic, we removed the SUSATs from the LSWs and placed them on the bonnet of chiefy's Land Rover, as instructed.

At some point, someone got in said Land Rover and drove off back to Lossiemouth. Oops! Rest of day searching range roads for lost SUSATs. Last one handed to us by a postman, he found it on a public road as he was driving past!

Kevin Bell

Round about the same time as Steve Mullan's last. I was on 48 Sqn shooting team. Was training at Fort George. Shooting away and a Nimrod flew low and slow down the Moray Firth, west to east. That was the one that came down in the drink, just off shore opposite-ish the Skerry Brae. The order came at the range, "STOP!" First worry, although the AC was well out of range of 5.56, was that we'd put a round or two through it. Unlikely we'd hit it, as it was an air defence sqn and couldn't hit a cow's arse with a banjo!

Si N Becks Lloyd

Late 80s on II, we poodle off to Warminster for the day on the ranges, me driving the four tonner. Shooting done, we start the journey back to H. Half hour after getting back, called to see chiefy. "Right, explain what happened on the four tonner on the way back."

Cue quizzical look. "Errr no idea, Flt, what did happen?"

"Right, who was mooning out the back?"

"No idea, Flt. I was driving, couldn't see the back of the four tonner."

Chiefy realises the stupidity of his questions and tells me someone mooned at some old dear following the wagon on the way back. Turned out to be the wife of the lt col in charge of Warminster camp, who took the wagon registration, phoned her hubby, and it got traced back to the sqn.

Cue sniggering from me, quickly stopped with a look from chiefy, but replaced by sniggering from cpls and sgt also in office. "Fuck off, Lloydy," says chiefy, breaking into a smile.

David Jeremiah

While on 19 Sqn, on the way to the ranges, can't remember which one. Mick was map reading, concentrating on the map, he glances up and shouts at the driver, "Turn right now," the driver turns right and so does the whole convoy, following Mick. We ended up in a farm yard!

Mick on glancing up from the map saw a sign: 'Range'. We spent an absolute age turning the vehicles around in the small farm yard, when we get back to the junction the sign read

'Free Range Eggs'. As you can imagine, it was a long time before he lived that one down.

Andrew Paul Jones

Bisley, Group SAM, 2005. The highly successful RAF FP Centre Shooting Team (all Rocks) are getting in a little competition range time before RockSAM. We were a good, no, a *great* team; we were cresting on a wave. But after an unfortunate unavailability of a regular and seasoned shooter, we brought in a 'replacement' who very nearly became our downfall. This then SAC replacement is still serving and is now a JNCO and am sure he is quite proud of this tale.

Now, like all gunners, he likes a drink and at times didn't seem to have an off switch, for a few nights on the trot he drank more and more until he got a gypsy's warning from the team captain. The reason for this was he came back from the bar, arousing us all from our slumber, only to swamp his own bed before getting in it and going to sleep.

So after his gypsy's, like most of us, he again pushed the boundaries, this time returning from his night out as we were awakening to go to the range. Pissed up, he prepped his rig and tried to dress himself. Well combat jacket, webbing, body armour with high-leg boots is never a good look with your jeans still on, especially as in your pissed up state you have managed to bungie up your jeans too.

Well, the said gunner was sent to bed and we loaded our transport to go to the cookhouse for breakfast, leisurely arriving at the range in good gunner 5-mins-before timing. Only to get verbally abused by a very angry flt lt RCO and det cmdr, ranting and raving that if us Rocks didn't square ourselves away he was going to RTU us all back to Honington.

Little did we know that after we left the RAFSAA clubhouse, thinking our drunken cohort had gone to bed, NO! He had taken it up on himself to get a lift to the range. Still adorned in his range kit and bungeed jeans, he had flagged down the only other service man he could find and said in a heavily laden alcoholic-odoured voice, "Gi'me a lift to the range, you Guin fuck. My mates have forgotten me." Well, as you can understand, said RCO told him to fuck off then came head hunting us to extract his frustrated revenge.

Geoffrey Herschell

Another one about Youngy. The 2IC threw him off a range in Senneybridge and told him to double to his next range. Half way there the sqn WO caught him up and started bollocking him.

He told him nothing he could say would get him out of the shit he was in as this charge will have been his third in two months.

Youngy replied, "The 2IC will be in deeper. He has just sent me off a range, wandering around on my own with a weapon loaded with live rounds and two full magazines." Funny, he wasn't charged and the WO gave him a lift to his next range.

Si N Becks Lloyd

Sennybridge Ranges. Get to range and boss gives his scenario and tells us this is a grenade stalk with two of us lobbing them. Yours truly and one other, I forget who, do the crawling and being covered by everyone firing into the target. I throw my grenade and the boss is stood right behind us giving his 'educated' critique as my colleague follows suit straight after me.

We get down, as it's a bit close, and the boss is still waffling his arse off. We look at each other, thinking the same thing, and yep, double boom, followed by a yelp behind us and, "Man down." Look round and the boss is on the floor with blood streaming down his face. It took me and my mate all our strength not to laugh out loud.

OC and OC ranges pitch up after a short time. OC ranges asks "You okay?"

"Yes, Sir," he replies.

"Good, now tell me why you're fucking throwing grenades on a non-grenade range!"

"Errr." More subdued mirth from the troops.

Turning to sqn OC, "Well you can both explain when you get back from the hospital, *can't you?*"

Simon Stanton

Remember one certain Sennybridge, live firing section attack. Cos it was so cold we had a rum ration before it. 90% were youngsters so I ended up with a pint of rum. FS Caisley and I was on the right flank, a blizzard came down so the GPMG didn't know when to traverse. We were running with spouts all around us, the flight was dancing all around, all I thought was *Wow*. Until the debrief.

John Berwick

1980, s busy year for 15 Sqn as we went to Germany on TACEVAL then off to Cyprus then Ireland and then once we came back, Crusader 80. Out of the year, I think we were only at RAF Wittering for three weeks out of the year.

Anyway, we went to Cyprus for 17 days, the point of the exercise was to see if we could get there and once there we were up in Akamas Ranges and doing beach landings on the RCT landing craft. The whole of A flight were to do a beach landing. We sailed out in to the med, seemed like ages, then sailed back in to the shore. We are all lined down each side of the landing craft, ready to disembark, but first the RCT guy drops the door, steps out, and with a big stick checked the depth—it was too deep. He tells the guy to take further in. Door drops again, pongo used stick to check depth, says to Flt Macgonagal, "It's fine to disembark," so the cpl and the OC A step off the door into the water and fucking disappear. It was about 7 foot deep, the lying fucking pongo says he must have hit a rock on the bottom. They take it further in and we all get off. It was by this time between 5 and 6 foot deep—remember we are in LFO with boots and bungees and the old DPM. We hit the water and some of us just managed to have our heads out of the water, some of the short arses had to hold their breaths. By the time we hit the beach, because we were wearing LFO, our webbing filled up with air and just took our feet off the sea bed and made it harder to get ashore. When we did get to the beach our combat trousers filled up with water due to the bungees at the bottom—we looked like Michelin men full of sea water. C Flt were defending the beach and were rolling down the hill pissing themselves laughing at us. We were exhausted by this time, but was great fun after as we hit the beach bar and all got pissed.

A few days later, up in Akamas Ranges, A Flight advance to contact with 81mm firing over the top of us and the GPMGs on SF roll firing over the top. Anyway, we ended up in the mountains, this is in Jan in Cyprus' rainy season, and it was freezing out. The whole section was trying to get under Paul Collins' poncho to keep dry and sleep. The following day, continuing with the advance to contact, Andrew N. aka Buek was GPMG gunner and was going up a hill and slipped near a whole belt of ammo when live—lucky no one was shot. Was great training and time there and hard graft.

John Ross

Early days in the reformation of 51 Sqn RAF Regt at Lossiemouth, we found ourselves at Garelochhead doing live firing. A certain gunner known as Martin and a flt cmdr known as Mac were tearing down the range road in a Landy only to thump a range sheep! Now, said sheep was not dead but in a bad way and being an ex-undertaker, said gunner called Martin took the shovel from the bonnet 'to finish the job'. After the first thump to the head, Martin walked away happy the job was done, only to hear it bleat again so he returned. This happened another three times until, in a frenzy of blows, the sheep succumbed!

Now bloodied and in a red mist induced grin at having completed the task, Martin takes a step to the ditch to drag in the body of the sheep only to look up and see two pongos in a sentry position 15 feet away, shaking in fear at what had happened before them! Martin points the bloody shovel at them and shouts, "You ain't seen nothing right?" Before jumping in the Land Rover and doing one.

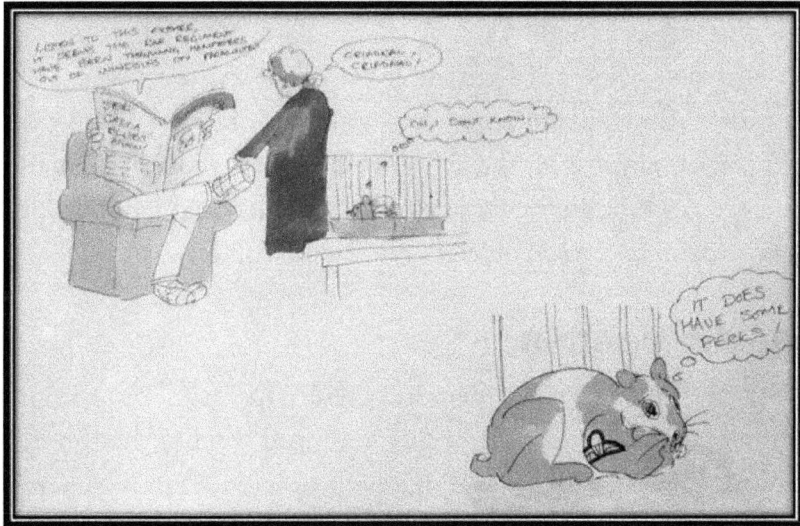

Steve Mullen

While on 33 Sqn (Pumas), some of the station Guins had been invited to partake in a March and shoot over in Denmark. A few of us Rocks were 'invited' to bolster the team. So, me, Spence Rockett, Stephen Snow, and Flt Lt Mcivor headed off over on the ferry to take part.

Competition went well, can't even remember where we came in the competition but the after party was celebrated in true regt style with the Rocks having a skin full and then proceeding to show some of the female talent what was what. I got acquainted with a particularly beautiful, leggy Danish FS and Snowy was later spotted with a different young lady.

Anyway, the next day we were due to leave. I just made it back to our accommodation in time to find the boss flapping because Snowy was missing. Turns up half an hour later, winks at me, and tells the boss he's not going back! Boss proceeds to have a meltdown as he believes one of his guys is going AWOL right in front of him! Turns out Snowy had leave booked but let's the boss stew on it for while! Snowy spends his leave with the young lady.

Anyway, sometime later, while on ops in Kosovo/Macedonia, Snowy receives a hand painted oil painting, showing an abstract of his relationship with the girl he spent a week with in Denmark. She had tracked him down to Kosovo somehow and sent him this bizarre painting, which duly got hung in our office!

Martin Cannon

That just jolted the old memory. Pre-NI trg, late 70s, 15 Sqn. On a range somewhere, probably Stamford. End of the shoot, I was up in the control tower, had just ordered, "Safety supervisors show clear," and was waiting for the thumbs-up from three NCOs, a cpl on each flank (Coddington and Oswald) and my sgt, Roy Lobley, in the middle. Got thumbs from the two cpls on the flanks, but I couldn't see Roy who was right underneath me. I stood on a chair to see better over the control panel just as Roy who, realising the situation, was shuffling backwards, thumb in the air, looking up at me. Unfortunately, he took one shuffle backwards too far and fell vertically, feet first, down into a fire trench, thumb still aloft. Didn't do his back any good, but had the whole range in stitches!

Neil Horn

Still got a 'temporary cap' on my front tooth after an argument with a SUSAT on an IBSR, 27 years ago. Being beasted by Pete Kelly, hit prone and tooth impacted SUSAT, hurt like crap, but I knew it hurt less than a further beasting from Pete! Cap was meant to last a few weeks, never did get it done!

We were first J Course to have the SA80. I think we invented the requirement for the magazine release shroud. Doing an IBSR, PBSR, TBSR with bang, click, followed by (Mick Knight), "Fucking forget something … Sir," got really, really tiresome.

Gareth Burton

Stanival at Tain Ranges north of Inverness with 16 Sqn. It's Mick Buckland, first Rapier ex as a DC. After a few days of settling in and tracking the live bombing going on, the FS picks myself and Andy Vyse up and we head out to visit Mick. Proud as punch, he meets us and guides us in. After getting the brews on he decides to show us around. "What do you think of my camouflage for the Rapier kit, gents?" We look on in total silence. He has used old range targets and his site was positioned at the end of the range. We quickly picked ourselves up off the floor to quickly assist with throwing them away. Phew. Thankfully no casualties but much laughter though. Mick's a legend, fair play.

Des Kennady

One shoot, SAC 'Jones' was having a bad day, couldn't hit anything, so we decided that the blokes left and right of him would lend a hand! At the end of his ten rounds, it came over the tannoy, "Congratulations, Jones, you've got 12 out of 10!"

Michael Marsh

34 Sqn, Cyprus, 1972, and we are on the range after a good shoot tidying up. FS Bostock has tasked me with collecting all the

flights field telephones, which I have chucked into the back of an RL Bedford. I found some Don-10 wire just short lengths and connected two together. A quick twist of the handle and the bell rings, so I pick up a phone and answer, "Hello, 34 Sqn B Flight, SAC Marsh speaking, how can I help you?" Bostock looks over towards me and I continue, "Flight Sergeant Bostock, yes Sir, one moment Sir, I will get him for you now!"

I turn to Bostock and say, "Chiefy, it is for you, the CO, Sqn Ldr Flack!"

He walks over and says, "Hello, sir, Flight Sergeant Bostock. Hello, hell-lo, hell—Marsh, I am going to screw you, you little bastard!" But too late, I had already started running and was at least fifty yards in front! However I let him catch me at the one hundred metre point. Knackered and both out of breath he started laughing and gave me a playful kick up the arse! Yeah, he should have known it was not the CO, after all he sent me to collect the damn phones. Good laugh and I bought him a beer later on!

Neil Horn

Otterburn field firing and 'dry' training on 66 Sqn. Was night of a 'dry' B Flt attack on A Flt's harbor. All going swimmingly well, me with Flt HQ, with the GPMG SF and 51mm to the rear in support. Can't remember who was 'platoon sgt', that stuff was never John Cloughton's thing.

Anyways, Sqn HQ Flt had their own cunning plan and on a hill to our left flank, in the dark, there was a few figures in the gloom skirting along. With the help of my two drivers and sgt we hoisted the IWS over to view (remember that beast of an 'individual' piece of kit). It was OC HQ (Steve Griffiths, I think) and a few bods, obviously the recce group planning some secret flanking manoeuvre. Our only options to thwart this were to turn the 51mm and put some illumination on them, but that would plunge the main attack into chaos.

Ahaaa, like all prepared gunners, we had mini-flares in every friggin pocket and pouch. My 2 SAC's, "No fucking way, Sir," was probably sensible! So me and Sgt X prepared about a dozen mini-flare launchers, left them to operate the 51 whilst reigning 16mm flares down on Sqn HQ! Amazingly accurate at about 300m! We managed to get warning shots to land about 5 yards in front of them and continued to chase them off the hill. Some shots were a little awry, scattering the 'scout team'. Could hear them cursing for miles.

Dave Robinson

Used to love doing the firepower demo for the basics. Well except one time, when I was firing the 9mm pistol. Missed the fookin tiles with every round. Walked off hanging my head in shame.

Gwyn Moggy Morris

Otterburn, '93? I was the regular Rock on 2624 and we were on the anti-tank range being filmed by the crew of Countryfile. It was decided that a certain auggie, ex of 3 Para Falklands Conflict, would be the best person to be filmed firing the 66.

After the cameraman was advised that standing immediately behind the firer would be a good way to get cooked, said gunner aimed and fired. Everybody watched in anticipation as the rocket made its way into the distance and sailed majestically over the top of the target! This was of course followed by cheers, clapping, and calls of, "Wanker," by the assembled troops, followed by, "Cut," by the director and sour faces of the TV peoples. To say John Craven didn't appreciate our humour would be an understatement!

Albi Pinnion

About boots, 63 Sqn were down the Falklands, possibly '83, there was a march and shoot competition, we came second. The boss at the time was a major general, he was appalled that we were all wearing DMS boots that were literally falling to pieces, our stores had been told they were for army issue only. Things changed very quickly when he told his aide de comp that every Regt man would have a pair of high boots within 48 hrs or else, and a second pair within two weeks. The problem was sloshing about in the fuel re-fuelling everything, etc., the boots simply rotted, no matter how much polish you put on them, and we all knew the falling plates scores had been altered so the resident infantry won the march and shoot!

Robert Booth

Sennibridge Ranges. We are to carry out a flight in attack in respirators during a gas attack. So we are all lying in wait along the edge of a wood on a very hot day. The Flt Sgt is in charge of the 2" with the CS mortar rounds. He is going to lay down the CS then we are to attack through at 90 degrees to the barrage after cease fire on the mortar. First rounds start arriving, the shout goes up, "Gas, gas, gas." Then the cloud starts forming of CS, when suddenly a person appears running downwind trying to get ahead of the cloud following the mortar fire line.

Turned out that flt cdrs that leave their webbing lying about unattended have their canisters removed by grumpy SACs. We were all laughing so much at his coughing and spluttering that the attack was never completed.

Robert Booth

Was fortunate not to be the gunner of the Charlie G, but unfortunately the number two with the rounds on my back. Crawling forward into position downhill on a live firing exercise at Sennybridge. The rest of 51 Sqn A flight are behind the crest of the hill, waiting to assault through after we have hit the tank at the bottom of the hill. Load, aim, shoot, kill the tank.

Rest of the flight commence attack over the crest of the hill, when all of a sudden there is crack and impact into the ground not six feet away. The safety officer next to us is screaming to stop, we can hear the flight cdr screaming his head off as well. But the gunner and I were too busy checking to see if we were both still in one piece. First experience of being under fire, pity it was our own troops.

Dan Archer

Whilst on PCBC, we each had 2 HEAT rounds a piece. Problem was three of you were on the firing point and took turns at being the No1, No2, and a third as observer. After being there and firing six rounds in quick succession, you came out punch drunk and deaf!

Also remember Charlie Rigby firing the only HEAT round on the J Course. The round went over the top of the target and landed about 100m away intact! Problem was it was in about 6 feet of snow, which made finding it very interesting! Happy days!

John Stowell

Whilst at Warminster and on the anti-tank phase, we were receiving instruction on the Charlie Gee from the Black Watch guy (Smudge Smith) on the squad. He stresses the point already mentioned about fingers clear when closing the Ventura and then demonstrates the loading drill, but, instead of the expected metallic clunk of the Ventura closing there was a sickening and dull squish. Yes he had trapped said fingers. Credit due. He continued with the lesson but now spreading blood over everything he touched. The worst part of it was trying not to laugh.

It was near the end of his lesson whilst summing up that he stood facing the class in the at ease position, with a film of sweat on his now sickly grey face and the blood dripping onto the floor between his feet that it got too much for me and I started to laugh followed by the rest of the squad. I was then instructed to leave the room by the squad instructor who later told me what a naughty boy Biggles had been. He did have problems keeping his own face straight whilst doing so.

Ian Moon

There had been a misunderstanding on the range. We were briefed that the shoot was an ambush. So in best RAF Regt tradition, as soon as the targets appeared they promptly vanished in a withering hail of fire. When the smoke cleared, the range warden in his tower was pissing himself laughing. Thought it was the best thing he'd seen in ages.

Flt Sgt John Geddes and the pongo zob taking the shoot, however, were less than impressed and after professionally unloading us (not that there was anything left to unload), John then went into one of his specials, as is usual in these circumstances, everyone was having trouble keeping a straight face, especially the likes of Stuart Reeve and co.

However, the ultimate Monty Python 'fwee Bwian' moment for us came mid-rant as his face changed colours yet again, when during aforementioned rollicking, instead of saying that was a fiasco, he came out with something along the lines of, "that was a fecking cafascifo." We're so sorry, John. We couldn't take any more. And in scenes reminiscent of the famed 'Biggus Dickus' Monty Python scene, troops were pulling obscure faces and avoiding eye contact as they tried to stop themselves laughing. Of course the troops barely concealed mirth and the shoulders rising and falling only enraged poor old John even more. They were great days though. RIP, John.

Steve Mullen

III Sqn, field firing at Sennybridge, section attack, someone had decided we had to throw the grenades at the dummy targets rather than post them. Throw was from a knee deep water filled ditch about 15m away. WO standing with me as safety and as I throw, rifle slips down, hits my arm, and I mong the grenade into the same ditch we are standing in around 5m away.

The WO and I look at each other, realise there is no time to climb out, and just drop to the bottom of the trench! Bang! No one hurt.

"Right. Throw the next one without fucking it up," says the WO.

Paul McCarthy

I was helping out Pete when he was DSC 15 Sqn by doing the BATSIM for their field firing package, at Otterburn, I think. The ammo indent for the BATSIM was screwed up as they gave us all electric detonators and very few flash dets. It wasn't a problem as I had my demolition safety officer tick and was stage 5 plan and conduct, so I robbed the flash dets out of the range dems box for the BATSIM. Reason being I'd use an electric det for a blinds charge if necessary. The sqn had the new frag grenade that had the safety clip, which retained the fly off lever that you had to flick off before pulling the pin. Anyway, the LAC (had to be!) crawls up with the Kav, pulls pin, and throws grenade. No bang. FUCK! Wait the 30 minutes and crawl forward for a look. No safety clip or fly off lever around. FUCK!

On close inspection, there is a tiny bit of stone wedged between the striker and the percussion cap that looks like a fart will dislodge it. Crawl back about a metre to get the charge out of my pocket and get the electric det out to tape onto the det cord cradle. Get that done and then splice the det to the black and tan that I'd dragged out behind me as I'd crawled forwards to do the initial check. Crawl forward again to place the charge so it is a gnat's pubic hair away from the blind and positioned so it *will* blow the blind. Crawl back to the shell scrape where the Kav and the LAC are and get the Shrike out of my smock. Connect up the black and tan and, cos I'm all heart, I let the LAC press the button for the bang. Made the lad's day.

Robbie Robinson

1 Sqn, early 80s, at the defence range. Things are not going to the two FS's way. With a big bollocking all round, 30 guys was made to stand and watch the two give a lesson on the shagging shamooly. "This is how it's done, its simple, any moron could do it." Then proceeded to fire said weapon … into the trench they was standing in. He was holding it upside down and *us morons* was not going to tell them.

Neil Horn

Otterburn on J's in '88. One blind, RCO goes forward, L2 cannot be found in the long grass and crap on the range. We end up, full course, line abreast, doing the Basil Fawlty goose step trying to find the damn thing. Lots of sphincter twitching!

Andy Devine

GDT Leuchars running a 25m range for aircrew. 15m Walthers at the ready gives the command, "Four rounds standing, three rounds kneeling, at your target in front go on." 1 pillock, sorry, pilot decides to blast off all seven rounds in about 2 seconds. Rest of the group complete the shoot, unload, and show clear. We dress down to check targets and as I work my way to his lane with the usual wisdom about group size, etc. I mark up the one shot hit the target and ask him why he only hit the target once?

"I wanted to see how fast I could get them off."

"Oh," says I. "Well head back up and place your pistol on the table and see how fast you can get of this range."

"What?" says a confused pilot.

"Go back to the sqn. Tell the wg cdr you failed CCS and why."

"But ..."

"Go away, sir. Now!" Completed the rest of the day, with the other aircrew. Guess who was back the following week sitting next to the wg cdr. Think he was orderly officer that Xmas.

Robbie Robinson

3 WRAF officers turned up for a course in blues, shirts, and I'm pretty sure stocking and sussies. Why, you ask? I advise they go and change into DPM. "No, Cpl, we are going straight to the mess for exchange drinks and will not have time to change."

"Okay, Ma'am," and all the classroom stuff done, made our way to the CS chamber. Yes, you are ahead of me, god were they uncomfortable in all the wrong places.

Next day range, they arrive in DPM. They even made a big thing about it. It did not take long to figure out they was still pissed. In fact, two of them had only a few hours' sleep. I refused to allow them on the range, more orderly officers. I loved the job.

Fraze Barkaway

St Mawgan, we had a WRAF officer, a flt lt who was OC Portreath. Now to understand this fully, the lads at Portreath were a dream as they had to be permanently live armed guard qualified so we saw them every three months and they were shit hot.

She turns up for CCS, having not done it for years somehow, and complains within 10 minutes that the PowerPoint is out of focus. It isn't, she's so fucking fat her cheeks actually prevent her from seeing properly. Time progresses and she gets the mandatory TP prior to WHTs. Watching this fucking whale floundering on the mats with her lads doing lightening mag changes and shouting, "Magazine!" etc. and doing the further stoppage drills, broken firing pin, etc. is just comedy.

Needless to say she failed her WHT and demanded to know why. I gave her the sheet and said, "Go ask the flt cdr to explain it." To give you an idea, it had 'attempted to fit the mag backwards'.

Anyway, CBRN after lunch. Fat fuck can't fit in an extra-large NBC suit so I'm told, "Gas the bitch anyway." Normal hilarity in the chamber as she fucks it up and attempts to dash out the door with me heaving her backwards with the cursory, "No fucker leaves until I say so."

By the time I've got them back to GDT, I hand the course over to my oppo to do the DCCT shoot. And the boss calls me in, sat in his office is the station tayloress, I get fat fuck in and she's measured for a special made NBC suit and handed a written warning to sort her shit out.

24 hrs later I'm stood in front of the stn cdr as I've been accused of bullying! I explain my case while he's pissing himself laughing to the point he's banging his fists on the desk and sweating like a blind lesbian in a fish factory when the phone rings. He manages to compose himself and takes the call, he loses it in a fit again and slams the phone down. All I get from him is, "Gym. Ped O, Fat Cunt failed, ran into wall on bleep test. Cpl B, fuck off, I can't take it anymore ..."

Gareth Glover

One of my first ever range days as a sprog Lac. Zero shoot done, legged it down to the butts to be told 3 right 6 up. No probs. Got back and did exactly that. To the rifle of a gunner who shot at Bisley. Ended up doing press ups in an ice cold puddle all afternoon. Didn't do it again though. *Per ardua.*

John Corr

I remember whilst on the ranges, some of us got the honour to lob a grenade. The adj (Wobbly) was running it, with the CO nearby watching. I threw mine, got it spot on, but the just silence. The CO and Wobbly then go down, Wobbly puts the det cord round it and then they both head back towards the pit. Wobbly breaks into a bit of a lollop and I hear the CO say, "Walk, an officer never runs from danger and we have two minutes." 30 seconds after it's been lit and literally, just as they both enter the pit, there's a big old bang.

The CO ducks, looks at Wobbly and says, "You're a f****** c*** and so are you, Corr, for throwing it."

Wobbly and Gunner Corr both reply in unison, "Thank you, Sir."

Mick Sweeney (RIP), who was in the pit helping run it, said, "I owe you a pint for that."

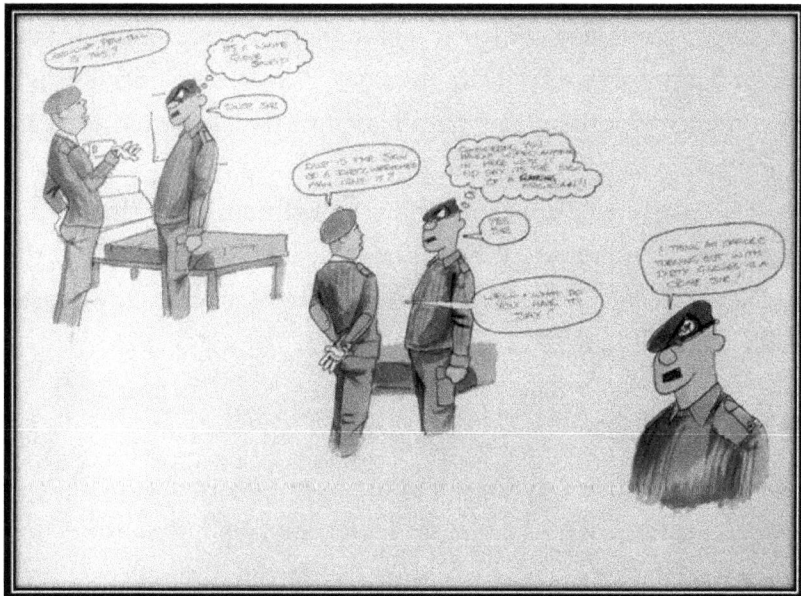

Andy Bates

19 Sqn, shooting team, late 80s. One of the 'joys' of being at Brize was that it invariably involved traveling some distance to get a day on a proper range. One Friday, someone had got us a day at Mere

(somewhere near Warminster). Dutifully left at early o'clock and spent the day honing our skills and turning live rounds into empty cases until the range shut at 1600 before blasting back to Brize in a couple of Land Rovers.

As it was Friday, and wanting to avoid the usual traffic bottle-necks, we opted a back road route to Swindon. I was driving the second vehicle and was getting slightly concerned with the speed, etc. that the lead vehicle was doing and noticed (by the road signs) that a hump back bridge and sharp left bend were approaching so backed off accordingly. As I crested the bridge, we saw the first truck in the middle of a field of cows! Luckily no one was hurt and nobody had been coming the other way up the road! The vehicle was reversed out of the field and one fire team set about 'repairing' the fence and tidying the hedge whilst another fire team used a tow rope off my rover to pull the bumper of the front offside wheel to allow us to resume the drive back to camp (in a more sedate manner!).

Once back to camp, some more formal repairs (with an FBH and IRR green and black paint) ensued. It was a late start to the weekend but we got away with it! That range day paid off, we eventually won the Lloyds Cup.

Dan Archer

I am not too sure if I should admit to this but many, many years ago I was a member of a Maxeval team and was responsible for taking officers on the 30 m range to ensure their green card reflected their ability! I arrived at the range, which was open and ready. I signed range orders and got things ready (ammo, etc.) for the first four to arrive.

They duly turned up and I took them through the practice. Each fired about 10 rounds and then left the range. Due to lack of time and needing a quick turnaround, targets were not checked.

Once the detail had left, I awaited the next four. It was at this time I heard a voice saying, "Can I come out now?" To my horror I realised the range warden had been in his shed at the bottom of the range throughout the practice! My heart missed a beat and he appeared no worse off for the experience. We agreed not to mention it! How different things may have been as they could have had a chance to practice their first aid!

Michael Marsh

1977 RAF, St Athan West Camp, 25 yard range and just done SNCOs and officers on SMG firing. Had a few rounds over so decided to fire them off rather than take them back. Loaded the mag with ten rounds of ammo and started to blast away.

Suddenly big flash, muffled explosion, and everything goes black. Cannot see a thing so pull back cocking lever and remove magazine, drop mag on floor, apply safety catch to safe and feel into breech and realise there is a case in the breech. So I stand there with weapon pointing down range and shout for Colin my corporal. He comes in and sees there is a problem. I explain situation and he examines magazine, which has six rounds in it. So seems I have had a premature explosion, which is why I am unable to see.

Colin rings for ambulance and doctor arrives some eight or ten minutes later. By now I am getting some sight back and have placed the SMG on the table and asked for an armorer to come and inspect. He looks at ammo, and then hightails it to the phone, comes back and tells me I have been using some dodgy Indian ammunition and they just received a memo not to use it and withdraw from use.

Doctor examines eyes and washes them then covers my eyes up with gauze. I am taken back to SSQ on East Camp. I was kept in overnight and monitored then placed on light duties for a fortnight. Eyesight returned to normal within forty or so hours.

Ammunition was destroyed SMG unplugged with *four* projectiles in barrel. Seem four rounds went off prematurely and insufficient force to push out of barrel. Crap ammo or what?

Robert Booth

I have no live rounds, empty cases, or misfires in my possession, Sir. Or did we? Can't recall the sqn but they were based in Germany. Maybe someone on the sqn can fill in the details. But after arriving for an exercise with 51 late 70s and enquiring after some mates that had been posted out there. We were informed that a couple of them were not available. Not available due apparently to being incarcerated for the duration. They had been at a live fire range, done all the declarations and were on their way back to base along the autobahn. Upon finding a belt of some fifty rounds still in one of their webbing pouches, they decided not to face the wrath of the sqn WO when they got back and loaded the GPMG and emptied it into the banking from the back of the Bedford as they drove along. Apparently it was the carnage of all the civvy vehicles on the autobahn weaving all over the road that caught people's attention and dropped them in it.

Dean Montgomery

Laarbruch, B Flt 1 Sqn, about '85ish! Flt deploys to Arsbeck Ranges for the day, an hour or more in the direction of Bruggan and Wildenwrath I think. Anyway, numb nuts here sleeps in to be awoken by Sgt Paddy Wilson (RIP) knocking my front door down. He gives me 10 minutes to get my shit together and off we go in one of the Flt LR's. On route Paddy concocts this story that when he got to my place, I was burying a pet dead bird in my back yard and I had to do it because my daughter was so upset! Like a twat, I agree to go along with this and subsequently tell my FS this bullshit story. Thinking I had dodged a 252 or worse, I crack on with the range practices and do the necessary.

We get to lunchtime, I had just finished cleaning my SLR when the FS shouts me over. I start to bimble across and get bollocked to get there at the double, I receive the hair dryer treatment and called a lying little c**t. Clearly Paddy had bubbled me, so my FS issues my punishment, "You can fucking walk back to Laarbruch, leave your rifle, webbing, and helmet there, and fuck off," he says. I head off toward the range gate, which is some distance, just as I get there he shouts me back. Me thinks I knew he was fucking bluffing, so I gets back to him, he says, "Now give me a fucking range declaration and fuck off!" So I oblige and off I go, hoping I pick the right route so the flt can pick me up when they go by.

About 15 mins in, a LR screeches past and slams on it brakes. A cpl and SAC rock from 37 Sqn Bruggan appear and ask where I'm heading. "Laarbruch," I says.

"We're off to 26 Sqn," they say. "We will drop you at 1 Sqn compound." You fucking dancer, spent most of the afternoon playing table football with the lads in the sqn canteen! Can't remember who the 37 Sqn guys were but they thought it was as funny as fuck.

Rob Andrews

SF course, Akamas, Cyprus. Weapons firing weapon stops, change barrel lay barrel down load new belt, weapons firing. SAC Andrews thinks, *Where's all this smoke coming from?* Looks down to see the barrel bag spontaneously combust. Moral of the story: don't lay a red hot barrel on top of a canvas barrel bag. DOH!

John Stowell

At the armoury one morning, picking up grenades and 66s in preparation for going on the ranges at Feldom. The armoury staff handed us an ammo box full of old gun cotton primers and said if we could get rid of some or all of it then it would do them a great favour. So we arrive at the grenade range, set up do the safety brief and demos and off we go. The target that day was one of those very large monster truck tyres. Eventually the inevitable happens and we get a blind. So after the customary wait the boss gets the demo charge sorted and says we can get rid of some of that stuff. Off we go with all in hand.

The boss lays the charge next to the grenade and starts to pile the gun cotton wads onto it until there is a small pile. Once satisfied, he lights the fuse and we retire and take cover behind the throwing bay wall. Next, the thing goes off. After the debris had stopped falling and the dust had cleared, we peered over the wall (must have looked like a couple of them WW2 American Killroys) the scene must of been a bit like the aftermath of the first nuclear test at Christmas Island with a large crater where the impact area used to be and no sign of that giant tyre. "F*****g hell," the boss said. "Do you think they heard that at range control?"

"Range control?" I said.

"They are probably wondering why all the doors and windows just fell out in Darlington!"

So we spent the next hour or so trying to fill the crater in and bringing what was left of the tyre back. It had been lifted outside the grenade range boundary fence. Great days and great fun. The armoury staff were pleased too.

Carl Carrier

Back in the early 90s, before everyone had iPods and the like, we used to all sing on bus journeys. One particular trip from Hullavington to Lyneham, to use the ranges there, we were singing, "We are saaaailing …" All the LAC's had collected the pistols that day (as well as the gimps, LSWs...) and for some reason, singing along, waving their hands, with pistols, in the air. Scouse Larkin turns round at the front of the bus and sees what's happening and, well let's say he wasn't too impressed, and not about their singing abilities.

On arriving at Lyneham, all the LACs are made to run up and down for what seemed like a life time with the LSWs above their heads. I used 'their' because for some reason I was sat at the front of the bus and was not involved, but I was an LAC so there was no point in trying to point this out, "Tab on Carrier."

Also reminds me of the time Moonface was cleaning his gat in the back of a four tonner when he opened his rifle up and the spring shot out the back, middle lane of the M4! DOH!

Graham Spike Thompson

3 Sqn, Op Pennant Hythe and Lydd Ranges, late 90s. The sqn had recently been taken over by a portly bespectacled sqn ldr with a love of painting. He quickly became known as the fat controller. We would be working our nads off whilst he worked on his latest water colour.

I should have known someone was up to no good when during our first range of the day the troop shelter blackboard had the biggest pair of parachute wings drawn on it with, "Gorman is God" (previous OC) written below it.

I can't remember the two wg cdrs who came to visit us on the ranges but as FS D Flt I meet them with the OC and take them into the troop shelter to chat to the troops. The OC has his back to the blackboard and as I look over his shoulder I can see the most artistic chalk drawing of the fat controller sat at an easel painting whilst Thomas the tank engine is crashing in the background. The title, "The Fat Controller paints whilst the trains run off the rails."

I looked around to see two wg cdrs trying to hide their amusement as it was in full view to them as their shoulders twitched and they stifled laughter. I don't know when he saw it, but we weren't his favourite flt.

Robbie Robinson

On some god awful ranges in Germany when on 1 Sqn early 80s. Two of the finest FSs was contemplating their evil day's work whilst siting on a long drop shit house. Two thunder flashes was dropped into the long drop. Sadly the contemplating FSs did not get out on time. Nobody saw a thing …

Richard Hawkes

Whilst on 51 in the late 70s, support weapons were down Boscombe Down, well we were on Sailsbury Plain doing what's we do best firing mortars, anti-tank and GPMG work. Well the anti-tank and GPMG were doing their thing, and the mortars were doing their thing, the finale shoot had finished, and the flight commander went over to see the pongos firing their mortars from the back of an APC. So we dug a trench and put the oggies in, we waited and waited for the flight commander to return. No flight commander, so I decided to set them off, said and done. Back came said officer, asked who had set them off, I owned up, he looked like he was doing a war dance saying, "I wanted to set them off!"

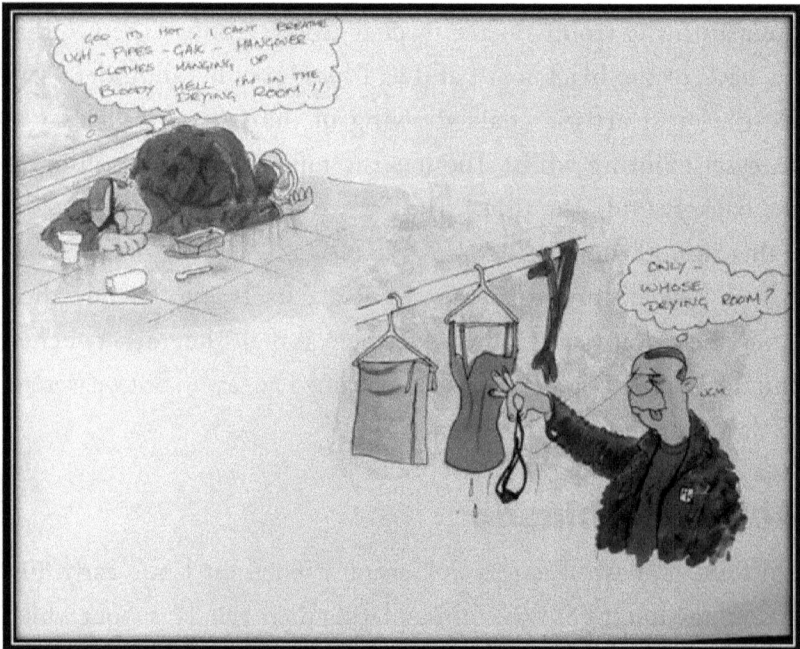

Bill Hayes

It's strange to think that all the accepted wisdom for military recollections hardly ever include the topic of training to fire one's personal weapon. The relationship between the infantryman and his rifle is symbiotic, it is part of him, part of his psyche. He is familiar with every scratch, scrape, and blemish of its surface. He has kept it, swum with it, run with it, and cleaned it, time after time after time. It works for him if he looks after it, a perfect training vehicle for a woman, except nothing can train any man to cope with the distaff side of the race.

I decided to punctuate my little stories with odd snippets of ranges after realising that some if the best episodes had been on ranges. It also lends itself to reminiscence because of the many and varied different ranges and training areas, ranging from a field in Belize where we stuck a few targets up and blazed away with our rifles for a good couple of hours, cathartic was not the word, to the delights of the Catterick and Feldom training areas and ranges.

In the distant alleyways of my life there loomed large an event that would reduce strong men to drink and weaker men to contemplate a future in a distant northern province of Canada, the Lloyds Cup. The premier shooting competition in the corps was visited on us every single year and was a serious matter. At least it was a serious matter for our COs. It could spell the difference between a further promotion or the commencement of a search for a security managers job for De Beers or other such prestigious organisation. Organising such a shoot was also one of the two open chasms into which more junior officers could fall, the other being the Station Firework Display, which for some reason always went wrong (a modern day risk assessment in today's air force would ban them completely).

As time has passed, the manner of the conduct of the Lloyds Cup shoot has changed in line with the training methods. The annual personal weapons test was the last persona I recognised before my retirement and I have no doubt it will have changed since. The test mirrored the changes in range construction and the gradual arrival of technology on the scene of military training. When I was a lad it was known as the Phase 5 Rundown. This was as it stated running down from 300 yards to 100 yards and firing at the ranges in between. Then advancing the last few years to close with the enemy and kill him—the stated doctrine of all British infantry since Oudenard onwards.

Every man jack on the squadron participated, even the flightless birds who fixed the wagons, did the leave passes, and screwed up the radio sets. The average of all scores decided on the destination of the cup (and the officers promotion roster) each year. Simple really except the devil was in the detail or, to be more precise, in the range booking.

Every rock knows that ranges are not simply classified on their facilities for firing. Such intangibles as a good scoff, open all hours also helps, as does an uninterrupted supply of beer for those not unlucky enough to be planning ranges, prepping ranges or guarding everybody. Decent accommodation is not necessary for a good range camp, the tin huts at Willsworthy Camp spring to mind, where I once passed a week range firing on Dartmoor. Despite it being the height of summer in the rest of the UK, Willsworthy remained a universe apart with all four seasons often happening twice a day. Keeping dry and warm was important and the sole means of this were the coal stoves in each of the cattle sheds where we slept. As a consequence, the troops went on the ranges smelling and looking like wee Geordie pitmen coming off shift down Paradise Drift.

So ranges were a very complicated equation and not entirely recognised by the rules of the Lloyds Cup. The reason for this, I suppose was either a simplistic view of life or one of those officer type thoughts that good troops would manage to equalise any anomalies. Whatever the reason, the squadrons in the southern half of the UK always won it. Us lot in the north never had a chance despite being on the edge of one of the most extensive range complexes in Northern Europe. It was not unusual for the troops to deploy at the start line complete with scaling ladders and crampons for the ascent ahead. The names of those pleasure centres like Deer Park and Whipperdale fail to mask the long remembered pain of those days. Deer Park in particular was almost vertical between the start and finish and because the range was up hill, each individual firing point had to be built up so that the last 5 yards was 20 feet higher as well and actually had wee sets of steps cut into the side of the elevating mounds. By the time us unfortunates got to the firing point (under strict timing conditions), seeing the target became somewhat of a second place to garnering enough oxygen into the lungs to sustain life.

Failing the delights of the Catterick Range complex, you might be unlucky enough to draw the reserve range at Battle Hills. I have been on many ranges in my life but the memories of Battle Hills is a horror story in a league of its own. It is the highest range in UK, above the A66 and the town of Brough. A winding road led in to the depths of northern Pennines but anything north of the entrance of the ranges was the marked on a fairly empty map as 'here be tygers'. The range was dilapidated and the unfortunates who were wardens eked out their miserable pittance by topping all manner critters on adjoining homesteads. Range discipline was always difficult with the range road in the centre but the weather was always the killer. Battle Hills would be booked for three days for a shoot that normally would take one. Mist was the staple diet that in reality was low flying cloud. Range officers would need runners to be able to see either end of the firing point and more than once I have seem a battle hardened young switched on officer carted back to Catterick by Land Rover gibbering and frothing at the mouth after a session here, especially if the mist lifted unexpectedly and he discovered he had been firing for ages with the butt's flag up— and a couple of the range wardens wandering back into the butts after topping a couple of reluctant sheep at Cowheugh Farm just down the road, with the year's mutton ration humped over their shoulders, waving to the troops. There was a huge inclination to turn their lights out permanently but common sense (and large and wise NCOs) guaranteed the continuance of their sheep husbandry activities.

Some of the other ranges, like the new-fangled ones with targets that didn't need to be pasted up were beginning to appear at the end of the 60s and more and more became common. Strangely the troops preferred the old gallery ranges with some hours being spent in the butts pasting out bullet holes with manky paste pots that had originally been created in the run up to Waterloo and the paste just replenished annually with some pungent rubbish. Small squares of different colours were the texture of the targets and god help you if you got a nit-picker who could see from 300 yards away that you had put a ochre coloured patch on one that demanded a black one.

The most fun were on the field firing ranges like those at Otterburn or Sennybridge. Sennybridge is a name that strikes fear into most old rocks—a place of cold damp and wind, and that was just the billets. The 16th of Foot were encamped in Sennybridge, preparing for one of the many deployments overseas we got volunteered for and were honing up our battle shooting skills on an Individual CQB. This took the form of the usual recce patrol—you get separated from the rest of the patrol and have information that can save the free world but you have to get it back to base with a rough mixed bag of Russian Spetznatz. In those days we had no electronic pop-ups and all the targets were used on a pull system with handles and levers and spindles, a very effective but Heath Robinson effect. The guys who pulled the levers were protected by bunkers and were usually those of the flight who were injured or more intellectually challenged. One of these, of Cro-Magnon lineage, was installed in the main target of the range, a crosser about 4 feet up over a stream. The form was usually a SNCO and a trooper followed the hapless wit who was being exercised down the range. The SNCO controlled the range and the trooper carried the flags which indicated to the occupants of the target bunkers when to put their targets up and down—simples, hah!

I had gone down on one of the first runs and did my stuff well despite getting drowned when the crosser came up late and I had to take cover in the stream. Still I was top of the leader board and was grabbed by our Sergeant Mick, the Brummie, and I carried on from there. The boys had a good day and many plywood Spetznaz were dispatched with vigour but as the afternoon wore on several things became clear. Unless my mate, the google eyed Yorkie, could beat my score, I was going to win the kitty. We always had a kitty, it was a bit of an incentive, but the rules were complicated which never became apparent until it became complicated. Anyway, the other thing that was apparent was that Cro-Magnon man in the crosser pit was less than consistent. In fact he was like a black powder pistol, you pressed the trigger and felt the hammer go forward and then a wait of varying degrees whilst it registered and another wait whilst the info was processed and the lever located and pulled. It could vary between 10 seconds and a number of minutes and ex-pletives. Yorkie had a secret, despite the outward appearance of a beer sodden wretch with rugby league tendencies he was, in fact, a very good soldier, and, after getting his two mags of 7.62mm (and swapping the odd round into the other mag—you didn't think we were daft enough not to work out that two rounds per target meant you needed an even number of rounds in the box otherwise you got a stoppage in the middle of an engagement) cammed up and moved to the start line ready to boogie.

Yorky's strategy was a bit like mine, pick your next cover and get to it ASAP. All went well, even the mag change negotiated until two targets from the end. A huge boulder gave some cover to get the breath before crossing the stream, where the mover was located. The idea was to get the firer to fire one from the shoulder and one from kneeling as there was no cover at all. Off we went, the Yorkshire whirling Dervish moving at goo pace when I get the signal to raise the mover. Green flag waving to where I know the bunker is—nothing happens. Yorkie is now toes into the stream and Mick is signalling to me—too late out of arc, when the caveman lets go and down comes the mover. Yorkie executes and turn that would have had Jayne Torvill purring with professional pride and lets go a double tap—I stick the red flag up—the Fig 11 target rotates off the pulley and steel wire and there is the most horrendous scream from the bunker. As an experienced RCO myself of later years, I can only guess what was going through Mick's mind. The prescribed drills were carried out—unloaded and cleared and I was dispatched forward to see what the damage was to Piltdown Man. As I got close all I could see was him on his back outside of his pit covered in claret, hands to his head. Out with the water bottle and sort him out sharp. The upshot. Piltdown was not just dim, he was a lazy git as well and had got into the habit of wandering out of his pit so he could do some fancy handwork with the target, which meant he didn't have to patch the targets as he should have. The second of Yorky's shots had hit the small pulley wheel at the top of the target, completely destroying it, so the target had spun around crashing down on Piltdown's head, splitting his head open and a small cut spewing forth his lifeblood. He never whinged about the pain after that first cry and the opinion on the flight was that it was a case of no sense no feeling. Anyway, the end result was when the scores were added up and cogitated over in the back of the Bedford it was decided that the kitty (there is *always* a kitty) would go to me for the best score, but as I was driving the boss in the Rover and was not there to collect it, I was disqualified and awarded to Yorky because of his flair and getting Piltdown. However, he was immediately disqualified because he hadn't killed the slow witted numbskull and it was put into the pot for the night's festivities in the NAAFI.

Richard Hawkes

51 Sqn, was at Otterburn training area, each flight had done there bit, then it was a sqn in attack. The mortar section had laid on their targets, so we were stood down until the afternoon, so we got the mortar bombs sorted in the trailer with the mortar. I got the No. 4 position, so all I had to do was to get the bombs out of the trailer, get the bombs out of the tubes, and pass them to the No. 3 who checks the oggies for the right charge. Well, everything was going well until the last firing. I had done my job and had put the empty tubes in the trailer, I then went back to the mortar where the last bomb was handed to the No. 2 who was waiting for the order to fire. Order given, round down tube, off it went. We waited and waited, then we hear the explosion, not in the training area but in the sheep pens. I don't know how many sheep killed or injured, at least the farmer didn't have to send them to the slaughter house,

James Little

WI course, Warminster, 1980. On range with 12 GPMGs, we had all been ordered to keep 1,000 rounds for the FPF at 12:00. We were also informed that there would be no further orders for this. 12:00 getting closer and one by one the GPMGs went quiet. At the appointed hour, all guns fired, a wonderful sight as tracer, dirt, and other crap from a 100 metre square was disintegrated. So was a 10 metre square 45 deg to our left. 12 guns quickly check the direction of their guns. Well actually 11 guns checked. The 12th gun was now deserted and the three BDF troops were fighting, not arguing, no, *fighting* each other as they each said it was not his fault. DS must be used to this as the rogue gun still kept within the safety arc.

CHAPTER 5
THE AMERICAN CONNECTION

Michael Hobbs

After leaving the Factory, I had a very, very short stay in Bruggen, which resulted in me being sent home after a night out with the WO's daughter. Anyways, I was sent to West Raynham to do the Rapier course, and after that held over with TSF until 66 came back from the land of sand. While at Raynham, I would go out into Fakenham on a Friday night and drink at the Limes. One night, I got a little bit drunk, and was jumped by a few of the locals outside the pub. I was being beaten to a pulp by these guys, when all of a sudden the punches and the kicks stopped, and all I could hear was a lot of screaming and shouting, and this thunderous voice shouting, "Hey, you fuckers, leave him alone, he's one of mine!"

A few moments later, I was picked up, taken back to the Limes, sat down on a stool, had a glass of whiskey given to me, and told to, "Man up and hold these." Through bleary eyes, I held out my hand and was given two teeth. The guy who had given them to me was a Rock on a course, but I never found out who he was. He was a big Scottish bloke, with a nose that looked like it had been broken a few times, and shoulders you could land a Chinook on. He said to hold on to these, as they would be collected sometime soon, then he disappeared into the drunken night.

The following week, I was at the Limes again, and some civy bloke walked up to me and said, "I owe you an apology from last week," then smiled , showing two front teeth missing.

I smiled at him held out my hand and said, "These must be yours then," and gave him back his teeth. I never did find out who the jock Rock was …

Dave Pooley

ADS Dflt. As a Sqn we were doing several exercises with our U.S. counterparts based at Mildenhall. D Flt was to demo a wood clearance at Stanford training area to be overseen and filmed by

U.S. High rankers. Not a problem, get on a helicopter, a few laps around, debus all round defence, and as a flt clear the wood of any enemy, job done. Only one problem—no one envisaged a certain SAC taking the limelight for all the wrong reasons! He had put himself as GPMG gunner on our section and had more link around him than John Rambo! Looking very ally but also attracting the attention of the U.S. entourage. I must point out to those who don't know him he's not the slimmest or fittest of gunners.

The chopper lands, we all debus and spread out as a flight into the wood and proceed to clear it by sections. Our section, led by Cpl Dave Knight, was moving speedily through, broken down into pairs FM through the cover. All of a sudden, the sound of controlled fire was overcome by a GPMG burst of about 5min! Everyone stops and crashing through the trees comes said SAC, chin strap around his cheek, eyes shut, gasping for breath, firing straight up in the air trying to fire off all his link in a one go! Cpl Knight screams, "Get the gun off that prick!" Myself and Pete understand the order but are unable to move as we have massive stomach cramps and piss dribbling from our cocks from laughter.

Lister is in full private pile mode now as he's taken up a fire position on his back like some stranded giant tortoise, still firing aimlessly into the air. This has not gone unnoticed by the cameraman or the U.S. Ds.

We eventually strip him of all his kit and leave him against a tree with just his water bottle and continue the wood clearance. "No need for debrief, it's all on camera, thanks," chuckled the yanks!

Mick Failes

Many moons ago on some exercise (A1 19 Sqn) deployed somewhere but non tac (tracking ex maybe?). Anyhow, we had an LAC sat in a tracker shelter that we quite often used as a radio shack type thang (yank Sqn), he was on radio watch while the so called 'old sweats' did their best to amuse themselves cooking din dins and so on and so forth. Our DC at the time had a habit of shitting in blue roll and wrapping it up to carry around with him all day (ex para). It was decided, with loads of giggles, to give said blue wrapped turd on a tin plate to said radio watch LAC for tea. Try saying that after a few!

The whole crew stood around this tracker shelter (LAC inside remember) as the steaming hot grub was passed in (neatly wrapped in blue roll), after a few seconds, while we stood around, trying not to burst out laughing at our own cleverness, came from inside a loud shout, "What? No fucking brown sauce?"

Geoff, you are and always will be 'The Man'.

Tim Parker

Odd how your eyes can deceive you. On 19 Squadron, we were doing some field type training on Sennybridge and a night navex featured. The rains had cleared, leaving us with a cold, clear, very moonlit night. The route truthfully wasn't that challenging but whatever map appreciations we had done had not prepared us for a canal. The water was still and glistened in the moonlight but no bridge could be seen at all. To a man we stood around stroking our chins and trying to work out how to cross it. Not fancying a full immersion, I suggested throwing a rock in to see how deep it was. For want of a better idea, we did this. All were shocked when, with a crack, the rock hit wet tarmac. None of the eight of us had believed it to be anything other than a canal. Rapier wankers ...

Wayne Holliss

Whilst at RAF Molesworth the Rocks had the joys of living on the yank base at Alconbury and all that came with it. So one Saturday night, a rather pissed group of Apes decided it would be nice to liberate a yank flag, the one we wanted was unobtainable as it was the station flag and was put to bed each evening by the spams. This left us only one option—the flag outside the spam station cmrd's house. Now, being Rocks, we weren't just going to run up and grab it, no, we were going plan this one properly like.

So, an 'O' group was organised by the three of us, then off we went. Fully cammed up, due to the lack of cam cream, we used boot polish. We move with all the grace of a drunk bull elephant over fences and through back gardens till we reached our objective. Two of us keeping watched whilst the third team member made a grab for the flag. It soon became apparent that having it away wasn't going to be all that easy, especially in the dark and pissed, first me and then the other Rock had to help tear it down. So there we are, three pissed up gunners, in full DPM, covered in boot polish, trying to pull down a bloody flag. All was going well till the window opened and the light went on, followed but a loud scream and hysteria.

Off we run with said flag, back to the block, stuffed the flag away and quickly got changed back into civvies, sat down to watch the box, beer in hand as if nothing had happened. Very soon there's knock on the door followed by the deep voice of two MOD plod coppers, both demanding to know, "Where's the flag?"

One of the last deployments 66 did to Lakenheath was one of the funniest I've ever been on. We'd been out for about four days when the FS and his driver turned up for a refuel and a chat. So we all got chatting as you do and it put to us that another crew were looking to swap half dozen eggs for a bag of porridge if we were interested. Well, we didn't have any porridge so we left it at that. Anyway turns out that another crew did the swap so that was that. We later heard that when they went to make some egg banjos someone forgot to tell them that Nige had hard boiled the eggs.

Si N Becks Lloyd

Greenham Common det. We must all remember driving the short wheel based LR around. Then of course someone says, "Let's do timed runs around the site." So moi tries to do a good impression of a rally driver going into corners, etc. thinking I was the dog's bollocks. Like you do. No accidents or fuck ups along the way. Or so I thought.

Park up get out and my co driver says those immortal words, "Oh fuck."

"What?" says I. Took me ages to cut the barbed wire off that had wrapped itself all around the prop shaft.

Wayne Holliss

The battle of the AQ club, RAF Alconbury, late 1987. As most of the block did in those days, I was entertaining a young lady in my room, when I say entertaining I mean making love, Annie from Corby. There I am, banging away, when all of a sudden the door is almost ripped off its hinges, in walks a rather bloody and pissed off SAC Billy Bird. So being concerned at the state of him, I enquired as to how he was and what had happened. He informed me that he had had an altercation with some American gentlemen of a certain colour persuasion, all words to that affect. This of course couldn't go unpunished, can't have spams getting above themselves can we?

So, a block call out was initiated. Rocks appeared from every room, most in regulation fighting order of dessie boots, UJ shorts, and t-shirts. We formed up and marched in mob order to the AQ club, looking for said American gentlemen. Soon after arriving, we took the opportunity to resupply with beer, all of a sudden someone noticed we were the only ones in the club, which was most unusual, one of the guys looked out the window and saw that almost the whole club was surrounded by yank coppers with red and blue lights flashing, even had some leaning over car bonnets with pistols drawn, scary especially when considering how yanks like to shoot unarmed people.

So it was time for a tactical withdraw, which we did, loved the look on the copper's faces when we left the club, don't know whose arses were twitching the most, ours or theirs.

So I retired to Gunner Moore's room, we both sat there beer in hand, me wearing a set of mickey mouse ears, Steve in a sombrero. Next thing we knew the RAF station commander was standing there asking Steve what was going on and why we were looking for a fight. Well if ever a master class in bullshit was given, Steve Moore gave it, that poor Guin didn't know what hit him, he left a broken man. We never did get to sort out the yanks either

Stephen Headey

I remember when I was attached from 48 to Greenham and used to share the guard duty with the snowdrops. It was winter and, as per usual, guarding the perimeter and keeping warm next to the coal fires we had. Two hours before take over, used to use all the supply of coal so the buggers froze later on. Teamwork or what! Alternatively piss on the fire till it was nearly out. Mmm, the smell of burning piss. The smell of victory.

Andrew Paul Jones

So Greenham Common, mid-80s, not the cushy GAMA job of 501 but yet another 51 Sqn trip to spend another 2 winter weeks stagging on the fence. As the shift patterns changed on a weekly basis for this jaunt we gunners were doing 12 hour days back to back with Trade Group 8s finest, the Scuffers drawing the short straw with nights. As I say a winter tour so we had our braziers, a supply of coal, and a pallet of wood to burn.

As you can imagine one of the only legitimate ways to relive boredom was to tend your fire. But no, as we were using far too much, the order was delivered that braziers could only be used by the night shift and us gunners would have to suck up the daytime cold with our Arctic Parkers.

For those 'lucky' enough to remember, shift change was done by four tonner driving from post to post, copper off, gunner on. We gunners would leave whilst watching the copper eagerly set about lighting his fire to warm his night. Well, it was during a very bitter day shift that a certain gunner decided to be nice to his copper cohort and *prep* his fire. All day I, I mean, *he* spent pissing on the coal, splitting the pallet to make kindling and layering the brazier so it would catch fire with ease.

There was however a devious side to our young gunner friend as he tasked the north side mobile to bring him a roadkill rabbit, a rabbit that was coiled into a neat little ball and strategically placed camouflaged amidst the coal and kindling.

Now cast your mind back troops to the split screen 109 SWB Landy with its petrol fuel tanks below the seats, and most Greenham fence vets will remember the coke can on a wire we used to use to requisition a little petrol to initiate our fires. Well our friend got a little carried away with that can, let's just say, in the short time before the Scuffer arrived, more than one can went on to the 'prepped' fire.

So it's shift change, the four tonner is on its merry journey, pig off, gunner on with a parting comment of, "I've sorted your fire, mate, just needs a little petrol."

Three or four posts further a long and one word, "Fireball!" Still to this day I giggle thinking of a Scuffer with singed eyebrows monking because a gunner set him up, being warmed by a great fire but thinking, *What is that god awful smell?* as the burning dead rabbit odour mixed with the urine sodden coal starts to add insult to injury.

Mick Cundy

On exercise, 66 Sqn HQ at Rod and Gun Club Lakenheath. Rock decides he needs to go for a shit and takes his shovel. Three of us follow him, very quietly with a shovel of our own. He drops his NBC suit and kecks and does the business. We are behind him hidden by a bush or something and have slid our shovel underneath him and his deposits land on that. We then withdraw it. Oh! The look on his face when he cannot find any evidence of his actions. Nearly choked trying not to laugh.

Wayne Holliss

I remembering standing at the bar in the Falcon Pub in Huntingdon, as you do, when a fellow SAC rock returns from the bog crunching on something. When I asked what he was eating he replied that he was having a piss when he wondered what the square cubes in the urinal tasted like, so that's what he was eating—not a lot one can say about that really is there.

Gareth Burton

During a Wurly Gig Op on 19 Sqn at Salisbury Plain, we had been given a shite site on a steep embankment after day four. In order to get the launcher into position, Spike Thompson guided me to a perfect spot where I could use the FUT to winch the main frame up.

After I parked it up, I grabbed the winch to attach it to the towing eye, I noticed the wagon pass me heading towards the lads. I'd left the handbrake off.

I don't know how I did it, but I managed to race to the driver's door, pull it open, and yank the handbrake up in one movement. I made the coffees for the rest of the det.

Stephen Headey

303rd Molesworth, circa '87. Sitting in on a lecture being given by one of the master sgts on tactics (ha ha). To the left of me was a certain SAC (ex QCS) who shall remain nameless but was very good as a lawyer, if you know what I mean. Well this m/sgt was carrying on when I just noticed at the corner of my eye this said SAC was cutting the 303rd badge off his DPM jacket. We had been ordered to sew these on our jackets by our flt commander.

The lecture continued and by now this person was getting noticed as he proceeded to cut up this badge. The lecture ended and our flt commander, who was now ashen with anger, pulled the SAC to one side and asked what the hell he was doing. He replied, "Sorry, Sir, I'm not allowed to quote Queen's regulations but it makes very interesting reading, especially about insignias."

Two days later we were all told to remove the said badges from our jackets. You are a legend, mate.

John Berwick

Greenham Common mobile patrol in an almost new 3/4 ton Land Rover 1300km on the clock, bondoo bashing letting the back end slide. Suddenly Land Rover is sliding and goes into to slow motion and then up on two wheels, hangs there for what seemed like hours, and then dink, it falls over on to its side.

Two young gunners in it with me seemed to slide out of the wagon quicker than a Scuffer's warrant card. I get out a bit dazed as the PVR radio clocked me on the head, I gets out, looks around, I feel panic creeping over me as in how the fuck are we going to get this back on its wheels. Two attempt fail panic sets in and I can hear in my head is march in the guilty bastard, I suck up and push like fuck! Land Rover is back on its wheels, leaning at a funny angle, smashed window, and a flat front tyre. I drive it back to HQ, Spike Cook was acting sgt, he knew right away what had happened. I came up with a story that a smellie threw a rock, it hit the Rover, I hit a tree (weak, I know). Crash investigators found tracks and wing mirror, I was fucked. Kicked off Greenham, two weeks in Northholt, and £500 fine. Ouch.

Jonathan Brocklehurst

So I remember a sprog who was left behind on Stanta training area one day by an American called Sgt White (303rd days). Anyway, after being told to go stag on and being left, thought it had gone a little quite, as in nobody remembered said lac. Being a good LAC and remembering his training, stay where you are someone will come and get you, he did. A little time later (a long time), someone realised poor LAC wasn't there so sent a search party to find him. Didn't take long as said LAC was at the FUP.

The sgt, a ginger haired person, gave lac two choices (I love this bit, as it was said about three years later) "You can have my punishment or a charge," well fuck me, not rocket science for a LAC. "Right, run back to the squadron lines and we will say no more about it and I will give you a head start. *But* you have to run back and beat us or you're in the shit." Smart LAC starts to run back and comes to a T-junction, instead of turning right, he runs straight over, cutting out a big portion of the route. Anyway, cut it short, I beat said ginge back.

Now poor LAC back at sunny Molesworth gets pulled into the WO and gets a right ass fucking, you know the type, where if you were right you were not, almost very upset (understatement), gets told to get out after said ass chewing to see a ginger head walking down the corridor. LAC sees red and is angry upset and being lied too (poor LAC) and runs down the corridor, jumps onto the sgt's back, slaps him, pushes him into the side room, and does a runner straight to the FS.

Now picture this. Flight sgt working away when lac runs into the room, sits down and bubbles a lot. "Please, LAC, sit down, why don't you, and what the fuck is up with you?"

LAC: I have just beat up Sgt Ginge.

FS: "Really, oh well."

Sgt Ginger runs in with someone else and shouts, "That's him!"

FS turns round and says, "What was him?"

Sgt says: "He is the one that jumped me and beat me!"

FS: "I dont think so, Sgt Ginge. He was with me after seeing the WO."

Sgt Ginge argues.

FS: "Are you calling me a liar? And stand to attention when speaking to me!"

Sgt Ginge: "No, FS, I was just saying …"

FS: "Well say fook off and don't call me a liar."

LAC then gets five days in the block as orderly airmen.

A few years later on parade 1 Sqd, said sgt is now FS on B flight, he walks out for his first parade with a book, walks past all airman, stops at now SAC says, "Is that you?" (well, the whole flight fucking knew what had happened)

Said SAC goes, "Oh yes, Flight, I was at Molesworth." He dismisses parade and SAC gets called into office for three years of shit using the old line of 'my end of the stick or a charge'. Tosser. Again, he couldn't prove anything but didn't have the balls to be a man about it. Happy days, ginger wanker. The FS now WO. Funny thing, saw him at Honigton and he brought it up in passing, made me laugh.

Phil Swales

On A Flt 66 Sqn at West Raynham, I forget the det name, could be A3, I was the TC and we had a LAC, his name was Duane Barwood or Baz to all, a real happy go lucky lad, always smiling and always seemed to have rosy red cheeks. He blushed easily, bless him. He got married whilst on the crew, moved into MQs and thought it'd be a nice idea if we had a crew 'get together' at his house, meet his wife, etc. so one Wednesday evening the crew gathers at his, the sgt couldn't make it if I remember right, we all bring the bottles and slabs of ale, I bring two slabs of Tetley bitter. We're invited in, introduced to his wife, a lovely lass, she called me corporal. "Hey, love, no need to call me that, Phil's me name." She asked what we all wanted, there was Vodka and coke, Bacardi and coke ordered, I asked for Tetleys. Few mins later, she came in with a tray of drinks, all get given their ordered drinks, I get mine—a blooming cup of tea! She had brought me a cup of Tetley tea, in a cup and saucer! I thought it was a wind up but it wasn't. God bless her. Baz's face went bright red! We never let him forget that.

Baz, I heard, had remustered to MT. RAF Regiment 'Gunner' Duane Barwood was killed in action in Iraq. He left a wife and two daughters. Rest in eternal peace, Baz. *Per Ardua*. Once in, always in.

Wayne Holliss

Remember cleaning out my goldfish one evening whilst at Alconbury, so I put him in the sink after filling it with water, and went for a shit. When I came back some twat had pulled the plug and he'd gone, never to be seen again, time you own up, ya bastard!

Chris Pacey

ADS Honington, in the late 90s, we went into shift as normal to be told when we got there that this was the last day of shift and the last Nuke convoy leaves today. No more Nukes, no more ADS! So with that very secretive ambush information we set about preparing to see off the five (TCHD) cargo trucks, the NW Convoy Group (RAF Regt), and the Special Escort Group (Comacchio Group Royal Marines). We have a crack with the RAF MT drivers, Rocks and Bootys as we wave them off for the last time, or so we thought!

As the last SEG transit 4x4 is leaving, an unnamed gunner on access duty prematurely raises the hydraulic ramp barrier under the transit lifting it into the air and grounding it. We all hear the awful crunch and scrape as it hit and all and wonder has it fucked it? Yes it has! Turn around everybody, we can't go on the road minus half our escort. You can imagine the procession of HQ wagons making its way to the site to chew the boss and unnamed gunner (last 3 Mason) a new arsehole! The reek of gash cunt was palpable! On the fucked about list included: 33 Sqn Puma 2 aircraft standby for another two days, all the police constabularies from Suffolk to Aldermaston, NWCG, Guins, Commach, Lynham, RAF STO Centre, already at Lynham, and the Civvy reception team at AWE. All because of Mat

Mase's fat cumberland sausage finger! You are a legend and chopper simultaneously.

John Rhodes

Talking of Greenham, on the way to or coming back from the plain a complete numpty in a transit milk float decided he was going to force our Humvee off the road. Definitely not his brightest decision. As we drove into the distance, he was last seen careering downhill across a field.

Richard Barton

Home to Greenham when I saw a lady hitch hiking. Ever the beau, I stopped, thinking she was going to Basingstoke (petrol was cheap in them days). Anyway, she asked me to take her to the CND camp at the main gate to Greenham. No problem. Dropped her off then drove into camp. The look on the face of the MOD plod was priceless.

Patrick Bartlett

Greenham Common mid-November doing a swing shift. As normal, run out of coal for braziers so any wood lying around, pallets, etc., pickup and dutifully delivered to said braziers. Of course with RAFP taking over from us, made sure nothing left for them to burn.

Anyway came back from three days off to be paraded. "Okay, who knows anything about the builders timber gone missing?"

As normal, dumb looks all round, "When did it go missing?"

"Night of last swing shift."

"Not us, honest." Turns out the RAFP got cold in the night, burnt £8,000 worth of roofing timber from an office complex being built, but Regt of course first to get blame.

Colin Whitaker

Well. One day in December at Greenham Common, we were having a lecture in the cinema. I think about the accuracy on the tomahawk. Anyway, another SAC Rock Yorky. We decided to make a rising sun headband and stand in the entrance to the lecture and wish all the Yanks 'happy anniversary', as it was Pearl Harbour Day. Afterwards, when we thought about it, we were surprised not to get court marshalled or at least charged.

Whilst we were having the lecture, I decided to ask if the Russians detonate one of theirs first wouldn't the EMP make the tomahawk useless. The answer from one of the yanks was, "Er, yeah." I think we all sniggered a bit

"GOT TO GO NOW, THIS IS MY LAST TEN."

John Stowell

Probably not the usual subject post on this site but here goes. Whilst at Catterick on basic gunners '86–'89, I worked for several flt cdrs, one of whom was the American exchange officer Capt Zider. He told me the following story.

One of his previous postings was in Okinawa, Japan way. Two of his combat security police men were on a local area patrol one night and were set upon by some locals. In the scuffle, a knife was drawn and one of the policemen was stabbed. The other policeman then drew his pistol and shot the guy.

At the court of enquiry, this policeman was asked to explain why he had shot the guy. After doing so the court then said, "Okay, but why did you shoot him nine times?"

His answer was because the 45 automatic pistol only has a nine round magazine. Good job he didn't have an M16, eh?

Wayne Holliss

Christmas at Molesworth, 87, all the lads are called to the conference room. After a while, in walks Major Ed Herron OC the wing, closely followed by old one lung Phil Barber, "Okay, folks, just to let you know we had an alarm go off on the site. A man in a red jacket with a white beard has been seen, you need to be aware." We all thought, do we really need this?

The next thing we know, the door opens and in walks a black yank dressed as Santa, so muggings here looks up and says, "Sir?"

"Yes, Holliss, what is it?"

Then I come out with one of the best lines I ever said in the MOD, even if I say so myself, "I think your chimney needs sweeping, Sir."

Fuck me, you could have heard a pin drop, Rocks biting their lips trying not to laugh; yanks sat there as the remark goes straight over their head. Old one gave me the look of death and then the pointing of his boney old finger, followed by those words I heard far too often, "You! My office now!" No sense of humour him.

Molesworth, '87, me and a couple of other Rocks pull up at the yank stores in a Humvee, we go in and the yank tec sgt asks us what we're here for, so we tell him we're after some cam sticks. He then comes out with, what can only be described as music to a monkey's ears, "Sorry, folks, I have to go a meeting, the sticks are in the back, help yourself, and please close the door when you leave."

We did just that, never seen a Humvee loaded up so fast. Hate to be him when they did a stock check.

Stephen Headey

Molesworth 1988. Myself and Mad Tomo were dicked to doing the flag raising ceremony. Whilst waiting to put on the morning show, Tomo was engaged with Lewis Benassutti about the stars and stripes flag, when Tomo took the flag, threw it to the floor, and proceeded to dance on it. I pissed myself laughing, to which Lewis grabbed the RAF ensign from Tomo and did the same smiling as he did it. Tomo turned round and said, "Ha, that's not the flag of our country!" Lewis's face was a picture.

Kett Windsor

Okay, I will write a story and I swear this is the frickin truth, as the best I can remember, my time with the Rocks. It was in the land of jolly ole England in the early years of 1987. I landed on A Flt missile defence team with a mix of American security police and RAF regiment forces. We spent the first couple of days getting to know one another and partying in Huntington after work and just having a great time. Well about the fourth or fifth day we had a break in training and went over to the NAAFI for a coffee or soda.

While we were standing in line, a server girl came up to us behind the counter and asked us, "Can I get something for you all?"

Well this kind of small Rock (only about 5'5" maybe) replied, "Well, let's see!" He then proceeded to unzip his trousers and pulled his frickin dick out. It was about the size of a small battle ship and hung down to his knees. He bent down, gave it a kiss, looked at the server, and said, "Well if you can do that, luv, then I guess you could help me!" I was like, *Holy fucking shit, that was impressive* and one of my first experiences with the Rock mentality!

Tony Ryan

For my sins against humanity, I was posted to 501 at Greenham Common. It was during a night shift in the gamma during the winter of '83 I was tasked with going out to relieve the whiskey posts, which were huts/phone box type of structure with a sand-bagged emplacement alongside for when the doo doo hit the fan. This was 12 hours in this hut watching a temporary fence erected to keep the workman out of the operational part while they built other structures. There was four of these whiskey posts so you had line of site of at least one. They had an electric heater and a field telephone to all connected to each other. My job was to go out and relieve them for comfort breaks and food breaks, etc.

Well, there was two yanks taking the piss with breaks so I went to this one post and I was knocked off my feet by the volume of heat coming from the heater, so as soon as he was gone, I turned it off and waited till it cooled before spanking my monkey on to the heater and wiping my hoop on the ear piece of the field telephone.

Eventually the yank came back, offered his thanks and off I went to the next one down to relieve him. It took about 10 minutes before the phone went and the enquiry regarding the over-power-ing smell of fish coming from his heater. I did of course tell him of my crime as well as to sniff the ear piece. I could hear the vomiting from where I was, the guy then threatened to shoot me so a cpl was summoned to get this guy out of site as he had lost the plot, one of the lads had to finish the guy's stag. Yanks can't take a joke.

Wayne Holliss

Molesworth, 1987. My good self was detached from the mighty C Flt to go and play with the not so mighty A shite. So there we are, somewhere on STANA in this wood where we were to dig in. There was myself, the great Steve Moore, and a couple of spams who were to occupy the hole once it was dug. One of the spams being none other than the 303rds own soldier of fortune, Combat Dan the man, or as he was known to us Rocks, a complete bell end.

So, we dug said hole—when I say 'we' I mean me and Steve, the spams always having some lame duck excuse to disappear. As we start to make it comfy, Combat Dan pops up with his Bergen and pulls out a spice rack, not a small jar but a complete spice rack. So I look at Steve and he looks at me, both of us thinking the same thing. I believe it's still in the bottom of the trench 30yrs later.

Next comes out a six pack of coke, looking at me, Combat tells me he's going place them in a hole to keep them cold "Okay," says I.

That evening Steve decides to dig a sump and, forgetting where the cokes were, manages to put the pick axe through each one, oops.

Just before dark, we were giving a trip flare to put out, with the order that it was to be placed on a command wire. So Steve went forward to carry out the action, place it right next to the shit route.

After the 2nd day, the spams were really getting on our tits, and a plan was hatch to seek revenge. That night, I was on stag when Combat Dan decides he needs a dump, so out he crawls, armed with a bog roll, no weapon, and wearing a pair of PNGs. Well, when opportunity knocks, you need to answer, don't ya? I quickly woke Steve and informed where dick head had gone. So we waited for the right moment, watching through the CWS. Didn't have long to wait, Combat had finished he shit and was making his way back. As he reached the trip, Steve pulls the command line. POP! Instant sunshine.

Instantly Combat's PNGs became useless, he was wondering around totally blind, twat must of hit every tree in the wood. Well we were pissing ourselves, Chris Eden came over demanding to know why we had popped the trip.

Barrister at law Gunner Moore was straight in there to our defence, "Well, Wayne saw this figure creeping about out there and called a stand two, we had no idea that the twat was one of ours, as he'd forgot to tell anyone that he was going out there." He got a right bollocking and we didn't have to disarm that bloody trip.

Phil Swales

Don't know if I should mention the night of Feb, 1986, myself as a cpl in charge of a section of lads from different sqns on the outer wire at Greenham and an SAC, an old mate from 58 (name not supplied for obvious reasons), helped two young ladies over the wire. From the outside in, and spent an enjoyable evening in our rooms in them rotten old railway carriages. And yes, they did smell a little from the camp fire. Getting them back out and over the fence to their camp the next morning took some planning.

Alan Trevest

Greenham Common, '85–'86ish. Detached there with QCS as part of our 'green season'. One night I was with three guys conducting a mobile patrol around the fence line in a SWB LR bombing along the track, as you do, parallel to the fence, when we came to a gravel path leading to a crash gate which ran across our path. This gravel path was raised and the edges were angled so that vehicles could drive over the path and continue driving along the fence line.

As mentioned, we were bombing along and we hit the edge of the path and became airborne. Now the SWB we were driving had the spare tyre on the bonnet and around the spare tyre was a roll of barbed wire. As we got airborne I watched as the roll of barbed wire lift off the spare wheel and flew over the back of the LR. We flew over the track, literally, and landed on the other side and slithered to a halt. I looked at the driver, he looked at me, expecting a bollocking, I turned to the back and asked, "You guys okay?" to find one gunner pissing himself laughing and his mate nowhere to be seen. I said, "Where's ???" (Name escapes me) to which he just pointed out back and curled into a ball laughing. I looked out the back and there sat on the grass with a WTF expression was the missing gnr and a roll of barbed wire! Happy days!

Chris Vipond

Remember 66 at Sennybridge, walking through the camp a little bit dark, passed this guy in combats. He then turned and shouted to us, "Who are you?"

I replied, "66 Sqn RAF Regt."

He said, "Do you not salute captains in the RAF?"

"No," I said.

"Why not?" he asked.

"Because we don't have captains in the RAF."

Richard Barton

Deployment to Salisbury plain training area. I dig a hole, live with three Americans. Noise in undergrowth. I somehow manage to keep the Americans silent. The noise gets closer. Challenge given, "Air Force, stop or I fire."

Suddenly I hear running away noises. I report this on the radio and was instructed to put slap flare up (American shemuly). This I did, not knowing it was signal for *stand to* for an army battalion and mod cops, about 1000 people, all told.

I send another flare up. Americans report lights on hill and moving trees. That's passive night goggles for you ...

I was on one of the gates when the TA came past with five stalwart amphibious vehicles. The CND ladies let four go past then attacked the last one. Daft convoy commander then brought other four back and they were attacked too. All over by the time TVP turned up. Laughed my socks off.

Patrick Bartlett

Did a couple walking the wire, joys of being on eng flt, Rapier. Remember riding shotgun on the mobile patrol with a short wheel base LR, having a little off road fun as you do at night. Ended up stuck in one of the concrete water reservoir, god knows how. Interesting conversation with guard commander though. Got towed out in the end. Funnily enough, spent the rest of that one sitting outside a little hut.

CND Camp, Greenham. Picture courtesy of Alan Thompson.

Richard Barton

Emerald Camp, Greenham, had a large banner tied to the trees. One night when I was off duty, I did my own combat patrol. I evaded the American security patrol and entered the CND camp.

I borrowed the CND banner but unfortunately ignored the information board on disposal of used tampons.

The next day, the good ladies moved their site back about 100 yards.

Lent the banner to my sister in Leeds, where it was subsequently stolen.

At Greenham we used to have little guard huts with a brazier coal fire outside. One fellow, don't know if it was a Snowdrop or Rock, decided to put brazier inside the hut. Result: hut burned down.

Greenham. Home sweet home. Picture courtesy of Alan Thompson.

CHAPTER 6
CVRT THE BATTLE OF THE BULGE

Paul Johnson

The ones that I have are very funny stories. If you were ever on 1 Sqn, then you would know the tank ramps in the compound, right? Well some of the guys had just finished a small demo course with the engineers on camp. When the CO asked if they could demolish the tank ramps, "Yes," came the reply. They drilled holes in the ramps with the help of the new demo course, and filled the holes with PE, just enough to crack them, they asked the boys to put the charge in the holes and mark the holes so they knew that it was filled. They forgot to mark which holes they did, so the REs thinking that they weren't done put more charges in the holes … wrong.

The young SAC was chosen to press the tit just outside the gate, when this fricking big almighty explosion filled the sky. The station went on lockdown thinking we were being attacked, bits of ramp went flying everywhere, 100s of yards, bits went through the roofs of all the buildings nearby, car windscreens, windows, bouncing off car bodies—lots of damage. The boys pissing themselves laughing. The CO was marking time in the station cdrs office for the damage and not telling him what was going to happen. In some cases, the holes had 2–3 charges in them, what a bang it made.

Paul Geordie Cunnugham

58 Sqn, 1986, if the memory serves me right. Hull to Rotterdam ferry (the love boat). We boarded at about 1600 hrs, we were all sat having our meal when the order came from the boss (Sqn Leader Parker) all troops to be in bed by 2000 hrs. Well, after a few pints in the bop, it was decided to mutiny by way of throwing our 1250s on to the dance floor, all us old sweats started and the rest followed all except one cpl whose name will stay a secret (known as Corporal B. Astard).

Well, next morning FS Campbell had us all on the dockside screaming blue murder at us, I for one became a marked man there after. Happy days!

Anthony Wells

The Spartan Crush. It was in the early 80s on 1 Sqn at RAF Laarbruch and a young officer called Fg Off (Dave) arrived fresh faced from his JROC. Having recently received our new Spartan's (CVRT) the sqn set about the wind up. An old sweat SAC was to play the CO and all but the people involved were hiding in the sheds in the compound. Said officer was to manoeuvre the Spartan around the compound avoiding all vehicles.

Now an old car was parked in the compound belonging to the sqn WO or CO, can't quite remember, but the Spartan was doing well and you could hear left stick, right stick on, etc.

A few minutes into it, the SAC driver was to ignore instructions, as if comms down, and started heading towards the old car. All you could hear is left stick, "Stop!" at the top of his voice as he headed towards the car.

With great laughter, we watched the Spartan mount the car and a face of shock and horror on his face. Straight away the vehicle stopped and out came the sqn WO shouting and balling to the new officer and both were now off to see the CO (old sweat SAC, I think it was Davy Lowe) to receive a bollocking which we could all hear.

Once the officer had left the office and entered the compound, we all came out of hiding to roars of laughter and to see a confused young officer, and then it clicked, and he let out a large sigh of relief!

Mark Minary

CVR(T) story. 34 Sqn, A Flt, circa 1992. We were on a CVR(T) patrol, one of the areas we were to cover was the Akrotiri cliffs—

600' high! I was driving a Spartan, Pete was the vehicle commander, we also had Rob (Brummie) and Muz; there may have been others but I can't remember. Anyhow, it was the middle of the day and also the middle of summer and we spotted some scantily clad females down on Subs point. Pete says to slow down and eventually we come to a stop so that he could perv at the women through the sight in the cupola. Unfortunately, he couldn't get the required depression on the sight. "Never mind," says I. "I'll turn the wagon around a bit." So (and this isn't the cleverest thing I've ever done), I turn the wagon so the nose is pointing out to sea over the edge of the cliffs. Parking brake on and the lads were getting a cracking view. I decided that I want a go, so I hop out of the driver's compartment and jump into the cupola. We sat there for probably 20 mins or so, by which time I was bored, so I was laying on the bench seat in the back of the wagon. The rest of lads were outside.

Next thing I hear is a creak as the wagon starts to creep forward. The lads started shouting, "Freddy, get out, get out!" So I try and push the rear door open which is now uphill. I get it slightly open and the wagon jolts and the door slams shut again. "Freddy, get out mate, it's going over!" Fucking hell, one last push and the door opens. I leap out, fully expecting to be in free fall on my way down to the med.

My feet landed on the cliff top and I turned to watch in amazement as a lump of rock wedges itself between the drive sprocket and the first road wheel, stopping the vehicle in its tracks. Pete Hailstone had already deserted the scene by running off back towards camp. The rest of the lads were pretty shocked by the whole thing. None more so than Brummie, who was then 'volunteered' to get on board and reverse the thing off the cliff edge. I can remember him saying, "I'm not keen" as Pete Hailstone pushed him up onto the sponson plate.

I learnt a valuable lesson that day—don't be a c*nt.

Picture courtesy of Terry Merrygold

Tim Coad

34th flip flop and sandals Sqn. Decide to go out on patrol 20:00ish with Spartans and 2 LRs. I think the ginge was sect cmdr (but I refused his cmdr comms set). After an hour, we go around the edge of the salt flats and, low and behold, find a fully stacked Keo brewery truck sunk down to its axles and nobody there.

Oh dear. After dispatching the LRs to the hard standing with an OP screen, the obvious happened. LRs dispatched a few laps round said vehicle, we towed it out after, and of course reporting finding abundant vehicle to OPs and SBA police. Good flt party after OPs.

Dean Montgomery

Big Red, 1 Sqn, mid-80s. It was common to be away from Llarparks for weeks while participating in several consecutive exercises. Between exercises, the chariots were parked up in a non-tac harbour. One of the guys wanders off into the bondu with his spade, bog roll, and wearing his jack hifi (Sony Walkman), so two others also grab a spade from the front of the tank and follow him. Keeping out of sight they watch while the 1x1x2 foot deep hole is prepared for the compo laden dump.

As the dacks are dropped and prep made for the big release, the other two leopard crawl in behind and catch the huge turd on the spade and withdraw! Imagine the astonishment on his face when he turned to check, as you do!

Don't think he knows even to this day. Must be a few out there who could put names to this one.

Len Hames

So it's the early 80s and 58 Sqn are doing their yearly exercise at RAF Laarbruch, defending the perimeter, this is before we had CVRT. We had the usual trip over by ferry, then convoy on to Laarbruch, arrive safely, get the usual accommodation, miles from fricken anywhere, surrounded by woods. Settle in for two days, we'll get pissed for two days, then sqn briefing, followed by flight briefing, followed by section briefing. My section cmdr being Cpl Squash Warburton. I am the section signaller, the section GPMG SF gunner, along with Blondie Roberts, I am also the section's Charlie G. We get our briefing and the get our section briefing including our defensive positions, being the sections SF gunner me, Squash Warburton, and Blondie Roberts draw the short straw and get a fricken 45 degree angle grass bank right in front of the Bloodhound compound. As we get to our position, we are warned that our position is the most likely location that is going to get hit.

We manage to get the LR and trailer cammed up by reversing it into a wood, we could not even see it our fricken self. Squash kept coming to us to ask where we had hid the fricken thing. Anyhow, we decide to place the SF trench about 10 foot from the top of said hill and about 20 foot from the Bloodhound compound. After digging for about 4 hrs—which Squash did most, mountain that he was—we finally get to camouflage the trench up, which I must say was fricken great, you could not see the position at all, even from 10 feet away, Squash did a brilliant job.

We set up the GPMG in the SF role, do all our range cards, map locations, and range poles, relay all our hard work to the CP, and await our instructions. Whilst applying the finishing touches to our trench, dear old Squash informs me that both his signalling skills and SF skills are a bit rusty (big scratch of the head), "Never mind, mate, we will get by."

First day, all very quiet, no sign of any enemy movement. We all get a good kip, Squash doing his usual fout hour stint, he never fricken slept. Second day, we lose comms, dead as a dodo all day. Squash starts to flap as we are due a replen and as we cannot get any comms, he wonders how we are going to carry on (and what a carry on it was). No sign of any activity, no comms, no replen.

After about 6 hours, whilst Squash is on one of his marathon watch stints, he hears a wagon on a nearby road. Unbeknown to us, it's Cheify Acott out looking for us. He obviously knows our location, but Squash just keeps watching said wagon going backwards and forwards thinking it could be the enemy. The situation gets worse as comms are unobtainable and our water and compo rations are getting low. On the third day, Squash is now on the edge, he is quietly doing his nut in and ready to throw the ageing A41 down the bank. He starts wandering up and down the bank and looking for any other sections trench positions, it seems we are on our own, every time he here's a wagon, he jumps back into our immaculate camouflage trench and keeps stum. By this time, me and Blondie Roberts are pissing ourselves at every movement poor old Squash makes.

Day turns to night and it's now four days since we have heard or seen anything or anyone. Blondie Roberts breaks out the emergency rations. By the way, we had managed to get extra ration packs of which Squash knew feck all about, 2200 hrs and me and Blondie decide to get our heads down, crawl right down in the old green slug, and nod of into a deep sleep.

Squash calls *stand to* about 0430 hrs, he had let me and Blondie sleep half the fricken night without him waking any of us. I give him a bollocking for not waking us to which he just nods and says, "No bother, all quiet anyway." So it's the fourth day and we ain't heard a fricken thing from anybody (which didn't bother me or Blondie) but poor Squash is doing his head in, saying, "We should have heard something from the CP *or* one of our other positions."

"Quiet!" Squash *shouts* as we all hear a wagon going backwards and forwards up the nearby road. I look at Blondie and Blondie looks back at me, and with a wink, we keep stum, quietly pissing ourselves.

Squash hears the wagon getting closer, he jumps out of the trench and starts running towards the road. Just as he reaches the bottom, almost falling arse over tit, he stumbles onto the road only to be nearly knocked over and killed by said wagon. It turns out to be Chiefy Acott in said wagon, out he jumps, all 6'4" of him, runs to the front of the wagon to find Squash getting up and brushing himself down, "What the fuck!" shouts Chiefy. "I nearly fricken killed you!"

After ten minutes of cussing and swearing, Chiefy calms down enough to start asking questions. "Right," he says. "Get that fricken trench filled in, get your wagon loaded, and get back to camp ASAP, and follow me."

An hour later, Chiefy is sat in is LR waiting for us. We get finished loading, pull our LR *out* of the woods, drive down the track through the woods, and meet Chiefy on the road. "Right," he says. "Follow me, you little fuckers."

We get back to the Sqn HQ only to find that all the other sections and flights were cleaning their wagons and kit. "Right, you three, get fell in over there." He points to a four tonner parked up on its own, we calmly walk over to said wagon, smartly followed by Chiefy Acott. "Right," he says. "Get sat down there, fag break, and we will have a little chat … Okay," he says, "what the fricken hell went wrong?"

Well we start to tell him everything from start to finish when he says, "Hang on, Hames show me on the map your location." I point out the location, he looks at his map looks at mine, grumbles to himself, lights another ciggie, and with no warning, shouts out, "You stupid twat! You gave me the wrong map co-ordinates."

Puzzled, I look up sly glance toward Squash and say, "Sorry, Chiefy, but that's the location you gave us." Looking at Squash again, I said, "But I could have made a mistake."

Big grumble again another ciggiee, "What about the fricken radio? What frequency were you on?"

I get out my note book look at the frequency and reply, "The same one as you," and show him my notes.

"Twat!" he shouts. "Fricken twat!"

I reply, "What Chiefy?"

Scratching his head he says, "You got the wrong fricken frequency."

I slip another cheeky look to Squash and say, "Sorry, Chiefy but it's the same, look."

He compares both and says, "Well what the fuck went wrong?" *Big pause*, then he turns to us and says, "You do know we finished yesterday? I have spent the last two days looking for your position, you had no comms, nobody could find your location or your fricken trench. Did you think not think anything had gone wrong? Well?"

"Er no," I replied. "Just thought that was part of the exercise."

"*Get the fuck out my sight*! And get your kit squared away. Cpl Warburton, follow me," he says.

Three hours later, Squash reappears, smiling, saying, "Think we got away with that, boys, but don't know what the fuck went wrong."

Well I did say Squash's signalling skills were a bit rusty. Turns out his map reading skills were to, as for the location of our fire trench, it was out about half a mile according to Chiefy's copy. As for the radio, well that was my fault, I was out on that too. Oops! We got away with that one but only just.

Cheers, Squash! He took all the flak, he really is a great bloke and would not have a bad word said against him. *Per Ardua*, Squash.

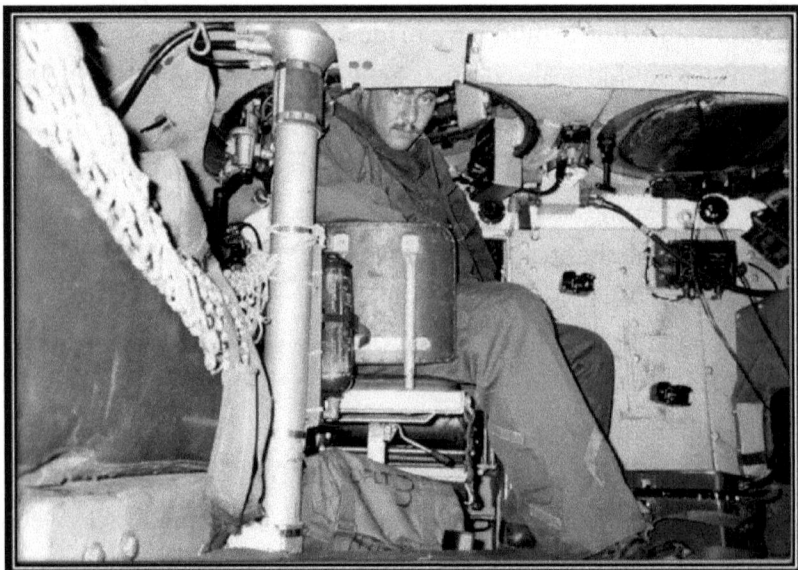

Picture courtesy of Terry Merrygold

Chris Parkes Snr

Around 1980/81, 6 Sect BFlt 58 were tasked with providing enemy force for Boulmer's yearly Taceval. Our Sect Cmdr Scott 'Geordie' Davies had been given the week's brief from their GDT staff (WO Rock). This included 'causing a disturbance/mini riot' (only 10 of us but greater disturbances have been caused by fewer Rocks, in truth). They weren't best pleased when we hurled half-filled canisters of 'Glitto' primed with TFs over the main gate causing airbursts and showers of white powder. Images of Guins rubbing their eyes and choking on the stuff. Nor did they appreciate one of our number (jock guy whose name fails me) sitting 'aboard' the station's rotating radar dish and randomly lobbing TFs on the clueless Guins below!

They must have thought they'd have their revenge when me and Clint Walker were set up by our own sect cmdr and captured during a perimeter breach. Refused to keep our blindfolds on, kept talking in their 'prison', making references to other incidents which were imminent (this duff gen apparently had them squealing to their seniors about the impending doom coming their way). We were expecting some harsh treatment, as earlier in the week we'd kidnapped some half asleep Guin walking to work (outside the wire, so it was easy) and knelt him sandbagged on a couple of pebbles before rolling the Land Rover spare wheel against his neck in a quarry somewhere near Newton Point. Rock WO merely asked us to play nice. Was a fun week, especially as we were given a fair bit of 'free rein'!

Ian Boyce

Summer 1990, the fighting 51st was out in Cyprus, topping up tans and running the CFT in the height of the Mediterranean summer (instead of doing it in the UK). The CG

(Barney Rubble) was paying us a visit and naturally spent a social evening with myself, Phil Marcer (Sqn WO), and a few SNCOs and lads in the sqn bar. Evening progressing rather well, bottles of Keo being consumed at a rate of knots, much banter, and I informed the group that Barney got stung on the bum by a scorpion in Malaya, when I was at JWS in 1972, much hilarity.

Things progressed and I realised that they might be getting out of hand when it dawned on me that I was throwing darts at Phil and Barney's feet. I thought this was a bit strange, as I had only had six pints, then realised it was six litres of Keo, so did not feel so bad.

We all survived the night and next morning Barney accompanied me and some of my lads on a whiz around the TAOR in a couple of rigid raiders, good cure for a hangover.

Martin Tomo Thompson

Somewhere in 85 I was helping out on a j coarse as a Spartan driver. Whilst going through the goal posts (these are literally goal post over the hole of the road) on the inner circuit up at the garrison, I kept slowing down when the officer said, "Go faster."

I replied, "If I go faster, the commander's lid will hit the top of the posts."

In his 'I'm an officer' voice, he replied, "I'm telling you to go faster."

So I did. The lid hit the top post, the turret span round like a spinning top, wrapping all the cables around the officer's neck. On hearing a choking noise, I turned around to see him turning blue while the other bloke in the section commander's hatch was pissing himself laughing. I was told to *slow down* then.

Stuart Robertson

For the lads who know about changing the sprocket on wheel on CVRT, especially the ring. This particular SAC who was sat in the driver's seat had asked and gave guidance to someone else in assisting in the maintenance. The SAC was the driver for this vehicle. The two sprockets rings were placed on the wheel, the SAC jumped into the driver's seat and told the other lad what to do. So in neutral gear, revved the engine, and pulled back on the stick and the assistant then tried to pull the track over the sprockets, nothing was catching and he carried on, still not catching, he continued trying for some time.

By now, a lot of the sqn in the compound were getting interested and decided to gather around this Spartan and watch in amusement. All knowing what he had not done. At this point there must have been about 40/50 people watching and the SAC's face was getting rather purple with embarrassment and he was getting quite flustered.

If only he had lined up the datum holes. Poor old Surgical Smears.

Robbie Robinson

The new cabbage head arrives on 1 Sqn in the early 80s, first day full kit inspection. The bay floor is laid out with all the tools of the trade and the large stone. He carries out the inspection and not once asks why we had a large stone in the kit.

The following week, sqn deploys on exercise in some god awful location. Come day two, we get a message over the radio *move to*. It was on the other side of the training area, plus we had just got lunch on, deploy the large stone, message sent, thrown a track.

Another CS was deployed, few minutes later, same message relayed back, thrown track. Up pops the cabbage head, noticing the track being replaced, and asks, "Is it a common fault?"

I replied, "Only when it's lunch time."

The new area is a shit hole and when we use the large stone. Still not sure he believed us thinking it was a piss take.

Darren Kitchen

One of Danny Boswell's LACs on 1 Sqn was told to return to block and iron his collars flat like the rest of the flight. A 10 min job. Two hours later, he returns.

"'Where the f*** have you been?"

"Med centre, Cpl," was the response. He had only tried ironing his collars flat while still wearing his shirt! He had the mark to prove it.

Robbie Robinson

1 Sqn, 1982, had just been told that we were on standby for the Falklands. One individual came to the FS and asked if one of us cpls could go home with him and tell his wife. As I came from the same area of the west midlands, I was given the task.

"No, he is not going," was the answer. "It's just a ploy to go on the beer." She was a lovely lass, and I was not going to argue.

Rolf Davis

34 Sqn, '84ish, Germany. How to get five gunners moving faster than a gazelle being chased by a lion! 34 Sqn on ex in coldest Germany 'Hohne Training Area'. Sqn in attack Spartans, Scorpions CVR (T)s, everyone's on final assault. Section Cmd 'Tim' bends down, strikes 'TF', goes to throw it and oops, slips out of his hand and drops onto the fuel tank inside the Spartan!

Five gunners out the rear door so fast never seen anything like it!

Haha, big bang, smoke coming out of vehicle, as we all piss ourselves in laughter. The driver Pete turns around, "What the f*ck was that?" We left the poor sod.

Geraint Jones

On 51 Sqdn, rear party, 1991, under the control of Chiefy Gus Dobney, not much to do apart from hangar sweeps and getting lashed in the scorps. On one fateful Thursday evening whilst drinking champagne and eating oysters with Catterick garrison's finest in the scorps, a small scuffle ensued over the last oyster, which resulted in a good old dust up with the pongos.

Casualties were moderate on both sides but Stevie Bannister's eye next morning on parade resembled a scene from *Rocky Part 1*. Gus Dobney asks, "What happened to your eye, Bannister?"

To which Stevie replies, "Well, Flight, I was watching a film called *Scum* last night and it got to the scene where the lad puts some snooker balls in a sock to twat the bully with."

Gus Dobney is now immersed in Stevie's explanation, "Aye, Bannister. Go on, man."

"He swings the sock and at that point I realised I have a 3D telly, Flight Sgt."

Dobney turns red and then purple. We think, *You're fucked, Stevie.*

Dobney replies, "You're a cunt, Bannister. *Dismissed!*"

Ian Willis

When 1 Sqn was back in St Mawgan, a certain Taff on SW Flt decided to have a midnight swim after a night on the ale. So off he trotted down to the closest beach, stripped off completely bollocks naked, carefully placing his clothes where in his drunken stupor he would remember them (*not*). He went for his swim, coming out on the opposite side of where he left his clothes. Thinking he had his clothes nicked, he then walks from the beach, stark bollock naked, through Newquay, past civvy police ,to the usual taxi rank to get back to camp. Taff was given a tea towel to cover himself up and the next taxi back to camp.

On arriving at the main gate, and the promise to pay for taxi as he was a good customer, he stripped off towel, folded it up, giving it back to the taxi driver. He then walks up to the Guin on guard, stark naked, and walking by holding his hands up says, "Does it look like I have any ID?" and storms on by to his room past the shocked Guin.

Fraze Bakaway

Exercise Sennelagger on 51, D Flt. We had a vile flt cdr who, for some god unknown reason, thought he had remote control tanks. We would spend hours listening to this anus over the radio. "41C advance, left stick, halt. 41D advance right stick, traverse right, halt!"

Absolutely bizarre behaviour. After a day of this, we parked up, BV on, Scoff on, etc. We were sat in the tank, helmets on, having a chat how shit it had been over the intercom when there is a clunk from the front decks and the flt cdr's head appears over the cdr's hatch and I can hear him explaining that he wanted to do more of the same in the dark.

I very gently started traversing the turret around, out of sheer boredom. In fine traverse, it takes a lot of turning to move it any real distance so didn't think much of it. Twat head finishes his brief with a RV time and place and leaves.

All of a sudden all hell breaks loose. So I stand up to see what's going on and find he's walked what he thinks is onto the front deck but fallen from the turret face-first off the side and face planted into the undergrowth next to us. Last seen on his way to hospital with first field dressing on his nose.

Our vehicle commander is in hysterics and can't work out how the turret got 90 degrees from where it had been. We had a good night sleep.

A mate of mine thought it would be a good idea to put two CS pellets in the flt cmdr's car cigarette lighter as an anti-theft device. The logic being if some knob stole it they would gas themselves. He didn't smoke so never used the thing, we all thought it was hilarious and thought no more about it. Months later, he turned up at work in a new fanny magnet and as we all ooo'd and aaaa'd at its leather and gadgetry. One of the lads pulled out the lighter and said, "Oh, you haven't installed security?" Dipshit turns white as a sheet as he realises some poor civvy is driving around in a new car with a time bomb fitted. Never did hear any more about it.

Kev Hunt

Remember being told of a story about 15 Sqn, during a freedom of Chippenham parade. As the Scorpions passed the Dias, they dipped their gun by way of salute. Some ingenious gunners had filled one of the barrels up with ping pong balls that went flying off down the high street.

Geraint Jones

I do hope you are not eating whilst you read this. Late 1990, myself and another brother Rock decide to partake in the joys of the Scorps one fine Friday evening, and after much ale and merriment, we both hit lucky and depart with a skank a piece to complete our skirmish.

The next morning, my conquest awakes (and obviously has trouble walking), wink, and enquirers to the whereabouts of her friend. "She'll be across the way in my mate's block, he's on 58," I reply, and duly escort her to the said abode.

On entering the block, things appear normal apart from the sickly iron and sweat smell in the air. On approaching my mate's room, the unmistakable evidence of blood is on the door handle and the door itself. Instantly we are thinking, *What the fuck is going to greet us if we open the door to his room?*

I knock, wait, hear movement, a sigh of relief. He opens the door. "All right, you Welsh twat, want a fag?" He is covered in his conquest's lady garden blood from his hair to his feet, nonchalantly offering me a period-stained cigarette. Well, it would be rude to refuse, wouldn't it?

The scene that confronted me in his room haunts me still to this day and is not really describable, I guess you can imagine …

Jez Eden

My very first day on my first sqn, Laarbruch, 1 Sqn, July 89. I swing into the compound to see a Spartan on its roof, next to a HGV low loader with a very dented roof to the cab (unlikely to buff out, I thought). Turns out that during loading, the driver didn't unscrew the butterfly nut which holds the throttle open. Drives forward, but can't stop, so up over the chap from 431MU who was marshalling, and then onto the cab of the HGV before rolling off sideways. The marshaller's femoral artery is severed and he has the wisdom to jam his thumb in the hole and save his life. Welcome to 1 Sqn! Best tour of my career.

Andrew Richards

'93–'94? Whilst serving on 34, we did rather well at rugby, all island champs a couple of times. In the lion heart whilst receiving medals from the CO McGowan, the lads went up, got the medal, and shook the big man's hand. Anyway, I'd had a few shandies and thought it would be funny to grab the CO for a snog post medal and hand shake, split second into drunken act, I saw out the corner of my eye Mr Kidd glaring at me, sobriety kicked in pretty quick, I made my excuses and left rapidly. Spent the next weeks ducking and diving.

Fraze Baraway

51 Sqn, Catterick. Run up to bonfire night, we had seen a humongous rocket for sale. This thing had a four foot wooden pole on it and the bangy bit looked like a bloodhound. Too much to resist so it was bought.

Normal Saturday night, spilled out of a taxi at the gate after a skinful up at the Scorpion and decided that it was a great idea to launch the beast over the camp and try to get it to air burst over the guard room just for shits and giggles. Sections of hoover pipe were stuck into the ground and with much 'left' and 'right a bit', it was decided that it pointing at the guardroom and the wind was factored in. Angle of sight was worked out for the trajectory with all the enthusiasm you would expect from pissed gunners. So it's all set up and can't fail. Fuse is lit and a safe distance retreated, with giggling gunners watching the fuse hissing. The pipe starts to tip down towards the ground and has dropped a lot as the thing whooshes out the tube, straight towards the Guin block. By a million to one chance it goes into an open window and we can see it bouncing around off the walls with a girly Guin scream. BOOM! The thing goes off and smoke is pouring out.

Pissing ourselves laughing we sprint into the Guin block and crash into the smoke-filled room where we find a fat, naked bird screaming and her naked Guin trying to put the curtains out. Fire stamped out, windows thrown open, and threats of, "You haven't seen us," and a fast exit to our block.

"Fair play, Pengy," said fuck all and nothing more was heard about it.

Duncan Ditch Hollands

A short briefing on Regt Sqn hierarchy—a Guin's tale. Having spent my first couple of years in the mob safely installed behind a desk in SHQ at Wittering, I was posted to 51 Sqn! Shortly afterwards, the sqn was off to Bruggen, exercising their war role. Ex glide over, if my memory serves. Half way through the TACEVAL, the adj (Ken Smith, I think) tasked Chris Moore and me to replen SW Flt with water, rat packs, etc. These were all loaded into the back of an RL. Loading done, I jumped up into the passenger seat resplendent with brand new '58 pattern webbing, tin pot, SLR, and puttees that must have come half-way up my legs! A couple of minutes passed with me wondering where Chris had gone. Suddenly, the door flew open, a hairy paw grabbed me by the yolk and dumped onto the hangar floor. No time to recover from the shock before Chris administered a few slaps and told me, in no uncertain terms, that Guins (especially sprog ones) did not ride in the cab next to him and that my place was in the back with the rat packs, jerry cans, etc. I got the message as it was sent in clear!

Anyway, I climbed into the back and took my place. Must have looked like a whipped puppy. Not content with that and to make sure the message had been properly understood, Chris then drove the RL at high speed across the bondu. Every jerry can and rat pack in the back of the RL must have bounced off my nut and the only thing that stopped me from flying out of the back was grabbing the tailgate rope! By the time we reached SW, I felt like I'd done a few rounds with Mike Tyson.

Despite feeling sorry for myself, I managed to put a brave face on things and unload the stores to a chorus of laughter from the SW blokes. That done, I waited next to the RL fully expecting to be told, "Get in the f@@king back, Guin!" However, Chris must have been content that I now understood the way of things because he let me sit in the cab on the way back!

Mark Halliburton

Back in '85 on ex in Germany with 51 Sqn, I was with Ian and Clive. I was the Spartan driver for Robert Kennell. In the woods around the airbase Bruggan, I went for a shovel recce. We were all NBC state without respirator on. I dug my hole. Dropped by duds and had a whopping steamer. Total pitch black. Wipe arse and pull duds back up. NBC straps back over my shoulder and tied up. Wondered what the smell was. Well I had only dropped my straps in the hole and shit on them not realising. I had to cut them off and use rope to hold duds up. But shit had got over some of my other gear, which I tried to clean best I could. But shit being shit, it was not good. Well you can imagine the faces of the team in the back of the Spartan as we drove along. Me driving with hatch open and the pleasant waft of shit filtering in the back. Must say I was popular.

Stan Hodgson

When on 34 about 80ish, there was an incident involving bored Rocks on an ammo truck and a thunder flash. Well it goes to say the journey was near its end, just got to the old 3 Wing building and the boys had the thunder flash and it accidently got struck so pass the parcel took place out the truck, and it flew. Only to land and go off under the station commander's wife car and full call out of the camp.

The outcome was a big hush up, I presume as I heard naught more, but a few will remember it of A Flt.

Anthony Rogers

Back in the early 2000s, 1 Sqn. I was dicked with being the block bitch to monitor the workmen go into all the rooms, everyone else was on sqn PT. So I thought that this was a billy bonus, no phys, and I could take the afternoon off work, double bonus. So the workmen come and do their jobs within 30 mins, cheers, easy. So off I slope back to my room to do my own PT of the one-armed kind. Happily snoozing a bit later and one of the lads starts banging on my door. So I open the door and he says, "Mate, you still got all the spare room keys?"

"Yes," I reply.

"Quick, mate, you need to get upstairs!" Rushing upstairs, we get to a room that has water slowly seeping out under the doorway, thinking, *Bloody hell*, I open the door. A tsunami of water and porn mags then comes flying out of the room the water was calf-deep in the room. So we wade in and turn off the offending tap and remove the brew mug that was covering the plug hole.

Turns out the room owner had been having a brew with the flight SNCO and other senior bods at lunch before they went to PT but the block water had been turned off. So the helpful SNCO had only been trying to clean the mug but as no water had appeared, put the mug in the sink, and left one tap on (minus the water at this point). Hence one very flooded room! The room's owner then returns to find prized German hardcore porn mags sodden. Operation 'save the classics' then begins, almost every radiator in the block had mags on them. Luckily, even though the water level was so high, his other prized porn video collection was saved by his locker door being closed and, I suppose, watertight.

CHAPTER 7
THE WHIRLEYBIRDS

Stephen Headey

33 Sqn choppers, late 80s. On exercise, 'somewhere in Denmark', located in a wooded area. As per normal, we were tasked with defence of the site and Darren and I set up a few surprises to the rear of the site other than the normal trip flares. This time we included smoke grenades in compo cans attached green string and pulled the pins. This was just enough give so the fly off lever would not pop and set at different heights. We also employed glow sticks buried in to the ground and strung in such a way that when tripped would rise above the intruders and stand out a good distance. Now we also employed the good old green string at different heights—neck, waist, and leg height. Finally, using old tripwire, this was deployed only 50m in front. We were ready.

That night we were informed that we were to be attacked by TA SAS. As per normal SOPs, they attacked just before dawn. Three smokes were tripped and we replied with automatic fire. The onus was now on the enemy and the charged trip flares now going off and gurgled screams as they were being bought down by all things green string and trip wire.

I was having difficulty to stop laughing as watching these guys getting really pissed off and falling all over the place. The funniest was seeing a guy who had managed to get a smoke grenade attached to him and it dragging behind him still belching out smoke.

At this point the DI staff interrupted and halted the attack. By now it was light and the enemy section reformed outside the wooded area, checked for injuries, redistributed ammo, and went back towards the direction they had come. Suddenly we heard another cry as their section commander hit another set of trip wires and was heard shouting, "F@#king tripwires!"

You just couldn't make it up.

Vinz Howard

Whilst on 7 Sqn, Chinooks at Odiham in early 80s, one our duties was as duty driver. Part of that duty was to collect the packed rations for any night flying that was taking part. For some reason, the aircrew rations were better than our as they usually included a pastie and boiled egg. Having seen the way the pilots shelled the boiled eggs by cracking them on the instrument panel above their head or on their helmets, you can imagine the witch hunt after I swapped the boiled eggs for raw ones and seeing the pilots covered on egg yolks just had to be seen.

Stephen Headey

Part two, 33 Sqn, choppers, still in Denmark. So the mighty 33 Sqn had now defeated the SAS all be it TA. Our Guins were feeling like Spartans. Now they were walking around proud as peacocks, patrolling with more vigour and spoiling for a fight. DI staff were now planning their next move. That night we had a brief suggesting that we would be tested again within the next 48 hours. This didn't worry our Guins as who could possibly beat them.

As per normal, routine continued and regular patrols were going out and dominating the ground. Second day, no enemy either at dawn or at mid-morning. Suddenly I got a call from one of our Guins who swore blind he had seen some movement in the ferns about 100 metres away. Myself and Kev went to his trench and he pointed in the direction of the movement. We had the guys stand to quietly. Both Kev and I decided we would move forward and do a quick recce. We sat in a depression and observed.

All of a sudden, 25 metres away, the ferns were indeed moving and this was not the wind. Slowly the movement came closer and closer until they were almost upon my position. Silently, there were two Gurkha's kitten crawling their way towards our site with only

LFO on. I lunged for one of them and Kev the other. Suddenly all hell broke loose and we opened fire at the rest of the section that was creeping up. Our Guins sprung into action, letting rip with everything they had whilst we dragged the prisoners back to our lines, bagged and tagged.

Once safely back, the section, who were now invincible, wanted to mount a counter attack and would have done if we had not stopped them. DI staff stopped the attack again and took away the Gurkha prisoners. The spoil sports. CO put on a few crates for a job well done by the lads.

Dan Smale

33 Sqn on exercise in Norway. Before going up to the final phase on the edge of the Arctic circle, weeks of build-up based near Voss, which just happens to be a ski resort. Used to volunteer for as many night shifts as duty driver as possible, which got you the day off.

Puma pilots on duty used to then take the off duty crew and any off duty Rocks and fly us up to the weather station first thing in the morning and drop us off. We'd time it so we got a full run down the mountain and were waiting by the top of the cable car when the first staff came up to open up the resort in the morning. They'd switch on the lifts and we'd get another clean run down before anyone else hit the slopes. Bloody marvellous. Heli-skiing at the tax payer's expense, got to love that.

Len Hames

18 Sqn Raf Odiham '82/'83. In respect for all our comrades who have paid the ultimate price for their country, I had placed a poppy behind my cap badge. I had been wearing it there for a couple of days without a single comment from any of our JNCOs or SNCOs or sqn officers.

A new zob had been posted in (a Guin). He promptly walked up to me with a wry grin on his face. I thought, *Here we go, a new zob gonna try and make a name for himself,* thought he was gonna try and bollock me for my dress or something.

Any way, he sticks a pointy finger out at my beret and promptly says, "What is that?"

I replied, "It's a poppy, Sir. I am wearing in respect for our fallen comrades," looking straight in his eyes.

He sharply replies, "Remove it now."

I paused, think to myself, *Time to take a gamble* and reply, "No, Sir. With respect, can you tell me where in Queen's Regulations it says I cannot wear a poppy behind my cap badge?"

Well stunned was not the word, thought my gamble had paid off but instead after a short pause he moves in for the kill. "Name Rank No. you're on a charge for insubordination."

Gob-smacked, I walked away, only to be challenged again by the famous shout of, "Airman, get back here!" I keep walking. "Airman get here!" Keeps walking. "Airman, get here right now!"

I now turned round and replied, "With respect, Sir, I am not an airman, I am a RAF Regiment gunner."

"Right," he says, "CO's office now." So off I go.

Five minutes later, I am outside the CO's office (who I know is on leave, because I was the CO's driver for that week). I was called in by the duty officer, who happened to be a certain sqn leader, a real old school officer. He asked, "What was the gen?" (his actual words) I quickly fill him in with all the details. After a few minutes of deep thought, he calls in the officer and looks him up and down and says, "There will be no charge, however I will deal with SAC Hames how I feel fit, thank you, you may leave." The young zob leave,s and after shutting the door behind him, the sqn ldr (Dick to his friends) says, "Okay, Hames, here's your punishment. First of all—coffee. Second—cigarette. Then you can drive me home." Waiting, I expect the worse. No, all I get is, "Now piss off. Oh, and leave the young officers alone."

Still did not find out to this day if it states in Queen's Regulations that you can or cannot wear a poppy, especially behind your cap badge.

Dave Capps

During a major NATO exercise, the German Army parked a Leopard tank for the night in a wood, locked it up, and went to the bar as was the way. A wayward patrol of Rocks from a certain tiger-striped helicopter sqn found it. As per the norm, if it's big and shiny, it belongs to a Rock. Padlocks on the hatches were duly changed and UNDER NEW MANAGEMENT painted on the side in large white letters.

Just goes to prove no target is insurmountable to a Rock when they set their mind to it.

Kevin Bell

Whilst on 'choppers', 33 Sqn at Odiham. I was the sqn duty driver for the week. Went to do the mail run, which included a stop at gen office. No parking spaces so I put Land Rover in stn cmndr's parking space. With Odiham being a small station, everyone knew when he was on leave. He was on leave at this time.

When I came out of gen office with mail bag, the idiot SWO was stood there with a look of glee. I explained the he was on leave and I'd only been there about 30 seconds. I spent a lot longer in the turd's office as he wrote out the 252. I should imagine he was roughed up by a Rock or two previously? Fair play to the station cmndr though, he apologised to me. Think it was loss of pay, as I don't remember doing 'restriction of privileges' at Odiham?

Steve Cameron

On 34 when a young, zealous officer straight out the factory was on a heli op with us. As the sea king came down (with that 15ft false landing), he shouted in typical public schoolboy style, "Fallow me, men!" and fell on to salt lake in typical officer style! Of course, not one of us mentioned it to anyone. Honest, guv.

Dan Smale

Detachment with 33 Sqn choppers, honestly can't remember if it was Denmark or Norway. Too bloody expensive to drink in town more than one or two nights of the week. So we're tucking into the cheap NAAFI booze one night when a young gunner (who can dob himself in if he likes as he's in this group) is either bored, skint, or just (as he usually was) mad as a box of frogs, announces that he will drink a pint of Asbach for a bet. Always happy to witness this kind of insanity, a few of us stump up a suitable wager. Being the gentlemen we were, I think we gave him a generous 10 seconds rather than down in one. Anyway, he finished it, collected his money, and announced loudly (if a little incoherently) that he was fine. Someone suggested he'd proved his point and had better throw up before he went into a coma.

"Fuck off, I'm f—lobberdobberdob …"

"Okay, lads, hold him down while I get my fingers down his throat." Didn't go down well.

Anyway his condition went south sharpish and the ambulance took him away for a good pumping of the stomach.

We later heard he'd woken up in a straitjacket after having taken a swing at one of the nurses. Of course, the last bit is just hearsay, unless you'd like to fess up, mate?

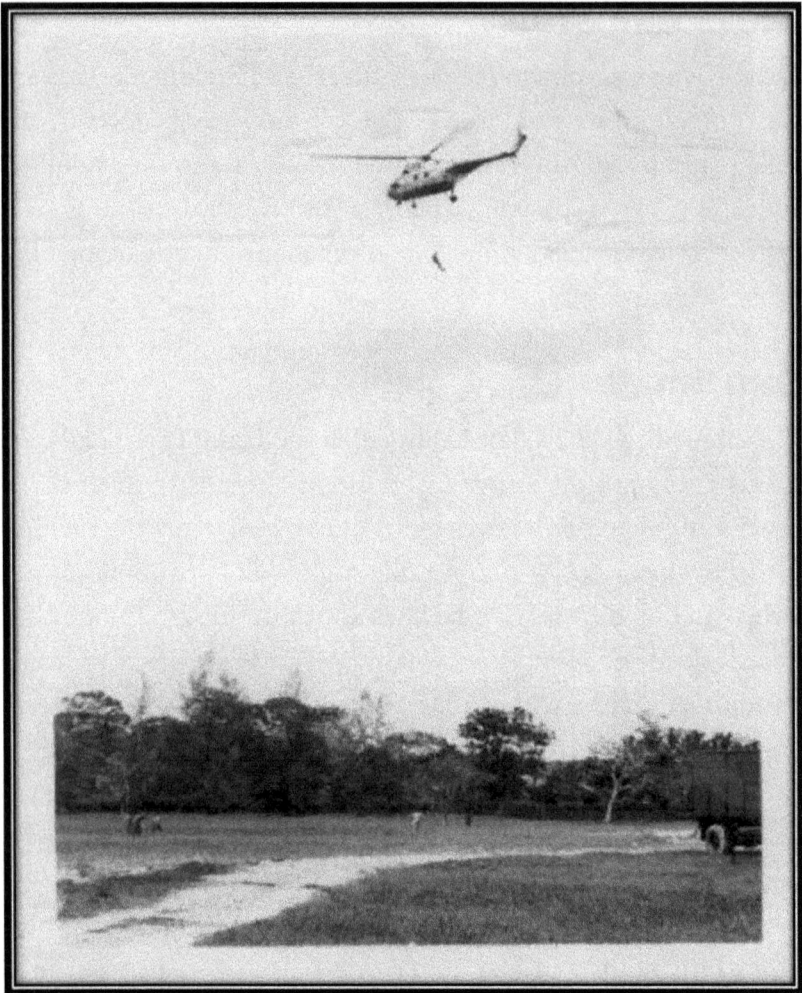

Picture courtesy of Bill Hayes.

James Little

Got posted to 72 Wessex Sqn in '79 as and went up on jolly's now and again. One of the 'aircrew' (winch weight) had a neat trick of joining a few safety straps together then proceeded to climb up the front wheel strut and tap on the outside of the co-pilots window—face of co-pilot was a picture. Aircrew's face was even better when he looked down to the crew cabin one time to see one of the passengers (Rock) holding a loose end of a safety strap. Aircrew glued himself to the wheel strut for a while and did need a change of jump suit.

Strap was a spare one but it had the desired effect.

Stephen Headey

Late '88 'somewhere in Denmark, 33 Sqn Pumas. We nearly started WW3. We had just finished a NATO exercise and were being awarded a large amount of wobbly for a job well done. Attached with us were the Luftwaffe choppers. Well you can probably see where this is going.

On our sqn, we had a techie sgt whose first name was Otto and his grandfather was one of the original nasty SS in WW2. Beer is flowing fast and furious and *zee Germans* are getting above their station. Well it's song time. They sing whatever and of course the Regiment sing our songs, all good fun. Then, from nowhere, Otto jumps up upon a table shouts at the Germans in perfect German, saying he will sing them a song his grandfather taught him. Otto then proceeds to sing the Krieg's Marine song perfectly to a stunned audience. Halfway through the Germans are shouting, "Nein, nein, nein," and pelting him with cans bottles and anything else.

Needless to say we all retaliated. Next morning, Otto on the CO's Axminster along with a few others. Great laugh though.

Len Hames

RAF Odiham 1982/83. Being as I spend so much time in the NAAFI, one of the guys says, "Why don't you join the committee?"

Well I had, as usual, had a few so I said, "Okay, I'll give it a go." Well, I end up being the entertainment's member who's responsibilities are, well, entertain the troops! So off I go, hiring all the discos, bands, comedians, and film nights. One night, as I am researching some DJs and bands, I come up with the bright idea of trying to hire a well-known DJ or maybe a radio DJ. I start phoning around, well this lasts for some weeks until going through all the old paperwork from the last entertainment's manager I find an old magazine with advertisements for radio DJs and come across an ad for Steve Wright the radio 1 DJ (this is in the 80's), it was for the Steve Wright DJ mobile show. Well, off I trots to the NAAFI office phone, gives them all the spiel about the camp and how the boys and girls would love to see his show and it would be a sell-out, cut to the important bit, fee and how much, his manager replies £300.

"How much?" I says.

He replies, "£300."

Pause. I say, "No. How about £200?"

He say, "No. £300."

I say, "Okay, look, how about £250. And I will get him and his crew a flight on a Chinook." Well he jumped at it and we come to an agreement, he posts off all the said info and contract to sign, it arrives days later I sign it and send it back. Job done, I tell the rest of the committee and they're shocked—how could a pissed up Rock organise this?

The date arrives, the NAAFI is booked, it's fricken buzzing in there, packed to the rafters. Steve Wright turns up with his roadies, they set up all his gear and get ready for a great night. Steve is dressed smart and has a really fricken bright blazer on, you know the one you would see back then at Blackpool, the numptees taking photographs and selling you them.

Back to the story, we're all having a great night, great music, great banter from Steve, then out comes the silly string, crazy foam. He sets it up behind the stage and calls me over. I take him a pint. He says, "Now we going to have a few fun and games," the big winner would get his jacket has a prize. I decide to up the game and suggest the 'dance of the flaming arseholes'. He says, "What? The dance of the flaming *what*?" I explain. He says, "Fricken great, never heard of that, let's get going." Off we go, I get some Guins to take part and of course a few Rocks. I somehow get to the final (fixed? of course not!) and a Guin called John Hawkhead (nicknamed Acidhead). Well it turns out to be a draw at the end because both of us kept crossing the finishing line at the same time, both have red, raw, sore, burnt arses and balls, a glass of lager goes down well—not down the throat but all over my burnt bits.

Steve Wright gets on the mic, pissing himself laughing, out comes his silly string and crazy foam. There are tins of it everywhere. The whole NAAFI is covered in the shit. He calls me and John up to the stage to present us with said jacket. He says, "A draw? Now what the fuck do I do?" Both of us covered in head to foot with foam, string, and lager look at each other and with a slightly pissed wink at each other, grab the said jacket and proceed to attempt to rip it in half. A sleeve each, rip it straight down the middle, half for me, half for Acidhead. We both jump of the stage with half a jacket on each, pissed, wet through, sore arses, covered in string and foam.

"Okay, okay," comes over the mic, Steve Wright says, "what a night. This is possibly the best disco road show I have done in ages." He said he has never laughed so much in years, "And as for my jacket, I never saw that coming. And as a result, I will waive my fee for the gig."

RESULT! I am thinking, *Feckin brilliant!* The only thing is now I have to break the news to him that because of gearbox problems, all the Chinooks are grounded, oops. I'm terribly sorry, Steve, but trust me, I will get you that jolly in a Chinook.

Jump to 2015, Steve Wright never did get his jolly in a Chinook, and I never found my half of that jacket, haven't got a fricken Scooby Do what happened to it, and I haven't got a clue how I ended up sleeping in the guardroom. To this day I still have not found out if I got arrested or not, apparently I walked into the guardroom, straight into a cell, and fell asleep. *What a fricken night!*

And I still listen to Steve Wright in the afternoon on Radio Two. I wonder if he remembers it too.

Steve Mullen

Whenever I hear the army slagging the Regt off, I think of the time that four of us from the Regt section on 33 Sqn flew into a foreign airstrip (Congo) in the middle of the night, lay on our Bergens under the turning and burning engines as the Hercules reversed and took off again, leaving us to secure the FOB. Pitch black, with locals appearing with AKs. Turned out nice though! *Per Ardua.*

Steve Mullen

Op Determinant, 33 Sqn Pumas, deployed to Brazzaville/Zaire. To stop the local kids from getting too close (no wire), we made a deal with them that if they stayed away from the choppers we would meet them on a little hill nearby and give them the boiled sweets from our rat packs—bribery, if you will. After a few days of this, the pongos declared that it must stop. Shame, as it worked well.

The very next day, army four man patrol (only one they did) with *camera crew* strolls to the hill and hands out sweets as part of a recorded 'look how nice we are'. Only thing is, I'm sure in the background you can hear Al Rush and me abusing said pongos as loud as we could!

Paul McCarthy

Mid-90s I was a cpl on 33 Sqn Pumas along with Tim McAlpin, Mark Nussey, Andrew John Starrs, and Brian Haycock to name a few. The sqn was getting ready to deploy to Bosnia with the UN and the pre deployment training was in full swing.

I was the RCO, running a range day at Ash Ranges (?) where the Guins were doing grouping and zeroing followed by application and advanced application of fire. We had a chf tech who was a fat fuck and dumb as shit. He was so fat, he rocked on his gut in the prone position. Anyway, the Rocks were bored so we decided to have some fun with him. I pulled the bullet head from a cartridge case and on the next check targets, pushed the head into the target before he got there. "Fuck me, Chief, haven't seen that in a while!" And proceeded to tell him he wasn't applying the marksmanship principles correctly, the buffoon swallowed it hook, line, and sinker and we repeated it twice more before the JEngO told him he was being made a fool of.

You could tell he was well liked when his troops were lining up to piss in the fire trench he was going to stand in for advanced application of fire. It had about a foot of water in it anyway and when he jumped in was heard to say that his boots were leaking.

Albi Pinnion

63 Sqn were chosen to play enemy for Laarbruch's tacteval. It was a flt attack in two Chinooks, at night time, each section had their tasks, everyone was dressed in fighting order, ladders were taken, pieces of wood individually numbered, and with the word, mine on them. Absolute pandemonium was caused, lads being engaged by 1 Sqn, police being taken prisoner. I'm not 100% sure, but seem to remember the runways were closed for 48 hrs, until every blank and all equipment was accounted for!

You could say it went too well, I'm sure others on 63 and 1 Sqn will have stories too add to this!

Albi Pinnion

Exercise Lionheart. Early eighties we were doing ops, for the choppers two days op, two days patrol, before crawling down the ditch to our op position, last three wham used to piss up against the fence, so I decided to connect the other strands of wire and not just the top one.

Electrified—MC. Sure as eggs is eggs, wham pissed up the fence before op duty. He realised it was me and tried to christen me with a GPMG. The Germans that came by every evening, to bring us food and beer and snaps, thought it most amusing and could not stop laughing!

Dickie Henderson

1 Sqn 1st Gulf. I was tasked with going on a Chinook to provide cover for the crew whilst they transported some Iraqi prisoners. After some intense low flying skills, we arrived and loaded the prisoners onto said chopper. Without giving too much away, these guys were not your normal Iraqi conscripts, and one or two where twice my size!

The flight was taking some time, and I noticed one of these guys kept trying get up off the floor. Full mag on and bayonet fixed on SA80, he got a few warnings to keep himself still. The flight went on. About twenty minutes later, I had a brief lapse in concentration and was looking out the back door at the beautiful scenery when all of a sudden this big prisoner suddenly rose from his knees at a rate of knots, screaming his head off. Fuck me, I shit a brick! I thought he was coming straight at me in order to get hold of my gat. I was up on the seat and had cocked a round up the chamber in a flash and giving this prick a load of verbal. "Get down on floor! Get down on the floor or I'll fucking drill ya!"

The airloadie came flying down the aircraft shouting, "Don't shoot, don't shoot, for fuck's sake, don't shoot him!" Airloadie got to the prisoner and let him stand up. I was still pumped and wanted to plug this prick when the loadie turned to me and said, "For Christ's sake, Rocky. The poor guy's only got cramp from sitting on his feet. You nearly downed a Chinook for cramp."

Well to say I was never asked back would be an understatement! Laughed about it later on though.

David Nicholson

Whilst on 33 Sqn SH Pumas, had some great times we some great Rocks—Mal Campbell, Tony Levy, Andy Ratcliff, Davie 'Sid' Simpson to name—but a few loads of exercises all over the place, this story involves a chief tech, he as the original Rock hater. Now to be fair, the Guins on the sqn were all pretty good and we all got on and had, I suppose, a healthy respect for each other. Plus, we had a pilot CO who thought we were great. But this guy hated us with a passion and never missed an opportunity to slag us off.

So while on exercise in Germany, a place called Bahmholder, huge American base, part of ace mobile force and all the NATO Helis in a joint op, all we were tasked with was driving the techies to heli site an do refuelling. There was five Rocks—me, Andy Ratcliff, Jimmy, and one other, sorry can't remember his name, and Cpl Kev Cavnagh—now out on time off, as we were working shifts, Kev had us doing fitness and weapon drills. Yeah, we had loads of spare time, our own block, techies didn't wanna share. Back to the chief tech, as I said, never missed any time in slaggin us off if he couldn't find us, he'd spout off we were prob pissed or on the piss. So one day after we'd dropped the Guins off at the site, we went back to the block, nothin to do till pick up time so Kev had us on a Bergen run then some gimpy drills. The chief tech had made it his mission to try an catch us on the piss or doing fuck all. As we were doing the gimpy drills, we spotted him creepin up the stairs to our block, his face was a picture as he strutted upstairs, expecting to see us drinkin or lying in our pits. He was faced with two groups in full kit, two gimpys, and Kev barking out the drills as he stood in front of us, both triggers were pulled! His face was a picture and as Kev asked him, "Yes, can we help you?" he made his excuses an fucked off, and never again slagged us off again. Have to say a lot of that was down to Kev.

Picture courtesy of Stephen Headey, Gulf War 1

Dan Smale

33 Sqn, 1982. Party on scaly quarters (pretty sure it was at John Bush's house) ends in the usual carnage and I end up jumping over a wall in the wee small hours and discovering (oh the irony) a bigger drop to a 'rockery' on the other side.

I'm in a fair bit of pain the following morning, so I ask one of the lads to drive me down the med centre. My ankle is swollen up a treat and they inform me I've just sprained it. Well I've had some previous with RAF medics, a broken collar bone skiing was diagnosed as nothing more than a bruise a couple of years earlier because the WRAF medical officer on detachment with us couldn't be bothered to do the paperwork to send me to a German civvy hospital for an x-ray. Ten days later, and on leave in UK by now, I'm told it is broken. Anyway, I take their word for it, take the painkillers, and hop off ("Sorry we've run out of crutches").

I hop around Odiham for about a week days till my boss tells me to get back to the med centre and have it checked again. This time they send me for an x-ray at Aldershot Military Hospital. Despite the fact that it is my ankle that's broken, evil grinning pongo orderly plasters right up to my balls 'for support'.

Fast forward a couple of weeks and I'm back at Aldershot Mil for physio when the plaster comes off. Back at 33 Sqn, the lads are packing their kit to go to the Falklands (before someone decides at the last minute to send 18 Sqn Chinooks instead). I'm getting changed for physio when in comes a Gurkha on crutches. He's broken his leg in six places (probably not jumping over a wall pissed). He clocks my regiment flashes and says he's met some lads in Belize, "Jolly good chaps, let's have a beer." Well I like a drink with the best of them, but it is 9am in the morning, so I'm a bit surprised when he pulls out a six-pack of Harp larger, but I make it a rule never to upset a Gurkha, so we get stuck in.

We head up to the physio and a big army PTI sits us down against a wall, bean bag over ankle, raise, lower, repeat. PTI turns his back and Johnny Gurkha is up on the multi-gym pumping the weights with his legs.

PTI is horrified, "WTF do you think you're doing?" he screams.

Gurkha calmly replies, "I get fit, go to Falklands, kill Argie bastards." PTI tells him in no uncertain terms that he is going nowhere, he's there for at least 6 weeks. PTI turns his back, Gurkha gets on the exercise bike … and repeat. A few days later, the troops sail, and no more Gurkha.

Stephen Headey

Bardafoss, 33 Sqn, '88. Exercise Hardfall. A few of the lads and I went down town for a few wets. It was snowing like mad and slippy under foot. Well the evening went well and as always we were now back out in the snow waiting for transport back to camp and I wasn't pissed.

Whilst waiting for some unknown reason this old guy starts trying to wind me up in to fighting him. He was obviously well pissed and was trying it on with anyone who would give him the satisfaction of a fight. He then started again at me saying he would take his rank off and we could fight. I said, "You are in civvies, you prick, I don't know who you are." He replied he was a warrant officer in the Army Air Corp. *Here we go*, I thought.

I noticed across the road two RMPs watching on and thought, *This isn't worth it*, and told him to piss off. He now became more violent and swung a punch which was easy to avoid and he fell on the floor. Just then, our transport arrived in front of the RMPs and I gave him a quick kick to his nads and jumped in.

Next morning, I was summoned to JENGO's office as he had heard that I was causing trouble downtown and a WO from the AAC had been assaulted and made a complaint. I denied this and the JENGO was threatening to charge me but I had an ace in the hole. This was all witnessed by the RMPs and they confirmed my story of an arsehole of a WO trying to fight with anyone. JENGO apologised to me.

All of a sudden there was an almighty bang of metal hitting metal. We rushed outside and saw that a Land Rover had collided with a Puma. One of the engineers opened the driver's door and guess what the prick of a WO fell out of the rover, still pissed, shouting obscenities as the RMPs dragged him away. I took one look at him and pissed myself laughing. Later found out he was three times over the limit!

Bill Espie

Guin one—18 Sqn on ex in the north German Plain, six weeks of the old eternal triangle exercises. Rocks running all matter of crap duties with the old tricks—fill the elsan up with neat Racasan so the first aircrew who deposits one never goes near an elsan ever again because the splash back seared his jewels—kept stuff down to manageable proportions. We had a new chief magician in charge of the techies who thought he was the dogs. Told us one morning that from now on his men would burn the wet pit every day.

"Suits us," said the Hooligan whilst telling me and McBride to keep our eyes on them. So early in the morn after getting the birds off for the day's tasking, chief and his mates of flightless birds trogged down to the pit. It was roughly 5 feet by 8ft, about 6 foot deep, in the wood. Two jerry cans of paraffin was dutifully onto the pit and the burning taper thrown in, result naught, not even a sizzle, to the great disappointment of the chief. We shall have to try some more. Another 10 gallons of paraffin and still naught, so he decides he will use some petrol but not a lot so it remained manageable. Unbeknownst to him, MacBride and I had been watching and had each appropriated two jerry cans of aircraft fuel. None of your mambypamby Avtur, this was Avtag the old Wessex flew on—white spirit based.

So we slung the 20 gallons in when the guns were searching for a chit to get petrol and then down they came with 5 gallons of petrol, dropped it in, and tossed in the lighter taper. Slight difference. From out of the pit rose a huge fireball, rapidly ascending into the sky, blowing trees with three feet trunks aside like saplings in the wind, and leaving all the sightless birds with fricasseed eyebrows and black faces, to which the Hooligan remarked, "Obviously far too technical for the Rocks to do it, best you guys keep on trying."

Vyv Walters

Ok. In 1981, I had just got my third and was posted to a chopper Sqdn 33 Pumas, to be known as AMF (Ace Mobile Force WTF!). A good mix of rogue Rocks including Cpl John Bush (RIP), Cpl George Haywood, Cpl Simon Morris. SACs George Quirk, Dinger Bell, John Talk, Dave Hall (RIP), Nobby Hainsworth to name just a few. We were doing some morning Guin training on the sqdn. At the end we were left with a few TFs, and smoke grenades. John Bush and Dave Hall said, "We'll get rid of these TFs, Sarge, to save taking them back."

"Okay," says I, thinking they'd go to a safe area we had and set them off. All of a sudden all around the office was quiet, I went to look what these vagabonds were doing when all of a sudden, *Whooooooosh* over the top of two hangars went this rocket, which consisted of 4x TFs and two smokes. They only landed in front of the CO's frigging Puma which was part of a line of nine Pumas. He was a lanky thing called Wg Cmdr Tim Jenner (his name is engraved in my head for life). The boys, under the guidance of John Bush, had taped all that lot together, put it down a small water pipe, you know, just like a friggin mortar and though JB *thought* it would only go up in the air.

The phone was ringing even before I could get back to the office. I was summoned to Jenner's office and given the best bollocking of my life and he wanted whoever was involved charged by the end of the day (five Rocks in all). "I don't do 252s," I said to him.

He said, "It's either them or I charge you. Go away and think on that one." Newly promoted sgt, newly posted in sgt, what did I have to lose? Anyway, all the aircrew were weapon training and all had their own 9mm pistols signed out. I was walking back to the office red faced and pissed off with my lads, talking to myself when in the grass I spotted a 9mm pistol, *oh yesssss!* So I dropped my beret on the floor and the pistol fell into it. I took it back to the office. I checked who owned the pistol before locking it securely away until the shit hit the fan.

Two hours later, after trying my hardest to bollock the troops— ring, ring, another friggin call from OC 33. *Oh f**** is it another issue or was this my Ghandi's revenge? Heels together for the second time, I got the finger pointing wing co saying a pistol had been lost by the sqdn's 2IC and it was my responsibility to find it. Now I have never been one to suffer fools gladly and openly fought back with, "Personal weapons are individual's responsibility, Sir!" And it's a court martial offence if one loses one's personal weapon. To say he was at this stage livid with my comment was a bit of an understatement. As I sai,d I don't suffer fools gladly, so I said, "No problems, Sir, I'll call the snowdrops in and I will get the boys to do a routine search."

"No," said the CO, "get your lads looking. I do not want the police involved just now."

I said, "But, Sir—"

He said, "Don't push it, Sarge."

All afternoon, nobody could find the weapon. What a friggin day I'm having. Two more visits to the CO with his 2IC in attendance, I readily felt that I could turn this around. I called him just before knocking off at 17:00 and said, "Sir, have you got a moment?" I know he was pretty pissed with me at this moment. I went across with my mini Bergen on my back and said, "Sir, the lads have been looking all afternoon with no luck." He was just about to say, *Then call the snowdrops*, when I opened my Bergen and said, "I think I've saved you some problems here," and placed the cleared weapon on his desk. We went down the *Where did you find it?* route. I adjusted the truth a bit and said, "In the toilet, Sir." He was clearly relieved at which point I reminded him that we are all human and make mistakes and smiled and winked at him.

His exact words were, "You are trying too f*****g blackmail me, Sgt Walters? Get out of my office and make sure your troops stay squeaky clean cos I won't be so lenient the next time."

I smiled sweetly and said as I saluted, "Thank you, Sir. It's a clean slate for us both then," and quickly left the office, pissing myself with laughter.

A priceless tour, with some of the best Rocks around, but AMF (Ace Mobile Force) even had its own badge, WTF!

Anthony Wells

Clean white sheets and helicopter pilots!—Again, I Sqn in the early 80s and we were taking part in a helicopter (Tiger Sqn) exercise instead of QCS I think. On arrival at the heli site, we were immediately sent out to man the trenches, well we call them trenches, these had the old fuel heaters in as the Guins usually manned them. Well, when I say man them I mean sleep over the heater. Anyway, some of us were sent to the barn on site to crash out and set a QRF/HQ, etc. and told to get our heads down. Some of us had a look around as we were not used to such luxury and then we found it! On the top floor we found camp beds with clean white sheets, blankets, and pillows. Head down, we thought and dived onto the camp beds. About 5 minutes later, one of their officers popped his head up and politely asked what the hell we were doing on the pilot's beds and we were told to get off and out. *How rude*, we thought, and after wiping our sweating faces into the sheets, we were despatched to the barn floor or on stag. After a little light education by the onsite commander, we stagged on and thought of the camp bed heaven a few metres away.

CHAPTER 8
ENEMY MINE

Chris Pacey

Armament Defence Squadron in the late 90s and the sqn is playing enemy for the USAF at Eastmere FIBUA Village. Eight RAF Regiment gunners and 100 USAF SF. MILES Laser M4/16 rifles used by both sides. We watched them go into extended line and advance onto the village! We could not believe our luck, we mullered them down to forty troops in about 5 minutes flat. They then got their act together and put in some feasible attacks taking out some of our number, however at endex (called prematurely), we had four troops each. I think it had something to do with the fact that one of the last four Americans was a female! Words to the effect of, "Send that spunk bucket up here and we will call it quits," being mentioned. The American DS was pissing himself laughing at the banter but later said he could not face the humiliation of having his force completely annihilated by eight Brits so he called it off early! They were part of the PAVLOV/CSAR at Mildenhall, they considered themselves SF and had never met the RAF Regiment before.

They were quite hostile when we met afterward and we told them we were the stragglers from our main assault force and the main body were quite a bit better than us!

I later worked with USAF Captain Tom Minor, he was on that unit at the time but not on that day, he said word of the humiliation reverberated around his unit like wildfire. The name of the Regt went right up in their estimation and we were asked to play enemy several times after, albeit with some severe restrictions on numbers and ammunition.

Robert Booth

27Sqn Leuchars, Minieval. Eight of us taken in to the flight to be briefed on our limits, rules, etc. As we walked out, we all picked up a nice snowdrop hat off the coat rack. Once outside, we made for the first VCP we could find, put the hats on, and relieved the

Guins of duty. Once we had control we stopped the first big vehicle through and found it was hot lock breakfasts on their way to a sqn. So after liberating those we proceeded to put everyone coming up to the VCP into the back of the truck, once it was full we locked it up and left it outside the guardroom. We were told that was enough disruption for the day and stood down and forced to give the snowdrop hats back.

Mick Failes

Dunno about you lot but the one thing I loved more than anything was playing enemy. Did it for Bruggen once, met up with Ian Duffy (what happened to him?) who asked me to have a go at getting into the bomb dump. "Can't be and never has been done, Mick but give it a go. Use my push bike cos it makes you Guinnish." Two electronic steel gates with a checkpoint in between and I walked straight in. Yeah, I know, lucky, but that's not the point!

Robin Flack

2 Sqn on TACEVAL as enemy. Our brief was no attack before 0800 (yup, a Guin site). At 0600 we started our approach and by 0730 we were laid up ready for the off, happily watching Guins skipping around, preparing for the 'nasty men' to attack. On the stroke of 0800 (honest!) we hit them hard, as you do, and all outposts are overrun, tied and bagged.

Suddenly there is a shriek from inside the encampment from a distraught SL. "Feck off, feck off, put my men down, you're cheating! We are not ready! Go back and start again! That's an order!"

Thirty Rocks slope away to the sounds of, "Sorryeeee," giggle, giggle.

We wait 10 mins then attack from the other side of camp. "Feck off, feck off!" Yup, he's back. "That's not fair! You came in from the other side before, we are ready over there now!"

Our SL, who personally lead the attack and not known for his diplomacy, muttered loudly, "He was a prat at Cranwell too."

"I heard that!! Who said that?" Our CO stood up and was recognised. "Oh, it's you, might have known! I thought you were still with the Hooligans. Oh this lot aren't, no they can't be."

We just walked away, leaving a trail of tied and bagged bodies and a very upset SL. "Oh well, shit happens," smiled our CO. "If it hits the fan then the hooligans will get the blame … again."

David Bowen

Can't remember the date or who was with me but when Honington was a flying station we were given the task to play enemy on one serial. Four of us attacked the entry sanger to the primary site armed with the mark, one very sharp marker pens, we marked the guard's throats with said pen to simulate cut throats then took their NBC suits and weapons, took their places and on shift change, challenged everyone entering and then took the prisoner out of site. At sixty-three prisoners it was too much for the four of us so we legged it into the distance but the station was not happy that no one had noticed that almost an entire shift had failed to turn up.

Richard Hawkes

Whilst on 5 Wing, we went down to Lyneham for a TACEVAL. Well we decided to attack in three groups, so the group I was in attacked the airfield. Well three C130s were coming in so we opened up on them, well they had to stay in the air as they didn't think it safe to land.

We made our way to the perimeter fence where we caught the guard asleep so we took him with us and used him to get in the main camp, well of course we got caught, as per. About the three C130s, they were running out of fuel and had to land pretty soon, I don't think the pilots were too pleased.

Albi Pinnion

At Wildenrath, 1983, Rapier course played enemy for station TACEVAL. We were missioned to take out four hazs, got across all the barbed wire no problems and no challenges, the Guin in the dispersal entrance was taken out before he could raise the alarm. The hanger's doors were all secured, a door was opened, and the attack was spotted, too late, tfs and black tape, two were taped to each hanger door and struck as we legged it to cover. Guins came out of three of the four, far from happy, saying we had deafened them. A chief tech tried to bollocks us but I believe at the time Sgt Dave P. told him to wind his neck in, and praised the lads for good drills!

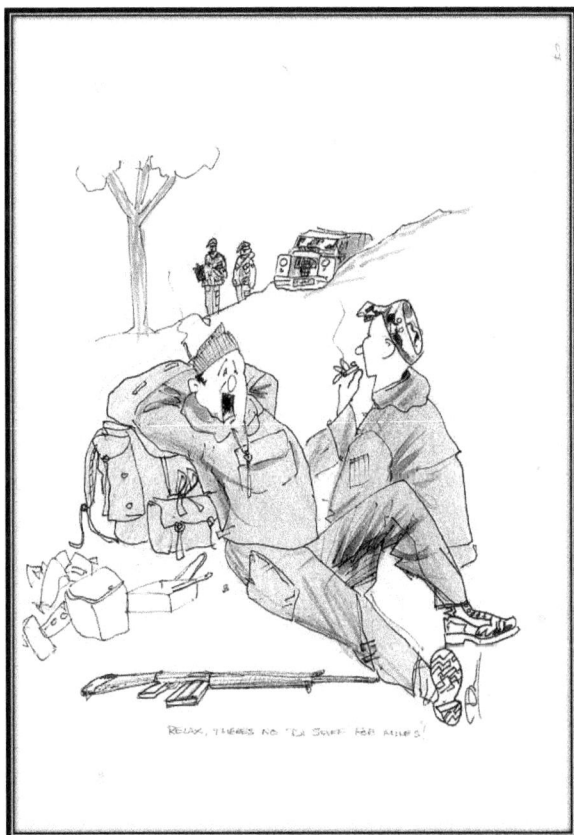

David Bowen

1987, at Wattisham again, had discussion with top brass about masking up during an air raid and was told no need in hardened buildings, as they were protected and filtered so I stated they could be breached or filters fail but was shouted down. So, on the next air raid was of the filter room of the WOC with L1A1 , pressurised spray CS. Yes, you guessed it, gassed 240 Guins and proved a point but was in the shite again and as popular as a turd in a respirator.

Also at Wattisham, with John Cromerty, we were tasked with putting in battle simms for an air attack on the bomb dump and 25 Sqn bloodhounds, so we places ten baked bean tins in a row for kero bombs, then John said, "Shall we make the last one a good one?" So we dug in a galvanised dustbin, put 15 gallons of kero in, then waited for the appointed time. We both run down the line, throwing in TFs, each kero bomb did as required, small explosion and ascending fireball cloud then the last the big one a 200 foot fireball cloud apparently up to 10,000ft. ATC assumed one of the bombing aircraft had ploughed in and stopped the exercise and called full crash response so there's me next morning marking time on station cmdr's carpet. Oh well, it was a good bang!

1987, during a station exercise at RAF Wattisham, we had arranged for 22 to attack the station. On the arranged evening, in total darkness, two SF C130 came in. 22 had agreed to hit three targets but wanted an ambush laid at the third for their training purposes so the station QRF made up of suppliers and stewards (Guins) were to facilitate the ambush with myself and John Cromerty as DI staff.

22 arrived at the third trgt and we went to start the ambush only to find the QRF had fucked off due to facing 22, leaving myself and John Cromerty to do the ambush, so John throws a thunderflash in 22's direction shouting, "Fuck off, you pongo bastards!" to which

approx. 16 thunderflashes came back our way, leaving me and John to tap dance amongst the exploding TFs in the dark with slight concussions.

Atky Atkinson

26 Sqn, 2006. I am tasked with providing an enemy section to test and evaluate the E3 detachment whilst holding at RAF Cottismore. All goes well through the week, apart from the occasional misinterpretation of the rules by some of the directing staff, using official passes to gain entry to the C3 facility and then robbing everything that isn't nailed down.

Last day arrives and the detcmdr decides that the blue jobs deserve a reward for a week well done and so a final attack against the accommodation area is planned. This attack will give the Guins the opportunity to blat off their ammo—should be fun! The attack commences at 0600 and after the first burst from the enemy almost every Guin on site appears and starts to return fire. Imagine my shock when mid-contact a grow bag wanders out of his accommodation wearing his towel and carrying his wash bag and proceeds to weave amongst the troops in contact to get to the shower block! Needless to say, I offered the jockey some constructive tips on his actions on drills. The final exercise debrief was fun too, although the blue jobs could understand my dismay!

John Stowell

Back in the late 70s whilst on 16 Sqn at Wildenrath, we were tasked with doing enemy for one of the exercises at Laarbruch. The powers that be had arranged it so that we could eat in the airmens' mess provided we wore the appropriate armband to show that we were not taking part in any exercise play.

It was whilst eating in there one time when there was a bright flash followed by a loud explosion, and thinking that there may have been a real time incident in the mess and possibly casualties, we ran to see what we could do. As we passed the coffee lounge, we saw a circle of Guins lying on their backs, legs in the air, and stunned and dazed looks on their faces with a large, mushroom-shaped cloud at centre now starting to billow out at the ceiling.

It turns out that this lot had taken refuge in there during the air raid warning that had just sounded so as not to have to wear their respirators and were all sat there with smug expressions on faces and talking about other general Guinly things when one of the 16 Sqn lads Ginge (real name witheld) decided this was not cricket and so put a thunderflash under the coffee table. It also burned a hole in the nice new carpet.

If memory serves, Ginge got 14 days in the main gate hotel for that one.

Rob Davies

Exercise Iron Chariot in W. Germany, '88?. Some bright spark in his infinite wisdom decides to strip down all the Land Rovers (no windscreens/no doors!), during a German winter. There we are, riding round, playing 'fox and hounds' with 1 Sqn, flashing our headlights in lieu of shooting them. Pretty soon this becomes hilarious and we end up just driving past each other and waving.

Anyhow, having stopped in a harbour area for a briefing, we take off, with me (the sprog driver) and the rest of my crew without protection in the back. Without windscreens it's hard enough to see but I wasn't wearing the issued goggles at time. Straight away, it begins to piss down with snow and as I pull out of the car park, I experience a white out and drive the stripped- down Landy straight into a deep gulley across the road. The Landy does a half turn but miraculously doesn't turn over completely. Everyone escaped injury that night but did I get a slagging!

Mark Minary

34 Sqn, Cyprus, mid 1990s. The island is having an Internal Security Evaluation (ISEVAL). A team of us from 34 is put together to act as terrorists and test various elements island-wide. There are various characters on the team including, from what I remember, Clubber Graeme Lang, Ginge Hopper, Rick Archer, Brummie Hughes, Joe Steele was the flt sgt, and I forget who the officer was.

One of the first serials was to do a drive by attack on the 12SU Salt Lake site. The copper on the gate shat himself and took cover, which was a good job because nobody had told them that the ISEVAL was happening and he was still live armed.

Later in the exercise, myself and Clubber, armed with an AK47 and something else, infiltrated Nightingale Barracks at Dhekelia (RMP were guarding) and we got a slightly different reaction—the guard deployed made ready and gave the challenge—Halt—Stamata—Dur. It was obvious from the lack of BFAs that they were also still live armed. I can't remember what I said to Clubber but it was some along the lines of, "Fucking hell, mate, they think it's real, best just surrender," which we did. They were still live armed—Joe Steele eventually arrives and gives us shit for surrendering.

Much later, the alert state on the island had gone up and eventually people had got the hang of issuing blank ammo (thank fook!). I had the task of attacking the SBA police station in Dhekelia which was being guarded by a Ferret armoured car and several fat Cypriot SBA coppers. I arrived, and with the use of only a 9mm Browning, I got the Ferret crew to surrender and then proceeded to give the cops the run around as they tried to arrest me. I shot one of them and then a huge fight kicked off as they tried to wrestle me to the ground. Eventually the DS said, "FFS, just let them arrest you, will you?"

By this time the poor Gollys were a dripping mess of lard. I got chucked in the slammer and processed as a terrorist. There are a load more tales to tell from that ISEVAL but some of the memories are a bit blurred now. Good times!

Dave Capps

RAF Newton, ads course, final exercise. Word had reached the students, i.e. US, that DS were allowing the enemy to listen in on our radio frequencies to aid them in their dastardly deeds. A plot was hatched to screw up their plans royally. Throughout the week leading up to the exercise, various huddles were to be found the accommodation block, muttering incoherently whilst much scribbling was done. The day arrives and a 12 hour exercise commences, come night time and the bad guys plan to up the tempo to keep us busy.

Things are ticking along as expected until the stroke of midnight, a voice is heard on the airwaves saying, "Topgun now, out." What followed can only be described as chaotic to those not in the know. The DS look on in disbelief as their well laid plans for mayhem crumble before them. Gone are the recognised call signs, to be replaced by such sobriquets as *Maverick, Goose, Viper,* and *Jester.* All the expected code words have vanished to be replaced by *Hard Deck* and *Angels.* The well laid plans are in disarray, the enemy are a shambles. They have no clue as to what is happening, the DS are trying to gain possession of one of the scraps of paper that mysteriously appear each time a radio message is issued.

Admitting defeat, they bring the troops back to the briefing room to try and unravel the hell. All is starting to settle down when the fire door bursts open and a Rock DS dressed in a flying helmet and dragging a parachute stumbles in screaming, "They got me, Mav!" The room once again fell into chaos and laughter. Said Rock DS somehow made the rank of WO! Lesson: never underestimate a Rock or group of, when you decide to play by your own rules. *Per Ardua.*

ADS again, our opposite shift is in the mire. Sgt on leave, FS off sick, and a brand new plod PO in charge. It was decided to send me to the sister flt to cover the sgt role for a shift. During a 12 hour shift there would generally be an 'exercise' to keep the troops on their toes, be it intruder, fire, or something else. The plod PO is eager to mix things up and takes me to the office to inform me that he would be running an intruder ex, with the standby shift providing the bad guys. No problem there. To make things more realistic he had arranged for the enemy to have blanks. Alarm bells are starting to ring and I try to explain that as this would be 'no notice', the troops on the ground would respond accordingly to being fired on. "Great," he says. I couldn't seem to get it across to him that this would involve returning fire with *live* rounds. No matter how hard I tried to stem his enthusiasm for the impending disaster, he was adamant about proceeding.

Having withdrawn to the control room, I made a quiet phone call to the Sqn 2IC, at two in the morning, advising him of the forthcoming sh*tstorm. Within 3 minutes the PO was cancelling his games and awaiting the arrival of the none too happy 2IC. Riot act was duly read, a severely chastised plod sulked in the office for the rest of the shift, and as a parting gesture, I was told to, "Wipe the f*cking grin off my face."

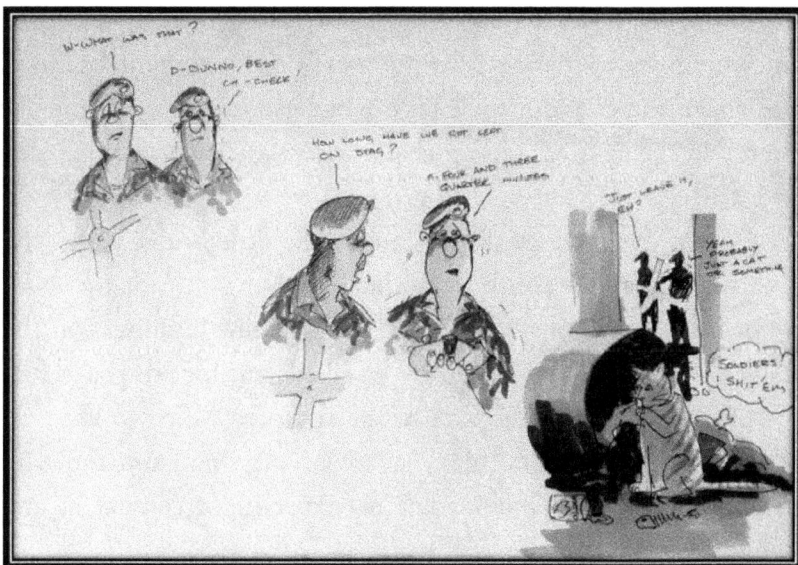

Atky Atkinson

34 Sqn, RAF Akrotiri, 1994 I think. Sqn is tasked with carrying out a hostage scenario exercise. Hostages are taken and held in a building on the far side of the airfield, 34 provides the inner cordon. Day 2 or 3 and the Hereford Hooligans turn up to take over the show. A demand is issued by the hostage takers that they require food for themselves and the hostages, so hotlocks are send to the inner cordon. SAC Smith is tasked with taking them in, needless to say he is not happy with the task but carries it out as ordered. The next day SAC Smith is called in by the SWO, "I understand you weren't happy with your task yesterday, Smith."

"Not at all, Sir. Why?"

The SWO then revealed that the hotlock container was bugged and it's all on tape, Smudge gobbling off about the WO and what a wanker he is! Smudge always did have a way with words!

Rob Andrews

Playing enemy. So, early 80s and A Flight 34 Sqn are playing enemy against the jock guards or Royal Sigs (pongos anyway) who are camped up in Paramali Village. We are based to the north and our mission, if we wish to accept it, is to try and infiltrate the village and take out their HQ, which was sited beside the old church in the centre. Step up Eddie as section leader, myself, and two others. Over the next few hours, we work ourselves down the west of the village until we can see the little bridge across the road that enters the south of Paramali. Staying clear of the road, we begin working our way toward the first few buildings on the outskirts of the village, keeping a good eye out for pongos as it is the obvious place for the first of the sentries. We reach the first of the buildings and nothing, so we keep going from building to building, further and further in, expecting a contact at any minute. Nada.

Eventually we observe their HQ and creep forward. Only 10 feet away we can't believe we have gotten so close without being challenged. Out come a couple of thunderflashes, which we strike and hurl toward the HQ. Then all hell breaks loose as the lazy fuckers wake up, yells come from all directions as they pop flares.

Having achieved our mission, we tear north through the village, blatting blanks off in all directions, laughing our tits off as pongos run round like headless chickens. All in, it took 4 or 5 hours to complete but what a laugh, one of the best nights ever, especially getting one over on the pongos. Apparently their zobs were none too chuffed that we made them look so shit.

Rob Davies

Playing enemy. I sometimes drift back to those heady days of my youth, when spending an evening outside, freezing my ass off in a trench was still exciting and exhilarating. I also remember the freedom we were granted over in Germany and look back fondly. SAC Bob Burton, the keenest man in NATO (whose ambition it was to start a support weapons section on 26 Sqn), was approaching his FT1 and was desperately badgering the flt cmdr (Wobbly?) to let him carry out a night time patrol exercise. Permission was given and he was allocated a section of 'volunteers'. I was asked if I'd like to act as enemy, and in my keen state, I jumped at the chance. Flt cmdr asked me to select a squad but I only needed my bro-in-arms, Jaz Yewen. Bob bombed up and briefed his section, whilst Jaz and I were told, "Take whoever and whatever you need. Just turn up at the pre-arranged grid, so Bob can recce your activity and then bump his patrol on the way back in."

Well, Bob and the patrol left camp on foot, in early evening, via the nearest crash gate, leaving Jaz and I a bit of time on our hands. A command decision was made, so he and I took the Land Rover to 'Little City' and the local schnell Imbiss. I stagged on as weapons guard in the Landy, armed with an SLR, Gimpy, several hundred link, trips, and thunderflashes, whilst Jaz, in combats and cam cream, popped into the schnelly for a special burger.

His visit was taking its time but eventually he returned to the vehicle beaming. His camouflage had been added to, by a local serving wench, who'd given him rosy red cheeks with her lipstick and his smile was further enhanced (if I remember rightly) by a serviette with her telephone number on.

Anyhow, after eating, we drove stealthily to our pre-arranged RV, where we sat up non-tac, providing activity and noise for Bob's patrol to report on. Several fags were smoked and the flask of coffee (and Asbach) was rattled a bit. We then moved on to organise an ambush.

I figured the patrol would be at their lowest ebb at the end of the patrol just as they returned to camp and set about two shell scrapes lining either side of the road, just outside the crash gate. Jaz and I set up trips either side, covering the acreage of barren, ploughed fields, and we lay on kip mats for what seemed hours. Eventually, almost hypothermic, through my IWS, I saw shadowy figures, despondently shuffling down the road to our front, assuming the patrol was over and within sight of their warm beds.

Suddenly, all hell broke loose. We triggered the trips with remotes (green string), illuminating and sky lining the patrol against the clear night sky. The individuals dived for cover but had none, with barren ploughed fields left and right. The flt cmdr dived headlong into the nearest cover (a manure heap) but this lit up with a strategically placed TF.

Jaz opened up with frozen hands on the gimpy and we strafed the area to our front. A lot of lessons were learned that night, the biggest of which was, in civvy street, we would've been on overtime!

Geoffrey Herschell

My first time playing enemy was on 19 Sqn in 1984 against RAF Lyneham. We were to be CND protesters during the day and military enemy at night. During prep at Brize, we were making signs for the protest: *Frankie says no nukes*, etc. when the IG walked in, "What the blazes is going on here?" he screamed. Nobody had told the future RAF Regt CG about the mock protest.

During the CND phase our flt cdr (a PO then, now a serving wg cdr) had a megaphone, he was saying such thought out protestations as, "Ban the bomb, ban the bomb."

I asked if I could have a go and started to chant down the megaphone, "1, 2, 3, 4, we don't want a nuclear war, 5, 6, 7, 8, we don't want to radiate!"

The PO took the megaphone back and tried to copy his LACs words of wisdom, "2, 4, 6, 8, we don't want a nuclear war … What were the words again, Herschell?"

Albi Pinnion

Same compound at Bruggen, we deployed there from Gutersloh to do their TACEVAL, we were unaware what the site was and challenged and had live armed guards with their faces in the mud. Only to find they were live armed when we removed and unloaded their weapons.

Could have gone very wrong if it was not for the Regt's aggression and speed at taking the upper hand. Caused loads of shit, and the guys that were disarmed got charged, poor buggers.

David William Ahearn

I think most of us have played 'enemy' against other stations. 16 Sqn did one against Laarbruch, middle of winter, dusting of snow on the ground. Because of our limited numbers, we were supposed to be taken to the guardroom, then released for the next attack. I get captured by the detached regiment sqn (possibly 58 Sqn) and get taken to the guardroom. The RAFP duty NCO tells me to strip down to my underwear out in the snow. I tell him to fuck off and the rest of the lads who are already under lock and key are giving the copper's stick and telling them to be careful as I'm a psycho.

Apparently they had a few big lads ready to do the deed. The lads who brought me in just tell the coppers to deal with it themselves and fuck off. Eventually they just shove me in a cell fully dressed and the rest of the lads are pissing themselves laughing. And when the boss turns up to collect us he had a few choice words for the MPs!

If my memory serves me right, he came out on an attack with some of us and was involved in a revenge attack on a couple of hapless MPs.

CHAPTER 9
ICE COLD IN BAHRAIN

'ALLOW THE PARTS TO SWEAT IN THE SUN'

Graham Spike Thomson

Gulf war 1, 26 Sqn. Saudi Air Force Base Tabuk. Moving every 24 hours as the Saudis can't agree where they want the Rapier siting. New Year's Eve, my fire unit is sited on flat desert with just a rise where the tracker is. Starts to rain cats and dogs in the afternoon and continues through the night. By early morning the water is ankle deep and sprog zob in the CP sends me prepare to move. "Confirm PTM," says I as we are up to our necks in mud.

"Yes," comes the reply. Soaking admin area packed away, 1 tonne winch needed to move the wagon and trailer. Order to move and we had to dig through mud to get wheels and generators on. All kit had to be winched clear of the quagmire. All crew members looked like mud men from Mars! Still raining!

Just as we get the last bit of kit clear, the CO turns up in a mass flap, "This should never have happened." After being debriefed by me.

The sprog zob surprisingly never sought advice. "What can I do?" says the sqn ldr. "I know, I will meet you and your crew at the chogie diner and buy you all breakfast." Off we go, CO to rip apart sprog and us to said diner.

The diner has two car parks, one left, one right, diner in the middle. We pull into the left, CO to the right. Bearing in mind, everything is awash at this point and the water is level with the raised concrete paths. CO gives us a wave and we all set off for central doors.

As we approach two U.S. AF, females leave the diner and turn left into the path of the CO. Being the English gent, he steps off the path into the water.

Fek me, all we could see next was his beret floating on the water as the chogies had dug a trench in that very spot he stepped on. We couldn't help him for laughing!

Finally we pulled him out and get into the diner, all the lads are getting their grub and the CO is stood at the till paying as a Philippino with a mop is running rings around him. The water was running out of his waterproofs.

He retired as a group captain and me a WO, every time we met up after leaving the sqn we always had a laugh about that New Year's Day, me more than him I must add!

Tony Paskin

Gulf 90 66 B Flight Rapier sight. Stag on. Think we had just finished tests and adjustments when kit alarmed on an incoming aircraft with no IFF. Wtf ? No comms. Turns out yank helicopter. Jolly green, I think Dave Capps, decided he was gonna scare us (we are still locked on), flew straight at us and then hovered with all lights full on about 30 feet in front of us. Sand flying everywhere, we shut the kit down.

He started to go so we turned the kit back on. Alarm wide target stupid American who won't put his IFF on! *FFS you prick*. He started dodging left and right and up and down and we all stood waving at him creased up. Late IFF did arrive eventually. Think some shit flew.

Jim Higgins

Getting arrested in Bharain with Wakey (John, I think) is a story I will write later. But the memory of seeing him dressed in his Fidi Dido shell suit, shouting to an Arab who is holding a dagger, "Your mother's a whore and your father smells of elderberries!" Nice one, Wakey, let's start this Gulf War for real.

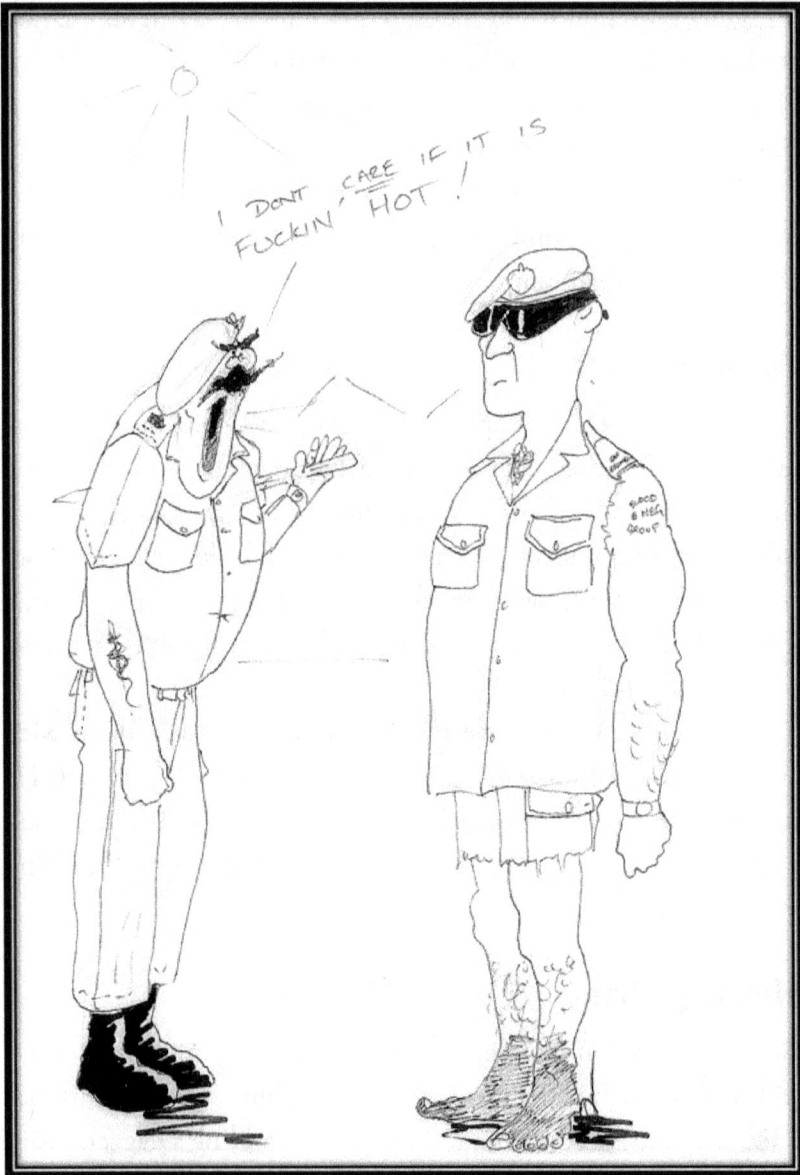

Fraze Barkaway

Gulf War, 1991, Tabuk. 51 Sqn had to man an OP on top of a HAS that overlooked the Rapier site that has its own tale to tell. Surrounding the HAS was literally a 100 prepped 1000lb bombs prepped to be loaded on to the Tornados to give Saddam a good kicking; these things were going at an alarming rate. On some of them were cheesy messages like, *Get some, MOFO*, and one had been signed by a load of nurses from Wegberg (still waiting for that bus).

Now a fellow SAC and I had been given a really good explanation of what these things do and how they can throw metal 500m in every direction by one of the Tornado pilots who would chat to us before they went off to wreak havoc over Bagdhad. So there we are on stag when my oppo suddenly announces, "Eyes on, I'm off for a shit," and off he trots down the side of the HAS.

Next thing some Guin is going apeshit and yelling disgust and horror. WTF? I leave the OP and arrive next to the two of them to see what's going on. Turns out my oppo was caught wanking on a 1000lb bomb and his explanation? "When this fucker goes bang, my jizz is going to spread for 100s of metres across Iraq. My jizz infested bombs are going to spread my DNA for miles."

The look on the Guin's face as he stood there listening to this with his torch lighting up a bomb that looked like seagulls had shat all over it was a picture. Oh well stag on!

Neil Horn

Arah Gulf 1 Bahrain and the numerous mortar attacks that we suffered. Well only one actually. Was the normal bright sunny afternoon (pre-conflict), not a lot of much going on, sun-bathing, hangovers, flt HQs driving around just trying to look busy, the normal stuff. All of a sudden (I was far side of airfield outside the wire), *Ka-boom* (repeat seven times). Wtf!

"Contact, wait out," then from Taff's site, BJ Beach, I recall. "INCOMING, contact, wait out."

Kind of all a bit lost in memory the next 5 or 10 mins before we were told to stand-down. Turned out, although they never 'admitted' to it, that the local Kuwaiti Defence Force had a little accident with one of the 2 40/70s they had on the airfield. I am no 40/70 man, but I recall 'ND with a full hopper' being the old sweat analysis. Missed Taff's site by a hundred feet at best, fortunately landing in the sea, causing no damage.

Anthony Wells

ISO container, gas, gas, gas. 2003, Gulf War 2, Ali Al Salem I was the CBRN SNCO for ground ops and the hostilities are under way. As part of the duties I was to be IC CBRN bunker (dug in ISO container) when a SCUD/inbound attack was called when off duty near the SNCO barrack block. Anyway the first siren goes up just after I had finished my stag and we all move (Guins mainly) to the shelter, head count, and all suited and booted full IPE.

After about an hour, we are requested to carry out sniff tests in our area. Now being the only Rock there and this being our first attack they obviously looked at me for guidance. So I called for two volunteers to help with the sniff test. I of course had no reply and when I shone my torch to the back of the ISO, all I could see were grown men cowering at the back, not wanting to come forward. I spoke to them and explained that we were not getting out of this ISO until it's carried out. I explained that I would do it and they were to watch and carry out first aid, using their aide memoire, if there was gas, etc.

So I went to the entrance and had a look around and I could see the locals moving about yards from our ISO, which meant no gas, etc. The Guins did not know this and out the three of us went to carry out the drill (no locals about now). You should have seen their faces as I did the drill and coughed and placed the mask down. It was stunned silence and no movement from the Guins, I blew out hard and told them what a fat load of good they would be if I was choking.

Anyway we went back in, reported all clear, and then I told them all to carry out their own individual sniff test and we eventually stood down and the ISO inmates, head down, walked past me in disgrace as they reflected on what had just happened. God bless them, gas, gas, gas.

Anthony Rogers

As small dit, out in Basra on tour in '04 and I and few others go to the Toucan Bar and start to use our beer chits. Bar closed, but the Movers Bar was still open, so myself and another, first name Gaz, move to this bar. Anyway, Gaz gets chatting to a female zob, after a while we end up talking about what we all did before joining up. She states that she used to be a holiday rep, so quick as flash I turned round and stated, "So there is a good chance we will see your tits tonight?"

Gaz spurts his drink out and she looks at me as if to say, *I don't know what to think or answer to that question.*

Anyway I cracked on, smashing the cans of wobbly, bit of blank spot after that. Next morning, FS swampy calls me over. I'm stinking of booze but trying to keep my composure (still drinks). Swampy turns round to me and states, "Get you heels together."

I think, *Oops, what did I do last night?* So my heels partner up, then swampy says to me, 'You were found wandering round the TDA last night by a Sgt (1 SQN attached sausage and bean). He had to put you in your pit. So, SAC Rogers, how much did you drink last night?"

Now bear in mind this is a hot country and I had not drunk much if anything for the majority of that tour plus, I get pissed quick as it is. I then think to myself, *Integrity is a value we as gunners hold sacred*, answers I, "More than three and less than eleven."

Swampy smiles at me and said, "Well, guess what? I hope you enjoyed them because your fucking dry from now on, understood?"

"Um, yes, Flight Sgt."

"Good, now fuck off on patrol." What a horrendous patrol it was, heat, sweat, flies, hangover, and *so* tired.

Stephen Headey

I was on CP duty at Razalgah in late January in GW1 prior to the air campaign. Picture this, 0100 in the morning, usual stuff RC, etc. so nothing to write home about. Suddenly over the radio comes an American voice announcing that we are under attack and there is 50 inbound missiles. At this point, the arse twitched a little. As I was the only one there, I ran to the tent and got the guys up and dressed in NBC.

Radio comes back to life with the same voice announcing, "All clear."

"Okay, back to normal, guys. Go back to bed."

Fifteen minutes elapse and again, "Air Raid Red." This time the score has gone up now 75 inbound. Rush over, wake the guys and again ready for the chaos to begin.

By now the site is a hive of activity with Penguins running round talking to themselves and panicking because they can't find their respirators or are busy swallowing NAPS.

Again over the radio, "All clear."

Another fifteen minutes elapse and here we go again. By this time the guys are fed up and just wait at the CP. Again, the same American voice declares, "All clear," and adds, "Sorry, guys, it's our missiles that's flying." Got to love our American buddies.

Paul Malpus

Kuwait desert, nice sunny day as you do, with Alastair, crawl up to the enemy position L2 out, grenade ring firmly on finger, pull the pin, check, over it goes, "GRENADE!" Nothing, looking at each other, any second now. Any second now … Still nothing. Shit!

Bob crawls up, "Show me the pin," all sat firmly still on my finger. "Bollocks, we've got a blind. Okay, we'll wait for 30 mins."

Then from my lips I say the dreaded words, "It could be worse. It could be raining!" Allah must have been listening and decided we were having it too good and decided to make me eat my words by hitting us with a biblical downpour. Oh how Al and Sqn 2IC Bob laughed.

An hour we lay in that puddle of a shell scrape. Oh and the fly off lever hadn't fully come off. We had to dems it.

Neil Horn

Just to show it is not just you enlisted who are debauched. I feel safe in telling this as it became public as you will read. Bahrain, 1991, the MoD were kind enough to deploy most of Ely Mil Hospital to a field ambulance set up just outside of Muharaq. So suddenly there was a target rich environment. I managed to attain a 'war bird' and fortunately she was only to keen to avail herself of the comforts of my room in the Sheraton.

Well the room was actually shared with OCA flt, but we were on opposite shifts. That was until returning to hotel one night with said nurse to find the door locked and chained from the inside with *Do not disturb* on it. Shit, OC A has the night off and was 'entertaining'.

Went back to lifts and enterprising nurse saw a little 'private' alcove where the shoe-shine machine was, "This will do." She set up holding the handles and the deed was done!

Anyhow, life moved on, until about two years later my wedding, not that nurse but someone I had met on return from the Gulf. Full church do, all the family there, big reception at the Golf Club. Bob was my best man and a bunch of officers from 66 Sqn (in the Gulf together). We were all at new postings, I was at QCS. All going well until midway through the best man's speech. Bob started to go on about, "We all knew Neil would end up at QCS, he always had a passion for shiny shoes, even on ops while entertaining he has been known to passionately demonstrate to nurses the use of a shoeshine machine."

You could have heard a pin drop. Grandma is wide-mouthed, new wife with a *WTF* look and all the boys from 66 laughing like drains.

A few drinks later and everyone forgot. Apparently my timing not being perfect and the swing shift officers (IG, Adjt Bob, and sqn OC) exited the lift to see OC B hammering young nursey who was bent over the shoe-shine machine. They kept schtum for over two years until my wedding day ... fuckers.

Neil Horn

On the duty free theme. 66 Sqn returning to Marham (then to WR) from Granby. All the sqn had a shit load of watches, gold, electronics that had been proffered during four months in Bahrain. In normal Rock fashion, it had been hidden everywhere; gold sewn into smock collars, cameras, watches, and walkmans rolled inside sleeping bags, all the norm.

On arrival at Marham, RAFP officer and customs bloke greeted the sqn. Plod was a good guy who some of us had drank with in the past. Bob and I met the guy and customs bloke, chatted and we came to an 'arrangement'. They couldn't be arsed searching the sqn, but had to be seen to be doing their job. 100 quid would cover the entire sqn. A whip round, currency didnt matter. Within about two minutes, we had a good handful of Bahrain Dina notes, job done. Now and again there is a good copper out there! Did the cash go to HMRC? Who cares!

Gulf 2 I was attached to HQ 1 Div. We proffered as many MREs as we could from the attached USMC. MRE were cordon bleu compared to the three squares of noodles that the div cook (I think that's what he was), mustered up every friggin day for months. Never ever did I desire boil on the bag more than centralised messing. There are many more stories about being attached to a div HQ at war, later. What a cluster fuck.

Chris Taylor

Myself and Barry were the two sergeants who were sent out to the Gulf on Op Granby pretty early on. After four months of training, the Americans on VCPs, weapon training, NBC, and a host of other subjects, and having supervised the siting and digging of holes for Mexe-shelters in tarmac because the Saudis wouldn't let us dig holes in their grass!

We finally got some help from 34 Sqn who had sent a flight out to Dharhan to carry out patrols and training for the Guins. We felt that having been sent out there at short notice (24 hours in my case and my youngest daughter was two weeks old), our work was done and we could return to UK. Speaking to our wing commander and we asked when we would be repatriated only to be told that he didn't know. So Barry decides to take matters into his own hands. He goes to see OC admin and tells him that our wing commander has told us to book the Friday flight back to Brize from Riyadh. "Okay, you are booked onto it."

He then goes to our wing commander and tells him that OC admin had told him to book us on the same flight. "Okay," says the Wing Commander, and before the two of them realised they had both been had, we were on an internal flight to Riyadh and then flew back to the UK after an overnight stay in a 5 star hotel!

Rod Jones

During the Gulf War, I found myself and the rest of the section on the pan near the Jaguars. Anyway, missile warning red, so we leg it into the shelter about 50 meters away and await the bangs. As we get inside, it's full of Royal Air Force chaps, all going through their buddy checks.

We get sorted and then the CT opposite me gives me the thumbs up as I must have been looking strangely at him, next minute, *boom, boom*. Just prior, the reason I was looking at him was because I couldn't work out what was wrong with his respirator, then it clicked he didn't have a canister fitted!

I then shouted to him something like, "I think you need to check your canister." He laughed. I then put my hand over the mount. He then realised that I wasn't having a little Rockape joke with him. The stink of urine and faeces will always stay with me as long as I live as I struggled to help him get the canister on.

CHAPTER 10
IT'S A GAS, GAS, GAS

Chris Pacey

NBCI 2000ish. Taff Jones, myself, and a couple of others head in two wagons to Winterbourne on a Sunday afternoon in convoy from Honington. Brew stop on the way and then arrive at the guardroom to be told to park as far from the annex access as possible in overflow car park.

Taff gets out busting for a piss. Finds a tall hedge and happily relieves himself. The hedge was at the end of the car park and start of the married qs. As he is in full flow, a voice says, "What the fuck do you think you are doing?!"

Taff looks around the hedge to see a man, his wife, and kids, dressed smart, coming back home from church! "What's your name and what course are you on?!"

"Cpl Jones and NBCI, Sir."

"My office, tomorrow morning, 0800, Jones!"

"Yes, Sir … Whose office do I need to go to?"

"The fucking RSM, Jones!"

We were pissing ourselves out of sight. Nice start Taff, we haven't even got in the building yet!

Derek Wagle

Deployed around Laarbruch from Bruggen one year—Sargie B you know the one! John had brought his goldfish along for the trip. It was so cold the water kept freezing so was constantly topped up from the kettle. DI staff turned up and a NATO officer popped into the admin area and spotted the goldfish suspended from a cam pole in its little bowl. "That's our chemical detector fish, Sir," says John. "It changes colour to indicate nerve agent."

Foreign officer wasn't sure but I remember looking at the DC who had that look of horror that only a DC can have when the SACs start!

Wayne Holliss

Anyone remember the fun and games when 15 Sqn did the Porton Down battle run (Rik Corrigan). Why HQ had to do it is beyond me, but we went and we did it, sort of.

Any way, that night the sqn was due to do a TAC harbour in the woods nearby, so we made our way to said area and put up our bivvies, etc. Now Porton wasn't new to me, having done a few detachments there for some experiments, etc., so I arrange a shower run for HQ with the pongo in charge of the block Id used before.

On the way back, we got chatting and decided rather than sit in the dark woods all night, we'd rather go on the piss, and so we did. The trouble is, it being an exercise, there was a lack of civvi trapping gear to be had, but undeterred and using our initiative, we troll what we had in our Bergens and set off.

What a fucking site we looked. Me dressed in green t-shirt, Ron Hills, combat boots, Pops para running top, Ron Hills, issued daps, the other lad dressed in a similar fashion. Well we hit the town and soon were in a pub pulling some pongo wives and drinking like there's no tomorrow. I even managed to get sticky fingers.

Soon it was time to go back as it was well after midnight, so we jump in this taxi, "Where to, lads?" he says,

"Middle of nowhere please, mate."

"What"?"

"Head towards Porton and we're tell you where to stop."

So we stop next to this gate in the middle of nowhere, it's as dark as pitch, and Pops decides to have a piss in the back of the taxi. I couldn't get out of there quick enough, I fall over the gate wetting myself. Then he tries to negotiate the gate. As he jumps off, he kicks it back into the taxi's headlight and smashes it. Oops.

Somehow we made back it back to the harbour area unnoticed. B Flt asleep again.

Come wake up time, we get told by Rik that two of the B Flt sgts are expecting us to cook them breakfast. Bollocks to that, we packed up and were ready to move before they were fully alert.

As we drove off we passed the two sgts, who looked on in total amazement at us, pointing to the 2 x 24hr rat packs and hexi blocks we'd left for them.

David Matthews

As I was the sqn NBC SNCO for 66 Sqn, I did a lot of teaching NBC prior to Gulf War 1. Never be away from your kit. Shit SA80 ECT. I had just done one of the first NIAD and cam courses. Now this day our NIAD was up and running on site. We had not yet moved into house. I was in the tent when along came my flt car.

We got briefing, etc. and we wandered down to tracker. When at said tracker, the NIAD went into alarm. Both of us went for our respirator. *Shit*, it was not there. Our webbing was in the tent. Two blokes running to tent to put it on. We lived to tell the tale but it taught me, and I am sure Neil, a big lesson. *Practice what we preach.*

Stephen Headey

I was at Odiham on GDT for a while. Anyhow, it's Friday afternoon and we have knocked off early. Sitting in my palatial, one man por-tacabin room, I and another guy from the balloon boys hoed in to a grate of Grolsche (oh memories). Well, two doors down one of the others guys from the balloon sqn had a habit of leaving his keys in his room door on the outside. We thought when he goes for a shower we will have a laugh. He nips off and we nip in to his room. The other guy screws his windows shut on the outside and inside I retrieve his respirator canisters. Now it just so happens that the lid of a Kiwi boot polish fits perfectly under a door.

So we are ready have tin and a couple of spare CS tablets. Just waiting for the victim. Sure enough, we hear him go in to his room.

Perfect. We rush out, the other guy locks his door. He shouts, "WTF are you doing?" I light the tablets and slide it gently under his door.

He starts laughing saying, "I've got my respirator, you idiots." Suddenly all we hear is, "Where the fuck is my canisters, you bastards?" Followed by, "Why is the window not opening?" Cough, cough, splutter.

Robert Booth

Getting an NBC lecture by a specialist team. All is going well up to the point where the demo of using the combo pen happened. Get into the lying position, the instructor says. He remains standing so we can see the demo, proceeds to place the pen against his thigh. Then a rather louder noise than expected and he collapses on the floor, screaming his head off. The other instructors at the back are all pissing themselves. They had swopped out the drill pen for a live placebo pen with full size needle.

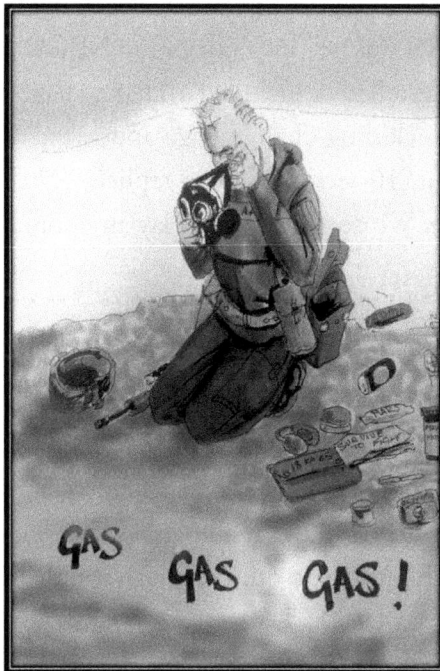

Stephen Headey

Mid-88, Moleswoth NBC lecture. Well now here is a turn up for the book. The Yanks are giving us cross training on NBC. So we are doing canister change exercises and are observing as they can't do theirs as their filters are internal. But here is the best bit. We then practice using combo pens whilst our brothers in arms use their combo pens.

All of a sudden, we hear a yelp as two big black Americans keel over. Somehow the pens they had contained the real deal Atropine. Ha, ha, both carted off to the med centre with Atropine poisoning.

Nick Day

One time, FRT had been ordered to 'set Command Code 22 and prepare defensive positions'. The two of us decoded the Batco message. We even went to the nearest site to see what they decoded. Same answer. Had a look at the Batco sheets, the nearest we could come up with, as it was nearing endex was, 'NBC Black and prepare' etc. Good old Zero hadn't included a 'change page' so I replied the same message, including change page and asked if that was what they really meant. 10 secs later, Zero replied, "No," and resent the original message. We decided not to play anymore and investigated rat packs.

Then there was a time a Buccaneer flew over Milltown during one exercise and sprayed B Echelon with something that smelled very much like AvTur. NBC Black declared rubber faces on and take cover. Apparently the Buccaneer had an emergency and needed to dump fuel in a hurry and did it all over us. No one gave a thought that an aerosol of AvTur is quite explosive and dry wood soaked with it burns very well ...

Steve Greef

Who else has done this? NBC exercise in '77 or '78, never wanted a dump until one puts those bloody NBC trousers on, off to the woods with shovel, as the bogs are lethal. Squat, do what has to be done, pull said trousers up, only to find they are full of what you have just got rid of.

Robbie Robinson

You asked for NBC stories, 1 Sqn early 80s, dug in on yet another exercise, on my crew was a certain gunner, now if you ever met this individual, you will not be surprised. I went over to his trench and he starts to tell me in full detail the benefits of the mark 2 suit compared to the mark 1. I listened and admit was starting to look at him in different way, but his last words were, "Plus the gap at the top of the trousers is bigger and makes it easier to have a wank in your trench." Sad bastard he was.

Simon John Spear

NBC related story from Gulf War 1. We'd driven in to the airfield to sort out a bit of admin, I decided it was as good a time as any to dismount the GPMG and give it a damn good clean. I may have got a bit carried away because it was stripped to its component parts and was looking like a belt fed weapon, if you'd just bought it from IKEA. The law of sod raised its ugly head and Saddam decided to test fire a couple of scuds. So, cue lots of people running around like headless chickens, frantically masking up, etc. and heading to the shelters.

My three so called mates were a bit more casual about the whole process but, in between giggles, wished me the best of luck in putting it all back together again as they waved goodbye and wandered off to the shelter. As luck would have it there was one of those over the shoulder sports bags handy so I grabbed that, threw all the bits in, and chased after them.

Of course, they were already in the shelter with about twenty odd other people all in full NBC kit and masks. I slowly walked past them all to a gloomy spot in the corner and spent the next 20mins slowly putting the GPMG back together whilst trying to identify my so called mates. The whole time spent f-ing and blinding about the jack bastards and whose stupid idea it was to strip it down.

Eventually they gave themselves away because they were the only three still watching as the gun got pieced back together and the fact that their shoulders were still rocking up and down from where they were still pissing themselves with laughter. Bastards!

Jim Higgens

Okay, some NBC from the 26 Sqn FRT Guins. Gulf War 1 in the paradise known as Tabuk. Driving along the highway and it is prayer time so all cars to a standstill. Scud warning comes over the radio so we adopt the attire, jump out of the wagon and over the ditch at the side of the road to land on some Saudi gents making prayer. Not happy chappies but think the SA80s slung around chests may have saved the day.

Lunchtime and in the blistering heat this FRT decided to eat chicken curry with the addition of some f*****g hot stuff bought at the local supermarket. Whilst savouring the last morsels, scud warning, fully attired we decided to look into each other's eyes and see who drowned first due to rising water levels aided by the bloody f*****g hot stuff.

Last but not least. A launcher or RT change at one of the sites. The crew had stored the wheels on top of the communal ISO and rolled them onto the sleeping ISO with a bit of a thud. Unbeknown to them, FS B was having a bit of shut eye. He immediately adopted the attire, ran into the communal bothy, shouting, "Mortar attack!"

only to be met by a bemused DC, FRT, and yank military police enjoying a quiet brew!

Laird Craig Cooper

This is more of a confession than a funny story. Way, way, way back, 2008, I had the pleasure of serving on a Tri service training team. While I was taking a unit of the Royal Signals through CBRN drills for their Matts test, I realised that I had brought along an empty tube of CS tablets, (it'd been a long week), not wanting to show myself up, I decided to adapt and overcome and find some paper to burn to create a smoky effect in the chamber.

After a while of burning and getting rid of the Daily Mail ash evidence, I let the first group in. It was quite smokey and they all stood there with their face wellies on looking at the Rockape that was stood watching them. After giving a quick brief on what I expected of them and what to do in the event of any effects from the CS, I got to the meat of the test.

While the first few were going through the drills, I noticed a couple of the lads were spluttering and doing the funky dribble. I allowed them to leave and carried on while in the back of my mind I was thinking, "You jack bastards," it was then I realised my major issue, I was not wearing my respirator throughout the whole thing.

After the third group had completed the drills, thirty lads in total, twelve of them had failed and had been let out due to more dribbling and eye watering and had to complete extra training before being allowed back in to complete the test phase. The thing is … there was no CS

Afterwards, quite a few of the guys were really impressed at my immunity to CS, one of them being the RSM. I decided to tell him that I wasn't immune but had only lit one tablet and that most people can manage one tablet without too much trouble. I remember him lining up and bollocking the failures saying that they had shown themselves and their unit up in front of a regiment gunner and that all the failures owed me a pint for allowing them to retake the test.

To this day I can only put to the fact that these guys were actually suffering from the effects of CS because of a residual build-up of CS in their respirators or canisters from the previous year's testing. Either way, the next time I was at the bar I didn't pay for any drinks, so it was win, win for me.

Robbie Robinson

GDT Machrihanish. Use to play Russian Roulette in the gas chamber. The boss' dog used to follow me in and just sit there. The Guins was sure I had not lit the tablet, so I would dare them to take their ressies off. Some did.

Phil Cameron

On occasion, I'd go into the chamber at Marham, light some blue roll to get some smoke into the air, I'd then bring in the Guins, get them to walk around, moving their heads, all the while saying the mandatory blurb of, "If at any time you feel the effects of CS, stop, shut your eyes, stop breathing, and raise your hand, I will then lead you outside, at no point resist the direction I'm leading you."

The amount of coughing, spluttering, and raised hands was a joke.

Tim Coed

Got used to CS so much was doing the usual in the (gas chamber) respirator testing facility, had all the Guins masked up with another in attendance, then knelt down with the big match to light up when a high pitch voice goes, "Sarge," as the dreaded smoke starts to swirl around my head, "Your not masked up."

"Don't worry," says I, "Nor will you be in a minute."

One dropped person later, my assistant drags out and is his usual self, "Whats wrong? He's just gassed himself, is he okay?"

"Yeah, he's immune to it now."

I'm inside with rest of the course looking at me as if I'm some sort of weirdo, just carried on with drills till he came back in with Cas. Did that on so many occasions they thought we were so mad and shouldn't even be instructing, the gayers.

Robin Flack

NBC story. On TACEVAL, Germany, sporting a full beard (excused shaving permanently). Approached by an examiner who tut tutted and said, "If a chemical attack was imminent, you would be dead."

I produced a razor from my pocket and informed him that I would shave it off. "Ha, no blade," he replied.

I produced a blade from another pocket and said, "I can assemble a razor and shave quicker than you can produce a proper chemical attack today."

TACEVAL assessors have no sense of humour.

ABOUT THE AUTHORS

Stephen Headey

Having served in the RAF Regiment for thirteen years on field, Rapier, USAF, and helicopter squadrons in various locations throughout the world helped make me the successful businessman and company director I am today.

The regiment gave me discipline and the fight to see things through, even when times were tough and I lost a limb, I never gave in. I credit this to the training I received in my career.

Today I am now the owner of an import company for British expats. This book was born out of wanting to help my fellow brothers in arms, and it was a pleasure to be involved in this from start to finish.

Tim Parker

Joining the RAF Regiment in 1980 helped shape me as an individual. The things I learned and did on the Queen's Colour Squadron and a succession of Rapier and USAF squadrons are very much a part of who I am today. Throughout my life, if a notion or observation strikes me, down on paper it goes, usually in pictorial form. I am flattered that many of the quick, rough, and ready cartoons I scribbled out on NAAFI breaks or slack time on guard are still retained today by many comerades. It is an honour to have provided old and new images for this work.

I've never fully turned my back on the Air Force, and despite an absence after twenty-four years regular and reserve service, I have recently come back to the fold. Watch out for more artwork.

GLOSSARY

9 mil	Browning 9 millimetre pistol
66	Throw away portable anti-tank weapon
181	Radar tracker in conjunction with Rapier
A41	Radio set
AAAD	All arms air defence
AG	Air Gunner
AOC	Air officer commanding
AIG	Artillery instructor gunnery
Aladdin	Cold weather heater
AM	Air marshall
Ammo	Ammunition
Auto jet	Atropine injector for nerve agent poisoning
Bergen	Army bag
BFT	Battle fitness test
Blank	Training ammunition
Batco	Battle codex used in secure radio transmissions
Beer chits	Money
CASEVAC	Casualty evacuation
Carl Gustav/Charlie Gee	84 mm anti-tank weapon
CFT	Combined fitness rest 10km forced march with full kit
Clansman	Radio set proceeded A41 radio
Claymore	Remotely operated or tripwire anti-personnel mine
Cam net	Camouflage netting
CPL	Corporal

CO	Commanding officer
CS	Tear gas
CVRT	Combat vehicle recce tracked
DZ	Drop zone
Flt Sgt	Flight sergeant
FG	Flying officer
Flt Lt	Flight lieutenant
Flt Cmdr	Flight commander
Gat	Personal weapon
GDOC	Ground defence operations centre
GD/GDT	Ground defence training
Genni	Generator
Glowsticks	Used to mark out tactical landing for helicopters
GPMG/ Gimpy	General purpose machine gun 7.62 mm
Groupie	Group captain
HALO	High altitude low opening (parachuting)
HEAT	High explosive anti-tank round
Helo	Helicopter
IG	Instructor gunnery
IED	Improvised explosive device
IWS	Individual weapon sight (night operations)
Kero	Kerosene
L2	Grenade anti-personnel
LMG/Bren	Light machine gun
L/R	Landover 4WD
M16	Semi-automatic weapon
M60	Belt-fed 7.62 machine gun
M203	5.56 weapon with grenade launcher
Macrolon	Car brand

Mag	Weapon magazine
NAPS	Nerve agent pre-treatment system
NBC	Nuclear biological chemical equipment
Noddy suit	Nuclear biological and chemical suit
OP	Observation post
Optical Tracker	Works in conjunction with 181 and Rapier
PB	Personal best
PE	Plastic explosive
PO	Pilot officer
POL	Petrol, oil, lubricants
PTI	Physical training instructor
Rats Rats	Enemy sighted
Rat packs	24-hour ration packs
Rapier	Missile defence system
Reserve	Spare parachute
Rock Ape	RAF Regiment Gunner
S10	Respirator
SAC	Senior air craftsman
SA80	5.56 mm both automatic and single shot weapon
Schmuelly	Single shot illumination parachute flare
Scouser	Someone from Liverpool
Scuffers	RAF Police
Scrim	Shredded sandbag used to camouflage on helmets and webbing
SGT	Sergeant
SHORAD	Short range air defence officer
SLR	Self-loading rifle 7.62mm
Smoke	Smoke grenade

SMG 9 mm	Sub machine gun
Spartan	Tracked recce vehicle
Static jump	Jumping from aircraft fully loaded (when hooked up, will open your chute)
SUSAT	Sight unit small arms trilux (rifle scope)
Sqn Ldr	Squadron leader
SWO	Station warrant officer
TAB	Tactical advance to battle
TACEVAL	Tactical evaluation exercises training for war
TF Thunderflashes	Used to simulate battle noise in training
Tilley	Fuel powered light/lamp
Tracer	Rounds of ammunition that glow when fired
Trip flare	Controlled manually or with trip wire for ground illumination
UXB	Unexploded bomb
Webbing	Equipment to carry spare ammunition, food, water, grenades, etc.
WO	Warrant officer
Zulu Time	Military time